# TELEVISION DISCOURSE

# Television Discourse

## Analysing Language in the Media

Nuria Lorenzo-Dus

First published 2009 by
PALGRAVE MACMILLAN

Palgrave Macmillan in the UK is an imprint of Macmillan Publishers Limited, registered in England, company number 785998, of Houndmills, Basingstoke, Hampshire RG21 6XS.

Palgrave Macmillan in the US is a division of St Martin's Press LLC, 175 Fifth Avenue, New York, NY 10010.

Palgrave Macmillan is the global academic imprint of the above companies and has companies and representatives throughout the world.

Palgrave® and Macmillan® are registered trademarks in the United States, the United Kingdom, Europe and other countries.

ISBN-13: 978–1–4039–3428–4  hardback
ISBN-10: 1–4039–3428–2      hardback
ISBN-13: 978–1–4039–3429–1  paperback
ISBN-10: 1–4039–3429–0      paperback

This book is printed on paper suitable for recycling and made from fully managed and sustained forest sources. Logging, pulping and manufacturing processes are expected to conform to the environmental regulations of the country of origin.

A catalogue record for this book is available from the British Library.

Library of Congress Cataloging-in-Publication Data
Lorenzo-Dus, Nuria.
Television discourse : analysing language in the media / Nuria Lorenzo-Dus.
p. cm.
Includes bibliographical references and index.
ISBN 978–1–4039–3428–4
1. Television broadcasting—Language.  2. Television talk shows.  3. Television broadcasting of news.  4. Discourse analysis.  I. Title. PN1992.8.L35L67 2008
302.23′45014—dc22                                    2008037604

10   9   8   7   6   5   4   3   2   1
18  17  16  15  14  13  12  11  10  09

Printed and bound in China

*In loving memory of my younger brother Miguel*
(1978–1999)

# Contents

# Extracts

# Figures and Tables

## Figures

## Tables

# Abbreviations

## Transcription conventions used in this book

| | |
|---|---|
| *CU/MS/LS* | camera close-up/medium shot/long shot |
| *MCU/MLS* | medium close-up/medium–long-range shot |
| *laughs* | paralinguistic/non-verbal features of communication |
| (vo) | narrative voice-over: off-screen delivery of talk |
| <u>word</u> | marked stress |
| WORD | increased volume |
| <slow> | markedly slow speech delivery |
| >quick< | markedly fast speech delivery |
| °quietly° | quiet speech delivery |
| ? | rising intonation |
| [ | simultaneous starting talk |
| = | latching (no discernible gap) between the end of one turn and the beginning of the next turn |
| (.) | short pause (a second or under) |
| (3.0) | longer pause, in seconds |
| mm, er . . . | filled pauses, hesitations . . . |
| (xxxx) | unclear portion of talk |
| an:::d | prolongation ('stretching') of prior syllable |
| wor- | syllable or word cut off abruptly |

# Acknowledgements

In the process of writing this book I have benefited from the help of various people and institutions. I am grateful, first of all, to the Arts and Humanities Research Council for a research leave grant, which enabled me to complete this project. I am also grateful to Kitty Van Boxel and Kate Wallis at Palgrave Macmillan for their advice in the preparation of this book. Colleagues in Applied Linguistics and Media and Communication Studies, both at Swansea University, have provided a most intellectually stimulating and supportive research environment over the years. My thanks go also to colleagues at the Universities of Canterbury, Victoria, and Auckland University of Technology, all in New Zealand, for giving me the opportunity to bounce ideas off them in the early stages of this project, especially to Allan Bell, Meredith Marra, Donald Matheson, Philippa Smith, John Read and Jim Tully. I am particularly grateful to Adam Jaworski and Kevin Williams for their helpful and constructive advice, and to Andrew Hoskins and Rob Penhallurick for their valuable suggestions on various chapters of this book.

At a personal level, I would like to thank Sonia Ferrer, Cristina Izura, Patricia Bou Franch and Gaynor Bracchi. My parents José and María Virginia have given me more than I will ever be able to thank them for. My sisters María and María José have always been there for me, as has Alejandro in recent times. The limited sleep and time that Clara's birth brought along two years ago has been more than compensated for by the perspective that her sunny personality has provided. Finally, Steve has continuously been a kindred spirit and loving pillar of support. It is to him that I am most grateful and to whom I owe the most.

NURIA LORENZO-DUS

Elsevier Ltd., for extracts from 'A rapport and impression management approach to public figures' performance of talk' (*Journal of Pragmatics*, 37 (2005), 611–35).

Granada Ventures and ITV plc, for permission to reproduce stills from an episode of *Trisha* (2004).

Granada: Comares, for extracts from 'The discourse of lifestyles in the broadcast media' (*Ways into Discourse*, P. Bou Franch (ed.) (2006b), 135–50).

Sage Publications Ltd., for extracts from 'Buying and Selling: Mediating persuasion in British property shows' (*Media, Culture and Society*, 28 (2006a), 739–61) and 'Real disorder in the court: An investigation of conflict talk in US courtroom shows' (*Media, Culture and Society*, 30 (2008), 81–108).

Every effort has been made to trace the copyright holders but, if any have been inadvertently overlooked, the authors and publishers will be pleased to make the necessary arrangements at the first opportunity.

 Arts & Humanities
Research Council

The AHRC funds postgraduate training and research in the arts and humanities, from archaeology and English literature to design and dance. The quality and range of research supported not only provides social and cultural benefits but also contributes to the economic success of the UK. For further information on the AHRC, please see our website, www.ahrc.ac.uk.

# Introduction

## 1.1 The broadcast discourse of television

This work marks the coming together of two of my great interests, namely television and talk. Of course, interest alone is not necessarily sufficient to justify a book. For me the rationale for writing this work now and in the way that I have done stems from my judgement that the study of talk in the medium of television remains comparatively limited and that a better understanding of what it is now is both important in its own right and can contribute much to debates about television as it may become.

This relative lack of extant research may initially sound strange, given the predominance of television as a medium of communication over recent decades. Let me elaborate. The study of television as a whole has actually been – and remains in the eyes of many – a somewhat dubious endeavour. Also, as Corner (1999: 121) cautions in respect of significant change in the British broadcasting context, the study of television can be seen as being 'caught in a position of double embarrassment [. . .] It has barely begun to make a full political, social, and cultural assessment of "television as we know it", yet its very object of study is shifting towards "television as we knew it" with some speed.'

Now is arguably one of those periods of substantial change in the international media landscape. On the one hand, increased competition has encouraged media providers to appeal, 'commodity-like', to specific viewers. Corner (1998: 95) refers, for example, to the process of hybridisation within the print and broadcast media, whereby elements from what previously were different conventions are combined, with the result that some traditional genres break down, 'including those dividing off "higher" from "lower" forms of demarcating the "serious" from the "entertaining" '. On the other hand, technology is enabling 'new media', which many argue will progressively challenge television's dominance as a communication medium. The advent of satellite and cable 'narrowcasting', as well as a seemingly progressive drift away from television towards the internet, are seen to pose, for example, questions about the social primacy of television.

Several implications ensue from the above, some of which are important to

1

the analysis of television talk, as we shall see in later chapters of this book. For instance, channel proliferation since the 1990s means that the number of programmes likely to be experienced by viewers 'out of time', despite being textually designed for particular schedule 'slots', has increased (e.g. Christmas episodes of recurring series being broadcast not only at Christmas) as programmes are recycled as repeats. This situation, which is likely to continue once we are 'fully immersed' in the digital era, may lead to changes in ways of expressing the referentiality of, for example, factual statements bounded in specific temporalities, such as house prices in a given property show.

Change is not *per se* a motivating factor for this book. There is already a considerable body of speculative research about the future media landscape and its drivers. Rather, *Television Discourse* is driven by a concern that the contemporary might be lost too quickly and with too little understanding to help not only current scholars to engage effectively in debates about how television talk may evolve, but also future scholars to look back and assess the impact of change on talk over time. This is why I shall examine recent and current forms of talk in specific television contexts (see Section 1.3 for my selection of these contexts).

This begs the further question of why talk is the feature of television selected for study. The answer lies principally in the relative neglect of 'form' in media research and in the general consensus within its study (when applied to radio and television) about the importance of spoken discourse. It is the latter that unites a wide range of disciplines studying 'media form', including literary criticism, applied linguistics, critical linguistics, cultural sociology/studies and media studies.[1] Spoken discourse (talk) is thus treated in this book as being responsible for generating the socio-communicative arena in which television images exist. True, it is television's distinctive ways of generating and combining images that most immediately engage viewers and secure their attention. It is, nevertheless, through its spoken discourse that 'television addresses its viewers and holds them in particular relations both to specific programmes and to channel and station identities' (Corner 1999: 37).

Given the centrality of the spoken discourse of television, it is surprising that it has not figured as strongly as it might have done in media research. There are a number of reasons for this, three of which are of special interest to this book. First, studying audio communication in media, especially sound, poses a significant methodological challenge. The multi-modal discourse of television requires competency in visual as well as audio and verbal communication (Tolson 2006). 'With speech', Tolson (2006: 5) further observes, 'there are methods for conversation and discourse analysis, but these require media students (and their teachers) to take some steps into another discipline.' The high level of interdisciplinary competence needed is thus responsible in part for the comparative scarcity of studies of television (and radio) talk over the years.

Secondly, research on media form has been criticised by some as too narrow in scope and, hence, as too limiting. Admittedly, to focus solely on texts at the expense of production and reception processes and practices undoubtedly risks missing important aspects of 'the whole picture' of television's communicative dynamic. Examining how television texts are produced is, indeed, a valuable exercise in its own right, as Born's (2004) work on the British Broadcasting Corporation (BBC) illustrates. Born's ethnographic study of this emblematic institution unveils, for example, the role of what we may term production forces in the consolidation of programme types such as docusoaps in the 1990s. Consider the following extract from an interview conducted by Born with the senior executive of BBC documentaries in 1996:

> We were trying to make very popular programmes and compete with the other side. But these shows [docusoaps such as *X Cars*] also act as valuable commissioning loss-leaders; they give me a lever to get through more serious stuff. Right now, we're making a special on Nazi gold. It's investigative, a dynamite story, front-page stuff, and very expensive to make. It's one of those things that might wither on the vine in this new BBC. Well, *X Cars* got me the money to do it. [. . .] It's a trade-off; it really is trading. (Born 2004: 437).

This quote exemplifies that there are some important factors shaping broadcast communication that studies of form (or of reception, for that matter) cannot access, but to which production studies are ideally suited. Similarly, studying how media texts are received/interpreted, or 'consumed', affords invaluable insights into many key debates in the history of media research, including the pervasive and thorny one of media influence.

As Corner (1998: 14–16) explains, much new work on media in the 1970s focused on 'language' – both on how the media used it and on the linguistic ordering of society and consciousness. Examples include the work of Lévi-Strauss in structuralist anthropology, Freud's analysis of unconsciousness, neo-Marxian concepts of ideology and the work of Barthes and Eco on semiotics. The early 1980s, however, witnessed a gradual but significant shift in media research – one spurred by the realisation of the extent to which the 'meaning' of media texts resides in acts of interpretation rather than in the texts themselves. Several lines of enquiry on the social conditions of interpretability established the implausibility of a direct media-text–influence link. Some of these lines of enquiry also, and importantly, denounced the 'negative bias syndrome' under which much research on media influence had developed. In Corner's (1999: 7) words,

> In this view of television power it is all high mountains – the varying contours of culture are ignored. In the context of the multiple, indirect ways in which cultural meanings are produced in a modern society [. . .] the general question of "influence or not?" risks banality. Enquiry into television's power needs to rid itself of some of the assumptions behind one of its key terms.

The issue at stake, in other words, is not whether television exerts a strong, misleading influence on viewers' minds and hearts. Instead, questions to be asked are: 'What kinds of power? How exercised? In support of what and against what other factors of social structure and action?' (Corner 1999: 7).

The third factor contributing to the comparative dearth of studies of media form also takes the form of a criticism: these studies too often drift into speculation about the complexities of signification, rather than centring on close textual description and/or engaging with the socio-political consequences of textual mediation. Some scholars, of course, have avoided this trap. The work of critical linguists such as Fairclough (1992, 1995, 1998, 2000), for instance, clearly counters the latter charge, for it is oriented towards the tripartite relationship that exists between texts, processes (design/production and consumption) and socio-cultural practices (how society and culture shape and are shaped by these texts). However, this has not absolved them from criticism and/or lament. Such work adopts a 'hermeneutics of suspicion', which assumes that language and the media are 'systems of representation that, in ordinary practice and use, misrepresent the reality which they re-present' (Scannell 1998: 256).[2] This critical approach to television, echoed in the traditions of critical theory and literary criticism especially, prompts Hartley (2004: 33) to observe that

> whereas many traditions of study in the general area of the arts have presumed some pleasurable investment by the student in the object of study, the textual tradition in television studies set out with the avowed intention of denouncing television and all its works [. . .] the successful student [of television] was the one who could catalogue most extensively the supposed evils associated with television, although of course these evils only affected *other* people, possibly because the students were not encouraged to watch TV themselves, only to opine haughtily about it (original emphasis).

Change, though, is in the air – and I am not just referring here to television's transformation in the era of digital, cable narrowcasting and internet platforms and the 'hype of speculation' (Geraghty and Lusted 2004: 1) that surrounds the nature, scope and development of such a transformation. Studies of media form are making a comeback.[3] Following the academic interest in language in the 1970s and the shift to interpretation in the 1980s discussed above, the 1990s experienced a quantitatively modest but qualitatively significant renewal of interest in the spoken discourse of broadcasting. Scannell's edited collection *Broadcast Talk* (1991) was the first and subsequently perhaps most influential academic book devoted exclusively to radio and television talk. It was followed by Fairclough's (1995) *Media Discourse* and Hutchby's (1996) *Confrontation Talk*. The former examined both print and broadcast contexts and, as noted earlier, considered media texts as one of three equally important aspects in the study of media discourse. The latter provided a detailed analysis of verbal confrontation in radio discourse. More recently, several projects squarely within a 'broadcast talk' research framework have focused on specific broadcast formats (e.g. Tolson's (2001a) edited volume on talk shows and Montgomery's (2007) monograph on broadcast news) or have provided overviews of the discourse of broadcasting (Hutchby 2006; Tolson 2006).[4]

*Television Discourse* builds on the momentum and the body of knowledge offered by all this research to provide – to my knowledge – the first book-length investigation specifically and thoroughly focused on television talk. It examines the relationship between the *what* and the *how* of the discourse of television. Using data from formats as diverse as make-over shows and political interviews, *Television Discourse* explores how television shapes and is shaped by the interactional exchanges that it features. It thus focuses, for example, on the interplay between the stories typically told in docusoaps (stories built around conflict–resolution structures) and the ways in which these stories are relayed in order to keep viewers switched on.

As such, *Television Discourse* is located within a body of scholarly work concerned with the analysis of media discourse, even if there is no single, overarching definition of the term 'discourse'. Indeed, discourse is conceptualised as, amongst other things, 'language above the sentence or above the clause' (Stubbs 1983: 1), 'language in use' (Brown and Yule 1983: 1), 'language use' (Fasold 1990: 65) and 'language use, whether speech or writing, seen as a type of social practice' (Fairclough 1992: 28).[5] Across definitions, one aspect recurs: discourse analysis does not examine language in the abstract but in use. The interplay between language use and the context of this use, however, is viewed differently across subdisciplines of discourse analysis.[6]

Within this discourse analysis approach, *Television Discourse* adopts a 'hermeneutics of trust' rather than of 'suspicion'. Language and media (television in this case) are seen as 'things that simply, routinely and ordinarily work (whether for or against human interests is not, in the first instance, at issue)' (Scannell 1998: 257). These two lines of enquiry need not, in fact, be seen as contradictory. As Montgomery (2007: 21) argues in the context of broadcast news, 'If we wish to understand and explain the news as a phenomenon we need thorough analysis of how it works. Criticism of the news is best conducted on adequate description of its discourse in which the full range of its communicative practices is captured.'

## 1.2   Who is talking to whom and when on television?

There is one aspect of television discourse that makes its analysis distinctive vis-à-vis that of other, unmediated, spoken discourse contexts: its double articulation. As Scannell (1991: 1) puts it, broadcast talk 'is a communicative interaction between those participating in discussion, interview, game show or whatever and, at the same time, is designed to be heard by absent audiences'. Television discourse is indeed explicitly designed and produced to be heard *and* seen by these absent audiences, which is why camera work, background music, screen graphics, language, voice quality, intonation, spatial arrangements in studio sets and performers' attire are all treated as meaning-making semiotic resources and, hence, as relevant to the analysis of the discourse of television in this book.

Consider, for example, the significant number of highly edited programmes on our television screens. The filming of each episode of property make-over shows on British television tends to last between three days and a week. Yet, its actual broadcast time is between thirty and sixty minutes, often inclusive of commercial breaks. Viewers are therefore presented with a strategically selected, arranged and articulated proportion of the entire filmed material for each episode. For instance, the 'moment of revelation' (Bonner 2003; Moseley 2000) or 'the reveal' (Spigel 2006; Heller 2007) – the moment during which the made-over property is shown to viewers and participants for the first time – is often synced with music appropriate to its interior decoration style (classical music for traditional properties, upbeat tunes for modern houses), rapidly inter-leaved long-range, medium-range and close-up shots of decorated rooms and ornamental items, and with flattering descriptions of the presenters' interior decoration achievements. Such a polished confluence of semiotic resources from different modes of communication (visual, aural, verbal) results from a range of decisions with regard to the discursive realisation of these shows.

The double articulation of television talk also makes its analysis challenging within traditional speaker–hearer models of communication, such as the one proposed by French linguist Ferdinand de Saussure in his *Course in General Linguistics* (1916). His notion of the 'speaking circuit' (1916: 11–15), unsur-prisingly given the time at which it was formulated, cannot account for the 'wittingly, knowingly *public*' (Scannell 1991: 11; original emphasis) nature of television discourse. The speaking circuit rests on the idea that concepts are transferred between two persons, 'A' and 'B'. Communication results when person 'A' encodes them through speech and person 'B' subsequently decodes them. Subsequently, more sophisticated communication models have been developed, including those by Shannon and Weaver (1949), Sebeok (1988), Sperber and Wilson (1995) and Goffman. The last one is especially relevant to our discussion of the double articulation of talk on television.

North American sociologist Erving Goffman did not set out to model spoken communication *per se* but a significant part of his work did investigate the particulars of how people talk to each other in given social encounters. In *Forms of Talk*, for example, Goffman (1981) explored the interplay between three general themes to investigate talk, namely:

- the ability of talk to be other- or self-referential, which he termed the 'embedding capacity' of talk;
- 'the moments, looks and vocal sounds we make as an unintended by-prod-uct of speaking and listening . . . acquire a specialized communicative role in the stream of our behaviour' (1981: 2), which he collectively designated as a 'ritualisation process';
- the 'participation framework' of talk, which he loosely described thus: 'When a word is spoken, all those who happen to be in the perceptual range of the event will have some sort of participation status relative to it.' (1981: 3)

For Goffman, the traditional notions of speaker and hearer were too simplis-tic. He replaced them respectively with those of the 'production format' and the 'participation framework' (for the reception of talk). He divided the production format into three roles: 'animator', 'author' and 'principal'. These respectively designate 'the sounding box from which utterances come', 'the agent who puts together, composes, or scripts the lines that are uttered' and 'the party to whose position, stand, and belief the words attest' (Goffman 1981: 226).

Goffman also identified the roles of 'ratified' and 'unratified' recipient. The former refers to the 'official' or intended receivers of a message, who can be either 'addressed' or 'unaddressed'. Addressed receivers are those 'to whom the speaker addresses his visual attention and to whom, incidentally, he expects to turn over his speaking role' (1981: 132). Unaddressed receivers are any of the other 'official hearers' in a given communicative exchange, even those who may not be actually listening' (1981: 133). Unratified recipients, for their part, are those non-official, unintended recipients of talk and can be either 'overhearers' ('inadvertent', 'non-official' listeners or bystanders) or 'eavesdroppers' ('engineered', 'non-official' followers of talk) (1981: 132).

Goffman stressed that production and reception roles are interactionally fluid. Interactants can – and regularly do – shift between them, engaging on each occasion in what he called a 'shift of footing': 'a change in the alignment we take up to ourselves and the others present as expressed in the way we manage the production or reception of an utterance' (1981: 128).

Goffman's participation framework presents distinctive advantages over speaker–hearer communication models but it is not without its own limitations. As evident in the above set of definitions, for example, he used the term 'participation framework' in his writings to refer to the production and reception of talk at times but at other times only to the latter. Also, Goffman did not examine in detail how the different roles that comprise given participation frameworks are actually enacted. This, as Levinson (1988: 221) notes, can pose a number of analytic complications because 'Having a set of participant role categories is one thing – but working out who stands in which when can be quite another, in a vastly greater plane of complexity.'

Subsequent studies of television discourse have explicitly taken on the task of understanding such complexity. They have sought to describe how participant roles and alignments are achieved in interaction, for they are not allocated unilaterally. Goffman's disaggregation of the traditional speaker role, for example, has led to a better understanding of how those 'doing speaking' on television may accomplish specific interactional tasks. Interviewers of politicians, for instance, have been found to be able to escape accusations of bias by formulating challenging questions in formally neutral ways. These often include shifts of footing, whereby interviewers retain, for instance, the role of talk animators but attribute talk authorship to a third party (see Chapter 10). Goffman's disaggregation of the traditional hearer role has also paved the way for more nuanced analyses of television interaction. His roles of the 'overhearer' or 'eavesdropper', for example, have been used to describe and examine the various parts played by television's non-co-present audiences – its viewers – in the performance of television talk (e.g. Heritage 1985; Heritage and Roth 1995; Illie 1999).

Goffman-influenced work at establishing 'who stands in which when' in television discourse has consistently upheld the need to include all those 'who happen to be in the perceptual range of [a television communication] event' (1981: 3). Yet, possibly because much of this work has focused on the actual structures of talk-in-interaction, it has seemingly assigned primacy to the 'local' over the 'broadcast' dimension of television discourse.

Thus, for instance, whilst separating author and animator roles within the talk produced by individuals on our screens has proved helpful, there is more to each of these roles within the double articulation of television talk. If all talk on television is explicitly intended to be heard and seen by absent audiences, then all of those talking on it are always its 'sounding boxes' – its animators. Programme producers, researchers, scriptwriters and so on are all its authors – the different incarnations of the 'agent who puts together, composes, or scripts the lines that are uttered' on television. This, which is evident in relation to dramas, soap operas and other forms of fiction programming, may be only implicit in a number of non-fiction programmes.[7] Moreover, because all television talk is primarily intended for absent audiences, and therefore does not benefit from their instant reactions to it, animation is both particularly 'self-conscious' (Scannell 1991) and varied, ranging from attempts to conceal it from viewers to those that make it fully explicit.

Similarly, being able to identify the various reception roles in which viewers are positioned within and across forms of talk on television has proved advantageous. But treating viewers either as overhearers or as eavesdroppers on the grounds of their physical non-co-presence is misleading, if understandable. In Goffman's participation framework, the roles of overhearer and eavesdropper are placed within the position of unratified (unofficial, unintended) receivers of talk. Since the nature and function of television is to broadcast, these viewers are by definition ratified (official, intended) receivers of television talk. They can therefore never be overhearers/eavesdroppers, however often they may be made to feel so in the current television climate of 'closeness' and 'voyeurism'. The standard term in much media research – overhearing audience – is thus somewhat inadequate, even if it has become widespread and for that reason also convenient. Hutchby (2006: 167), for example, suggests replacing it with the term 'distributed recipients' on account of the fact that talk on radio and television belongs to a 'broader category of *mediated and distributed talk-in-interaction*' (original emphasis).

## 1.3    Scope and structure of the book

*Television Discourse* examines a selection of television texts from a range of terrestrial channels and programmes broadcast in the US and the UK and, to a lesser extent, in New Zealand. These texts amount to a relatively small, but nevertheless representative, sample of a much larger reference corpus of video recordings of television programmes that I have collected and transcribed over the past fifteen years or so for teaching and research purposes.[8] In selecting specific programme types, I have sought to be as inclusive as possible within certain parameters.

First, and as in the 'broadcast talk research tradition', I have excluded all forms of fictional programming. This is because fictional dramatisations (soap operas, situation comedies, dramas, commercials, etc.) explicitly create their own worlds, putting boundaries around them through overtly scripted dialogue. The wealth of non-fictional material examined is rather diverse in nature but united in the 'sociability' (Scannell 1996) of its communicative ethos. Whilst different realisations of this sociability apply, news, political interviews, lifestyle shows, courtroom shows and other forms of non-fictional programming considered in *Television Discourse* are all in the business of creating relations, as it were, across the screen. They are also 'loosely' scripted to varying degrees. Television news broadcasts featuring interviews between a live news presenter and a news reporter, for instance, are known to include some questions from the former to the latter that have been prepared in advance (Tuggle et al. 2004).

Secondly, because *Television Discourse* focuses on contemporary television talk, I have largely drawn upon output that is 'on air' at the time of writing. On those occasions when output no longer on air is examined, I have selected programmes that are representative of a current programme type and that were (and remain in general) well-known in their country of origin and/or have been exported to other countries. In my discussion of storytelling in audience discussion talk shows, for example, I have used extracts from *Ricki Lake* (US) and *Kilroy* (UK). Both shows were taken off the air in 2004 for different reasons but had been very popular (inter)nationally: *Ricki Lake* had been aired on British television and Kilroy used to run some episodes in Australia under the series title *Kilroy Down Under.*

It is important to emphasise, moreover, that extracts are selected in order to *illustrate a range of points* rather than to provide evidence for points that support preconceived ideological interpretations. Data in this book is considered as being representative of wider tendencies. *Television Discourse* focuses on four particular features that recur in the reference corpus from which the extracts come, namely storytelling, closeness, conflict and persuasion. Although these features are interconnected to different degrees, they are successively examined in the four parts of *Television Discourse* for clarity of exposition. Each book part comprises an introductory chapter and two further chapters. The introductory chapter provides a conceptual background to the relevant feature of television discourse that the two subsequent chapters examine in relation to particular contexts of use, be it specific television formats (e.g. daytime talk shows) or forms of talk therein (e.g. confessional monologues). Chapter 14 explicitly interweaves the four features of television discourse and places them within a discussion of three emergent themes in the book: emotion, morality and reality.

*Television Discourse* is not therefore intended to be an examination of the talk of particular types or varieties of television programming. Whilst some chapters share one particular television format, they examine different aspects of talk therein. For instance, the discourse of the news is analysed vis-à-vis two features: closeness and persuasion. In the former, live interactions between newsreaders and news reporters are investigated against a television ethos of sociability (see Chapter 6). In the latter, sound-bites featuring politicians talking are explored vis-à-vis television's persuasion potential.

Connected to the above, the synergetic relationship between television and politics is the principal reason why the analysis of various forms of political communication in different television contexts features across parts and chapters of this book. To varying degrees, political communication has always involved the media, be it propaganda pamphlets, political radio broadcasts, press releases, political parties' internet sites or televised political interviews, to name but a few examples. But in most democracies nowadays, politics and the media have become so entwined that a new concept has been specifically coined to capture their mutually shaping relationship: the 'mediaisation' of politics. Broadly speaking, this either refers to the democracy-enhancing role of the media or, as it is used in *Television Discourse*, to the consequences of the colonisation of politics by the public relations (PR) industry. The policy elites' need to 'steer the masses' through persuasive communication strategies and the use of PR techniques are not new phenomena. Well-known past examples include the political oratory of Adolf Hitler and the Nazi propaganda machinery. Nevertheless, in the contemporary era the strategies for communicatively selling political ideas and images through the mass media have increased in number, range and sophistication.

From a political point of view, then, the media are potentially very useful. They can help to create consent and build mass legitimacy. A full gamut of PR techniques is thus deployed by politicians to project appealing political images (see Chapter 12) and to integrate journalists into the distraction machinery of politics (Louw 2005). From the media's point of view, journalists are far from innocent bystanders. Instead, and on the grounds of their claimed societal watch-dog role, they often play the part of a 'pack of wolves' (Partington 2003). They incessantly question politicians about their conduct and try to uncover flaws in the political process (see Chapter 10). They also engage in strategic acts of metarepresentation, through which they project particular political values (see Chapter 12).

Alongside 'serious' television formats, such as the news and those concerning politics, this book examines different formal properties of a number of 'banal' television formats, often collectively known as reality television. This term was initially applied to a sort of 'direct television' that originated in North America and which used footage of the purportedly everyday activities of people at the 'business end' of public service activities – police and emergency response workers. Programmes such as *Cops* (US) were, in the early 1990s, loosely imitated in other countries (e.g. *Crimewatch* in the UK and *Emergency Rescue* in Australia). They soon also diversified into multiple formats, from docusoaps (e.g. *Airport*) and reality game shows (e.g. *Survivor, Big Brother*) to make-over shows (e.g. *Extreme Makeover, Changing Rooms*) and talent shows (e.g. *Popstars, Pop Idol, The X-Factor*). The hybridisation that characterises the above and similar shows has produced certain terminological confusion regarding the broad category of reality television – some programmes, for instance, simply sit somewhat awkwardly with their labelling, others are hard to label. Bonner (2003: 3) uses the term 'ordinary television' to refer to a 'critically disregarded' set of programmes which 'operate as non-fiction', that is, which 'may be well scripted but [. . .] attempt truth claims'. The central characteristics of ordinary television include the 'direct address of the audience, the incorporation of ordinary people into the programme and the mundanity of its concerns.'[9]

Several aspects of the discourse of ordinary, or reality, shows are explored across the chapters in this book. This reflects not only their pervasiveness but also, in the highly intertextual medium of television, the provision by these shows of fascinating insights into the relationship between discourse, media and society. The discourse of today's lifestyle programmes in the UK, for example, echoes that of the 1960s DIY (Do It Yourself) shows. As Parts II and IV of this book argue, however, the instructional talk of the latter has been adapted in various ways to provide explicit practices of confession (see Chapter 7) and guidance (see Chapter 13) that may be seen as reflective and constitutive of the contemporary social practices of, respectively, moral surveillance and lifestyle coaching.

Last but not least, the Glossary and the Guide to Further Reading are intended to ease the passage of the reader through the following pages. Each of the chapters of *Television Discourse* is structured around a small number of video-recorded examples. I have thoroughly contextualised all the texts (extracts) selected for analysis for the benefit of those readers unfamiliar with the material. A summary of their co-text (the text before the extracts) precedes them, as well as an explanation of the nature of the programmes from which they have been taken. The extracts have been transcribed 'parsimoniously', that is, so as to render their analysis both meaningful and intelligible (O'Connell and Kowal 1995). Such an approach can be criticised for exemplifying a selective set of discourse features and, hence, for being biased. A transcript, though, is always an artefact of the analyst's own categorisation and selection processes and will therefore always remain an interpretation rather than a faithful reproduction of the primary data (Ochs 1979): video-recorded tapes, in my case. As Bucholtz (2000: 1439) argues, a reflexive transcription practice, as part of a reflexive discourse analysis, 'requires awareness and acknowledgement of the limitations of one's own transcriptional choices'. I agree with Coates and Thornborrow (1999) that, rather than being a problem, the latter is a necessity. There is no such thing as a perfect transcript – a 'true' written version of spoken interaction. Instead, transcribing is a partial, on-going process.

The transcription conventions used in *Television Discourse*, therefore, seek to facilitate comprehension (Cook 1999) but do not include more details than those required (Stubbs 1983). The transcription of linguistic and paralinguistic resources, for instance, has been slightly simplified from Jefferson's system (in Atkinson and Heritage 1984). The transcription of visual (including non-verbal) semiotic resources features prominently, has evolved from my own work on television discourse over the years, and builds on standard terms in the field as far as television's images and camera angles are concerned, such as medium angle, close-up, and camera zoom in/out. Although verbal, visual and sonic modes of communication are obviously realised simultaneously in my video recordings, they have been transcribed in parallel columns to aid readability. Starting from the left-hand side, the first column of each extract in the book contains a description of visual and aural resources: camera work, spatial arrangements, non-verbal signs of communication (such as gaze and hand gestures), the presence and volume of background music, and so forth. All of these are italicised. The second and third columns include the line numbers and initials of the speakers, respectively. The last column is the actual talk. Non-verbal behaviour appears occasionally in this fourth column in order to improve the readability of the transcript (for example, when the left-hand column already contains a significant amount of information) but remains italicised for consistency and clarity. An explanatory list of all the transcription conventions used in the extracts of this book is also provided on page xi.

# Part I

## Storytelling

# Storytelling . . . or the Entertaining Construction of Reality

> We dream in narrative, daydream in narrative, remember, anticipate, hope, believe, doubt, plan, revise, criticise, gossip, learn, hate and love by narrative. (Hardy 1968: 5)

Stories pervade our lives, so much so that storytelling is often regarded as an intrinsic aspect of the human mind. The ubiquity of storytelling owes obviously to its entertainment value but also to its importance in affording us a sense of ourselves in the world. Stories are discursive canvases upon which we paint our portraits – and those of others – for public evaluation. As sociolinguist Deborah Schiffrin (1996: 199) puts it, stories are 'a linguistic lens through which to discover people's own (somewhat idealised) views of themselves as situated in a social structure'. The practice of storytelling is therefore inherently partisan and its outcome always an artifice: the result of selecting and constructing material, and of discarding a number of alternative constructions.

Given that oral storytelling is one of the oldest forms of communication, why should it feature in an investigation of contemporary television discourse? The answer is twofold. First, television as a whole offers a kind of supernarrative – one that encapsulates different narratives therein (programmes), which in turn embed a number of discrete stories.[1] The entertainment value of storytelling at each of these levels is vital to keeping viewers switched on, which explains why television constantly searches for new ways of telling stories, as well as recycling old formulae. Documentaries, for example, have since the 1990s undergone an explicit process of 'narratisation'. Writing about BBC documentaries in this period, Born (2004: 431) observes that 'the concept of "the story" became ubiquitous among producers to the point of obsession: "getting the story right" and "finding strong characters" were prime concerns'. During this period, too, documentaries began to rely increasingly upon celebrities as on-screen narrators as a means to broaden the appeal of the stories that they told (see Chapter 3). Likewise, talk shows emphasise personal-experience stories. This follows and reinforces a contemporary trend towards considering first-hand experience talk as both a more enjoyable and a more valid form of talk than abstract argumentation (see Chapters 4, 7 and 9).

**15**

Secondly, television storytelling performs a clear identity-construction role – an ideological bardic function (Fiske and Hartley 1978). Through the stories told in travel documentaries, for instance, specific personal and social identities are constructed, which viewers are able to evaluate as more or less congruous with their own identities and the social groups to which they belong. Similarly, in talk shows, a concatenation of personal-experience stories around a given issue (e.g. unemployment) or identity (e.g. parenting) is used to construct particular versions of reality and specific identities, against which viewers may position their own day-to-day realities and identities.

Television thus uses storytelling to construct socially situated identities in enjoyable, cognitively simple ways. Whilst this applies both to fiction and non-fiction programming, the focus in this part of the book is on the latter: on story-telling in programmes which claim to show the 'world out there'. This is not because of questions regarding the veracity of storytelling *per se* in these programmes but because of the potential clash between their claims to depicting reality and the constructed nature of all storytelling.

The so-called 'assertive stance to reality' (Plantiga 1997: 40) claimed by a number of documentaries, for example, is premised on viewer acceptance of there being strong connections between cinematic record and reality. Several built-in signals encourage viewers to accept this stance. These include pro-filmic and filmic conventions that seek to increase the viewers' sense of being in the socio-historical world being shown on their screens. Pro-filmic or 'in front of the lens' conventions include location shooting, eye-witnesses being interviewed on-camera, presenters addressing the camera directly, and scripted, voice-over narration. Filmic conventions concern stylistic choices during filming, such as use of the 'natural lighting' (as opposed to the controlled lighting of feature films) to create ungraceful shadows, and of hand-held or shoulder-mounted cameras to produce jagged movements. These and other techniques seek to create an impression of actuality. They deliberately de-emphasise aesthetics to produce the 'discourse of sobriety' that is associated with documentaries (Nichols 1991).

Not all documentaries follow such a discourse of sobriety, though. Conventions from fiction are also drawn upon in some of them, such as recon-structions and the use of actors (rather than real people) as characters. Many natural history documentaries, too, introduce dramatic music at key moments and use sophisticated filming techniques. They also, as in for example fairytales, at times anthropomorphise animals, giving them endearing human attributes and names. The New Zealand documentary *The Secret Life of a Kiwi* (2003), for instance, portrayed footage of two kiwi birds and their offspring over a two-and-a-half-year period as an exciting tale of family survival whose characters were endowed with human-like attributes: the supportive male Joe, 'his' partner and diligent working mother Maggie, and their 'children', as reflected in names such as Snoopy.

Interestingly, the referentiality and propositionality of documentaries remains largely unchallenged, even when fictional conventions are drawn upon. In history documentaries, for example, edited black-and-white photographs and newsreel footage of past events and characters are used as devices through which viewers may access that past. Likewise, the speeding up of the life of a plant in the footage of many a natural history documentary is not meant to signal that the documentary in question is not truthful to that plant's life-cycle. Instead, it is treated as a production technique that facilitates viewers' 'direct' access to the wildlife world. The much-praised BBC documentary series *Planet Earth* (2005–2006), for instance, employed a range of filming techniques that were anything but 'sober': seas froze and thawed within seconds as an off-screen narrator described what was happening, close-ups from within holes underground showed in incredible detail how rare birds' eggs hatched, and powerful melodramatic music increased and decreased its volume to match the mood of the narration and the images shown.

As if concerned that all the above might jeopardise the belief that the documentary was accessing the natural world 'directly', however, each *Planet Earth* episode featured a final section ('The Planet Earth Diaries') which revealed some of the ways in which the world out there had been made 'directly' accessible to viewers. In an episode on Antarctica, for example, the Diaries section highlighted the cameramen's struggles when filming in the middle of a snow blizzard and their rescuing a baby penguin trapped in a hole. The latter was explicitly justified by the off-screen narrator on the grounds that the film crew had become emotionally attached to the penguins that they had spent six months filming in truly inhospitable conditions. By 'coming clean' about its 'meddling with' the natural world, *Planet Earth* sought to assert its realist stance further.

The idea of 'true' or 'realist' storytelling – the brief discussion above suffices to indicate – is far from straightforward as regards non-fiction television. As was argued in Chapter 1, all television output is designed and produced to meet the perceived needs of its main intended recipients: the viewers. This in practice means drawing upon and making use of the socio-historical world in different ways: editing those aspects that may not be sufficiently entertaining, highlighting others that may increase ratings, and so forth. In these circumstances, storytelling cannot be simply a matter of telling 'true' stories about the 'real' world. Nor can these stories be constructed in the same ways across all programmes. A particular form of talk, say the disclosure of personal information, may be seen to provide direct access to participants' real lives and feelings in talk shows. That same form of talk, however, may be seen to enable celebrities to perform a moralistic discourse and hence promote their professional careers in the context of a celebrity chat show. The remaining two chapters in this part of the book, then, explore storytelling in specific television formats, namely documentaries and daytime talk shows. This necessitates some words of introduction to both.

Talk shows, as their term suggests, fuse conversation and the interpersonal with mass-mediated spectacle. Storytelling in these shows helps to move guests' talk away from general discussions to emotional accounts. This has a voyeuristic and cathartic appeal, as well as the potential for entertainment. Concomitantly, storytelling is the principal vehicle by which individuals in the talk shows' studios may access the speaking floor. It is interesting to note that talk show guests regularly use two types of stories – personal and positional – to express their opinions and, through these, to construct their identities vis-à-vis those of other guests. Personal stories generally occur at the beginning of their speaking turns and tend to be preceded by discourse markers such as 'well' or 'well er . . .', which function as warrants for guests to access the programmes' talk and to 'legitimise any subsequent position they will take up in the debate' (Thornborrow 1997: 259). Positional stories tend to occur within longer turn sequences and to contain evaluations that both position guests and serve as 'pivotal utterances which contribute to the dynamic of the talk by enabling other speakers to respond with opposing points of view' (1997: 258). Through these personal and positional stories, talk shows construct particular identities and versions of reality in entertaining fashion.

Documentaries are in principle about truthfully recording the socio-historical world and are therefore sometimes structured as journalistic chronicles, written histories or legal case records, that is, as argumentative, factual texts (Kilborn and Izod 1997). Frequently, however, the discursive task of documenting the world is accomplished through storytelling. Nichols' (1991) and Winston's (1995) major studies in documentary form show, in fact, that documentaries are always narrativised. Similarly, Corner (1999: 56) notes that nowadays stories are used across documentary varieties, albeit in different ways and with different degrees of 'thickness'. 'To produce a good documentary', BBC documentary producer Marc Edwards also explains, 'you need a convincing story into which to weave the various pieces of recorded evidence. Without a story, there is no documentary.'[2] Consider, for instance, the sequel to the 2003 award-winning BBC documentary *Motherland*, entitled *Motherland: Moving On* (2004). This recorded a period of time in the lives of three black people (two British, one Caribbean), who volunteered to have their DNA sequences matched with DNA samples from other individuals across the globe. The documentary used a chronologically ordered, simple narrative structure to deal with the complex issues of national and ethnic identity arising from now being able to trace one's genetic ancestry back in time. Given the tendency of viewers to infer causality from temporal sequencing (Kozloff 1992), storytelling in *Motherland: Moving On* constructed specific interpretative paths for its viewers. Each of the three stories in the documentary had a point – a narrative evaluation or 'so what?' in Labovian (1972a) terms.[3] Internal evaluation was conducted by the three people concerned, who were regularly shown relaying their views and feelings on camera. External evaluation was conducted by an off-screen narrator, who commented on the significance of the events shown on screen – including the characters' internal evaluations.

The importance of storytelling in constructing a social sense of self was evident in *Motherland: Moving On*. Only two of the three people tested were revealed to have African genetic ancestry and, after meeting and interacting over a couple of weeks with contemporary descendants of their own 'genetic family', they extensively and emotionally reported on their newly gained identity. Their three personal-experience stories, moreover, acted as evidence-building case studies around the issue of the current and projected use of DNA testing.

For daytime talk shows and documentaries, then, storytelling is a crucial means to a range of ends: to build evidence-based argumentation, to position oneself vis-à-vis others, to present information in enjoyable, memorable ways, to intensify a sense of argument development, and so on. It is also a particularly useful way of seeking to assert the realism of these programmes, even in the explicit face of the use of both fiction (e.g. sophisticated filming techniques in documentaries) and overtly staged performances (e.g. stilted delivery styles by some guests in daytime talk shows).

In both television contexts, what is more, storytelling operates at two levels: taleworld and storyrealm (Young 1987). In the former, the programmes may be regarded as stories in their own right, with their own characters and plotlines. Its characters may be seen to be unaware of their being in a tale. They may be said to 'enter into it as real, engaging in a realm to be experienced by its inhabitants as a reality' (Young 1987: 16). In the latter, each programme may be seen to function as a discourse space in which discrete instances of storytelling take place – as 'an enclave of conversation, one orienting to another realm, the Taleworld' (1987: 15).

Let us consider these two levels – or realms – further in our chosen programme formats. Documentaries' taleworlds often use conflict–resolution structures. Initially identified by Franco-Bulgarian structuralist Tzevtan Todorov as the minimal plot for the archetypal realist fiction narrative, at its simplest this narrative structure goes from an equilibrium state A to an equilibrium state C through a middle disequilibrium state B. For Todorov (1975, 1981), realist fiction narratives revolve around finding order in a world temporarily in chaos – a process that involves five parts. The beginning of a narrative typically involves a stable situation or 'equilibrium' (part 1). This, Todorov explains, is next disturbed by some power or force, which results in a state of 'disequilibrium' (part 2). The following state involves 'recognition' that a disordering event has taken place (part 3). In the next state, efforts are made at 'restoration' (part 4). Finally, a 'resolution' emerges (part 5) that involves a return to a different state of equilibrium from that in part 1.

The popular New Zealand series *Heartland* illustrates the relative ease with which Todorov's narrative structure can be applied to the taleworld of many a documentary.[4] The stories told in *Heartland* used conflict–resolution structures to address contemporary national identity challenges posed to New Zealand society by a combination of post-colonial anxieties, such as the Treaty of Waitangi, the rise of Maori nationalism and various waves of immigration (Smith 2005, 2006). Each of the episodes began with scenic imagery of the landscape in the communities visited and a narrator's introduction that included historical information and interviews with some of the locals. This established the initial state of equilibrium, which portrayed the image of New Zealand frequently used in advertising: a land of outstanding beauty and friendly, down-to-earth people (Bell 1999). The disequilibrium state was next introduced by bringing up some problem (for example, high levels of unemployment) in these otherwise perfect communities. At this juncture, anxiety was raised through the recognition that the images and interactions in the initial state of equilibrium were not all that idyllic. Such recognition of the disordering event built narrative momentum and kept viewers' attention focused on possible ways in which the disequilibrium could be overcome. Three-quarters of the way through each episode, a resolution began to emerge and eventually prevailed. This resolution invariably entailed an optimistic prognosis for the country – a bright future for all New Zealanders. Through a narrative structure that was able to find order in a world temporarily in chaos, therefore, each of the episodes of *Heartland* created a sense of security in the audience. This documentary series emphasised that, with a bit of Kiwi spirit and acting together as a nation, internal differences and problems could be solved. The 'imagined' community presented in the *Heartland* taleworld reinforced a sense of belonging to a real multicultural community of New Zealanders with a positive future (Smith 2005).

Each talk show episode, too, can be conceived of as a taleworld structured around conflict and resolution. Indeed, a number of parallels between the narrative structure of talk shows and that of mythic romantic narratives have been identified. In both, for example, the story begins with an issue or topic that is seen to be causing difficulties for some people. These are the lay participants in the talk show and the inhabitants of the mythical kingdom in the romantic narrative.[5] The identity of some of these participants is constructed in talk shows to mirror that of the fairytale hero in mythic romantic narratives: a 'small child lost in the wood who by dint of only ordinary cleverness and great good luck manages to find her way home again' (Livingstone and Lunt 1994: 61). As in romantic mythic narratives, too, the taleworld of daytime talk shows is one in which characters embark upon journeys of discovery. Along these journeys, they encounter one or more villains. In the show examined by Livingstone and Lunt (*Kilroy*), the villains are the various experts in the studio. In other talk shows, for example in 'tabloid' talk shows such as *The Jerry Springer Show*, lay participants themselves are polarised into victims and villains.

At the centre of all the unfolding action, and regardless of the variety of talk show, is the figure of the talk show host: the mythical hero. A problem-free character, the host is in a position of superiority and, as the heroes of mythic romantic narratives, is adored and/or envied and has his/her judgements unchallenged. Towards the end of each episode, the host steps out of character and addresses the viewers directly. In doing so, the host provides a discursive bridge – a Labovian 'coda' (1972a) – from the show's taleworld to the show's storyrealm.[6] In shows like *Kilroy*, the host's coda generally consists of a brief address to camera delivered on stage and as though it were unscripted. In others, such as *The Jerry Springer Show*, it is designed as a distinctive, scripted segment of the show: 'Jerry's Final Thoughts'. It is performed to camera, off-stage and as though it were a brief homily. The importance of these codas is unquestionable. They, as per Labov's definition of a 'good coda', not only solve the mechanical problem of ending a story (a talk show episode) but also seek to leave the listeners (the viewers) 'with a feeling of satisfaction and completeness that matters have been rounded off and accounted for' (1972a: 366).

As storyrealms, documentaries and talk shows include a number of discrete stories about the world out there. The 'reportability' (Labov 1972a) or 'tellability' (Toolan 1988) of these stories is determined by set criteria, although a certain degree of variability exists to account for the idyiosyncracies of each show. Unlike most storytelling in free conversation, for example, talk show stories do not always need to be directly relevant to the programmes' discussion topics. Lay participants' emotional expression of their views may offset their telling stories that are only tangentially related to the general discussion in the studios. Nor do talk show stories always need to be new to all their recipients in the studio. Hosts are generally privy to the main – if not all – developments in the various stories prior to the participants telling them, which often makes talk show storytelling a case of host-directed co-narration (see Chapter 4).

The storyrealm of documentaries, for its part, revolves principally around the figure of the narrator, of which there are two generic types: heterodiegetic and homodiegetic (Kozloff 1992). The former detach themselves from the stories that they tell and also from the recipients of these stories (the viewers). Popularly known as 'voice of God', they are often off-screen tellers whose voices guide viewers through the documentary. Their physical detachment and general anonymity is designed to instil a sense of authority into their stories and, through this, to make truth claims about the socio-historical world.

As for homodiegetic narrators, they become personally involved in their acts of telling. In some cases, for example in some wild-life documentaries, they tell a story about a given animal species directly to the viewers through the camera. In others, they actually double as characters in the stories that they also tell. Homodiegetic narration thus blurs the boundaries between the documentary taleworld, the storyrealm and the world out there. Personal involvement – as opposed to the sense of detached authority of heterodiegetic narration – is the main means by which documentaries that rely on homodiegetic narration try to assert their realism.

This chapter has established the rationale for investigating storytelling in non-fiction television formats and has introduced the main theoretical underpinnings for its analysis in documentaries and daytime talk shows. It is now time to delve into some of the issues raised. The next two chapters do so. They examine how language, image and sound come together in particular instances of documentary and talk show storytelling to construct in entertaining ways specific versions of reality and particular identities. Chapter 3 examines conflict–resolution narrative structures in a British docusoap, paying attention to their role in presenting the docusoap taleworld as not only a truthful but also an exciting depiction of the world out there. It also illustrates different modes of documentary narration. Chapter 4 investigates some of the key semiotic resources by which lay participants and hosts contribute to the overarching narrative of daytime talk shows. Issues of tellability and co-narration inform most of the analysis in this chapter, as they are centrally connected to the shows' mediation of the world being talked about. The chapter also explores the connection between personal-experience storytelling and the performance of teller identities in ways that come across as 'authentic'. This takes the analysis into the discussion of a much-debated topic in studies of media (broadcast) discourse: authentic talk.

# Once Upon a Time in a Documentary

In the previous chapter, we saw that documentaries do not necessarily provide the most objective and accurate recording possible of the socio-historical world. Yet, many of them are visually, acoustically and verbally designed and produced as though they do.[1] To this end, they draw upon discourses of sobriety and fiction. The latter do not appear to jeopardise their truth/realism claims. Instead, they seemingly support them. It is against this background of 'fictional realism' (Corner 1995) that documentary storytelling is explored in sections 3.1 and 3.2 of this chapter.

Section 3.1 draws upon earlier discussion of the use of realist fiction narrative structures in documentaries. Through the analysis of several extracts from an episode of one of the pioneering and subsequently most successful ongoing docusoaps in the UK, *Airport*, this section explores how the mundane taleworld of the docusoap is transformed into an action-packed, suspense-ridden one. Section 3.2 questions the traditional distinction between heterodiegetic and homodiegetic narration as being necessarily marked by, respectively, positions of detachment and involvement. The data used in this section of the chapter consists of illustrative extracts from two popular BBC documentary series: *Planet Earth* and *Michael Palin's around the World in Eighty Days*.

## 3.1  How to make dullness gripping

Docusoaps began on British television in the early 1990s, although their success soon spawned copies in countries such as New Zealand and the United States (Roscoe and Hight 2001). These programmes share some features of observational documentary and of soap opera. Like observational documentary, docusoaps claim to record slices of naturally occurring life by allowing the camera to be around and to 'speak for itself'. And like soap operas, they are multi-part series that revolve around a number of recurring characters whose stories are interleaved (Winston 2000). Docusoaps typically deal with banal topics and the mundane working lives of ordinary folk. They are frequently based on life at large institutions, especially public services such as health and traffic control.

Major crises and life-changing moments, regularly found in classic realist fiction, are therefore not what docusoaps ought to be about. Yet storytelling in docusoaps often revolves around a number of 'major' conflicts (or problems) and their subsequent 'dramatic' resolution. Their taleworld tends broadly to follow, in other words, Todorov's model of narrative structure for fictional works. Why is this the case? And how is this model tailored to the demands of this popular documentary variety?

To answer the above questions, let us consider three extracts from the opening (Extract 3.1), the middle (Extract 3.2) and the closing (Extract 3.3) sequences of the first episode of the fifth series of *Airport* (BBC). The extracts come from two stories in this episode. The first story concerns an animal health officer at London Heathrow airport, Stuart King (K), dealing with an emergency call regarding a dog (Finn) which has escaped from its flight basket. The second story revolves around another Heathrow airport employee, John Cullen (C), who has been asked to look after the Irish Olympic team between their arrival at, and their departure from, the airport.

Docusoaps quickly introduce and dramatically evaluate the disequilibrium state in their stories. In Extract 3.1 (see p. 24), for example, and immediately after the opening credits, an off-screen narrator informs viewers of a looming crisis (lines 01–03). The disordering force of this narrative event – a dog running around one of the airport terminals – is readily evaluated as an 'emergency' (line 02). When the dog is next spotted 'close to the landing runway' (line 27), the narrator's evaluation increases the drama, as shown by his slow, emphatic delivery of its being '<a very se::rious matter>' (lines 28–29). The consequences of this disrupting force are equally dramatised: 'if it's not caught and gets onto the runway (.) all landing aircraft may have to be diverted (3.0)' (lines 29–32). A clever combination of verbal and visual devices increases the disequilibrium force of this event. The utterance 'all landing aircraft may have to be diverted' co-occurs with images of several airborne aeroplanes, thus implying that they are circling the airport as if waiting to land. Since the dog has not gone on to the runway at this stage, and no other similar 'serious matter' has been reported, these must be library pictures, which have been added after filming. However, their presentation alongside verbal commentary of hypothetical mayhem that is coded as contemporaneous to the time of telling means that these images contribute to dramatising the disequilibrium state in the story about the lost dog. As a result, the humdrum routine of a service company employee is transformed into a potentially dangerous adventure for a docusoap hero.

As for the story about the Irish Olympic team, it too is quickly introduced and dramatically evaluated. It starts with an interview to camera of John Cullen (lines 17–23). Cullen is unknown to the viewers at this stage but his uniform instantly establishes his identity as one of the characters in *Airport*. His evaluation of the Irish Olympic team's having a party in a British airport before departing on an Australian airline as 'rather strange' (line 17) and as 'a bit bizarre' (line 19) creates anticipation concerning the likely nature of the disequilibrium force around which this story will revolve. A brief cut back to the first story at this stage (lines 24–32) builds up the suspense before viewers are

## Airport (2000)

[The extract reproduces the first two minutes of the episode. N: narrator; K: Stuart King; C: John Cullen; D: Driver]

| | | | |
|---|---|---|---|
| CU – K, at wheel of jeep. LS – rescue vehicle through car windscreen. CU from left – K, smiling to camera as he drives. | 01<br>02<br>03<br>04<br>05<br>06<br>07 | N (vo)<br><br><br>K | animal health officer Stuart King has been called to an emergency at the other side of the airfield (.)<br>this is the only time I'm obviously allowed to drive on the runway (.) er (.) and also breaking the speed limit in a <u>big</u> way (.) so it's an emergency and I've got an escort |
| LS – rescue vehicle through windscreen. CU – K, to unseen interviewer. CU – steering wheel. LS – jeep drives away from camera. CU – aeroplane wheels touch down. | 08<br>09<br>10<br>11<br>12<br>13<br>14<br>15<br>16 | K (vo)<br><br>K<br><br>K (vo) | I can er (.) do it (.) er (.) just had a report that there's a loose dog running around terminal four (.) er (.) I think it's esc- as far as they're aware (.) it's escaped from the plane (.) I'm just trying to get over these as quick as I can (2.0) *(distant sound of jeep engine)*<br><br>(2.0) *(close sound of aeroplane landing)* |
| MS – C, to unseen interviewer in airport terminal building.<br><br><br>MS – tables and cake ready for party. LS – air traffic control building (ATCB); distant figures seen through windows of ATCB. LS – aeroplane lands.<br><br>LS – circling airplanes. MS – C walks up to coach terminal. LS – passengers disembark from coach. LS – C walks around airport. MS – airport terminal. LS – C outside coach. LS – C and driver (D) outside coach. | 17<br>18<br>19<br>20<br>21<br>22<br>23<br>24<br>25<br>26<br>27<br>28<br>29<br>30<br>31<br>32<br>33<br>34<br>35<br>36<br>37<br>38<br>39<br>40 | C<br><br><br><br><br><br><br><br>N (vo)<br><br><br><br><br><br><br><br>N (vo)<br><br><br><br>C (vo)<br>C<br>D<br>C | it's rather strange today because we've got the Irish Olympic team goin- or at least twenty five of them (.) and er (.) it's all a bit bizarre because here we are (.) at a British airport with the Irish team going on an Australian airline and we're also going to have a party for their departure at the gate (1.8)<br>Stuart's heading for the centre of the airfield as the escaped dog has been spotted by air traffic control close to the landing runway (.) a pet dog running around the airfield is <a very <u>se::</u>rious matter> (.) if it's not caught and gets onto the runway (.) <u>all</u> landing aircraft may have to be diverted (3.0)<br>John wants to track down his Irish Olympic passengers in good time for the party (.)<br>you haven't seen the Irish Olympic team in your travels (.) have you?<br>no<br><u>oh</u> (.) <oka::y> [. . .] |

returned to the story about the Irish Olympic team, only to find out that what was an unusual situation has now thrown up a problem to be resolved (lines 33–40). In lines 33–34, the off-screen narrator informs viewers that Cullen 'wants to track down his Irish Olympic passengers in good time for the party'. The verbal phrase 'track down' denotes searching for passengers, not simply waiting for them. It transforms Cullen's job – and hence his story – from routine to exceptional. Simultaneously, a long-range shot of passengers – not Cullen's – disembarking from a coach proves the narrator's commentary right. This is further confirmed a few seconds later when John is filmed asking a coach driver whether he has seen the Irish Olympic team, only to receive an unambiguous 'no' (line 39) from the latter. Within the opening two minutes of this episode of *Airport*, then, the disequilibrium states of the two stories are dramatically introduced and evaluated as, respectively, 'a serious matter' – potential chaos at one of the world's busiest airports – and the 'tracking down' of an important group of passengers.

Once introduced, and as in soap operas, the various micro-stories pursued within a single docusoap episode are intercut in ways that develop or reflect one another. Coherence across them is created by concentrating the whereness of the action around a limited number of locations and characters – in this case, around one airport and a reduced number of employees and customers. It is also created by quickly interleaving scenes from these micro-stories through a considerable number of 'narrative meanwhiles'. These present discrete events from different stories as though they were simultaneously occurring, interconnected events. In spite of its brief duration, for example, Extract 3.1 includes three such meanwhiles: lines 13–16, 24 and 32. The fast narrative pace that they set contributes to the illusion of viewers being able to access the 'exciting' reality of airport life as it simultaneously unfolds in various locations before their very own eyes.[2]

As an illustration, let us examine the first of these narrative meanwhiles. It occurs 22 seconds after the start of the episode and results from visual and sonic resources which create the impression of one story seamlessly flowing into another. In lines 13–16, a four-second pause separates a stretch of talk, in which King is heard attempting to restore the equilibrium in the story about the lost dog (line 12), from the next one, in which a new character is introduced (line 17). Visually, this moment of verbal silence is filled with a long-range shot of King's jeep driving away from the camera (lines 13–14), followed by a close-up of the wheels of an aeroplane touching down (lines 15–16). The long-range shot temporarily suspends the story about the lost dog by visually distancing one of its signifiers – the jeep of its main protagonist – from the viewers. And, as the subsequent close-up shot cannot logically be connected to this story (it contradicts the narrator's earlier prediction that all landing traffic may have to be diverted), the interpretation suggested to viewers is that they are now within a different story. Acoustically, the four-second verbal pause is filled with the sound of the engine of the jeep (the first two seconds) and of a landing airplane (the last two seconds). The sound volume in the first two seconds as the jeep leaves the scene remains constant. This creates a mismatch between, on the one hand, the increasing distance between the camera and its represented object and, on the other, the sound-track representation of this distance. Manipulating sound–image relations in this way also influences the viewers' relationship to sound, the volume of the latter remaining constant. The story about the lost dog is taken to an acoustic background during the first two seconds of the narrative meanwhile, making room in the next two seconds for a louder acoustic foreground of the airplane engine. Visual (quick change of camera distance positioning) and acoustic (sound–image relation manipulation) resources thus work in tandem in lines 13–16 to take viewers seamlessly from one story to another.

One of the consequences of the disequilibrium states of the several micro-stories in docusoaps being so quickly introduced is that a high number of suspense-building narrative devices are needed in order to maintain viewer interest in what follows. By the time the episode from which Extract 3.1 comes is halfway through, for example, King has found and put Finn the dog in a safe place and Cullen has located the Irish Olympic team. As in soap operas, though, these internal resolutions open new states of disequilibrium. In the story about the lost dog, for instance, once caught, Finn needs to be examined. During the course of the examination, it emerges that the dog needs to be kept in kennels for some unspecified time. This, of course, introduces a further state of disequilibrium: it is now Finn's owner who needs urgently to be found and told the bad news that they are likely to miss their long-haul flight.

Extract 3.2 (see p. 27), from the same *Airport* episode as Extract 3.1, illustrates the process of building suspense in relation to the story about the Irish Olympic team. In lines 01–02, and by 'eavesdropping' on a telephone conversation between Cullen and one of his colleagues, viewers learn of a new disruptive force: 'one of the Irish athletes has lost his passport'. Just as in Extract 3.1, when the off-screen narrator was quick to evaluate the potential consequences of having a dog running close to a landing runway, in Extract 3.2 the same narrator soon points out to viewers the hypothetical consequences of this new state of disequilibrium: 'if Gordon isn't able to travel (.) neither can his bags which have been checked straight through to Australia' (lines 03–05). Viewers are next offered a close-up of a concerned-looking Gordon as he answers two questions from an unseen interviewer. The first one has been edited out but we can infer it to be a request for an update, which Gordon provides in the direction of where the unseen interviewer is assumed to be standing (lines 06–08). The second one – 'how do you feel about that?' (lines 10–11) – seeks to elicit an internal (that is, Gordon's) evaluation of the latest disequilibrium state in his story, despite the very obvious reply that a concomitant close-up of a stern Gordon looking down already provides. The dramatic potential of Gordon's (non-)verbal evaluation is maximised through a quick juxtaposition of the previous close-up to a long, panning shot of Cullen ushering a high-spirited Irish Olympic team minus Gordon through the departure gates (lines 14–16) and to a party room (lines 17–19). A strong unhappy–happy contrast is thereby created, which is next used to introduce further suspense as the off-screen narrator announces a possible

**EXTRACT 3.2**

### Airport (BBC, 2000)

[The extract, lasting one minute and fifteen seconds, occurs half way through the episode. C: John Cullen; G: Irish Olympic team member Gordon; TM: Irish Olympic team members; K: Stuart King; N: narrator; UI: Unseen interviewer.]

| | | | |
|---|---|---|---|
| *CU – G. LS – C (on the* | 01 | C | I'm just going down to gate three (.) one |
| *phone) and G at airport* | 02 | | of the Irish athletes has lost his passport (.) |
| *terminal building.* | 03 | N (vo) | if Gordon isn't able to travel (.) neither can |
| *CU – concerned-* | 04 | | his bags which have been checked straight |
| *looking G.* | 05 | | through to Australia (2.0) |
| *CU – G looking in the* | 06 | G | unfortunately we have to take the bags off the |
| *direction of unseen UI* | 07 | | plane and they'll have to establish where my |
| *MS – two airport.* | 08 | | passport is |
| *officials.* | 09 | G (vo) | a:::nd <u><hopefully></u> we can get it [back |
| *CU – G looks down,* | 10 | UI (vo) | [how do you |
| *very stern expression.* | 11 | | feel about that? |
| *Looks up towards N.* | 12 | G | do you <u>really</u> want to ask me that? (.) |
| *CU – G, forced smile.* | 13 | | I'm smiling on the outside (2.0) |
| *LS – C ushers TM* | 14 | C | if you just go left (.) we need you at- we will |
| *through departure* | 15 | | need you at <u><gate three></u> <u>THERE</u> (.) leave the |
| *gates. To TM,* | 16 | | duty free alone boys (.) <u>leave</u> it alone |
| *laughing. LS – TM* | 17 | | (2.0) |
| *entering party room in* | 18 | N (vo) | John's got an idea which might yet get |
| *very high spirits.* | 19 | | Gordon onto the flight |
| *LS – animal reception* | 20 | | (3.0) at the animal reception building Stuart is |
| *building centre.* | 21 | | trying to keep Finn from getting into more |
| | 22 | | trouble (.) |
| *LS – K coaxes Finn out* | 23 | K | Finn (.) <u>come on</u> (.) <u>come on</u> Finn (.) there's a |
| *from back of jeep.* | 24 | | <u>good</u> lad (.) [. . .] |

resolution for Gordon's predicament (lines 18–19). Predictably, another meanwhile is introduced at this crucial point in the story (line 20), which takes viewers back to the story about the lost dog. The 'cliff-hanger' that this narrative meanwhile creates is common across forms of serial programming, notably in soap operas, where it is used to secure viewer attention in very competitive schedule slots. As Extract 3.2 has illustrated, narrative meanwhiles introduce a sense of action development and narrative pace in television formats in which 'banal' talk – mainly characters talking about themselves and others – tends to be the central activity.

Let us next consider Extract 3.3 (see p. 28), which corresponds to approximately the final two minutes of the same *Airport* episode and provides the expected resolution to the previous array of disequilibrium states. Long awaited, resolution in docusoaps is typically structured so as to bridge back to the events leading up to it, outward from the taleworld to the storyrealm and forward to future developments in the socio-historical world. In Extract 3.3, for example, Cullen evaluates aspects and characters in his story: 'feel sorry

### Airport (BBC, 2000)

[C: John Cullen; G: Gordon; K: Stuart King; N: narrator.]

| | | | |
|---|---|---|---|
| CU – Finn. | 51 | K (vo) | he's gonna stay here overnight (.) twenty-four |
| | 52 | | hour observation (.) er |
| CU – K, to camera. | 53 | K | but <u>hopefully</u> he'll fly out tomorrow morning |
| MS – K's rescue | 54 | | (4.0) |
| vehicle reverses. | 55 | | |
| LS – G at check-in. | 56 | C (vo) | GORDON? (.) <u>don't</u> worry (.) your secret's safe |
| | 57 | | with us |
| CU – G, to C. | 58 | G | that's ok (.) thanks *(laughing)* |
| | 59 | C (vo) | it <u>won't</u> go beyond Heathrow |
| LS – G waves hand at | 60 | G | oh yeah <u>sure</u> (.) see you guys |
| C as he walks past in | 61 | C (vo) | by::e |
| front of the camera. | 62 | G | thanks (.) see you |
| MS – C holding cake in | 63 | C | feel sorry he's lost his passport and he's gonna |
| right hand, to camera. | 64 | | get sent up about it (.) but they were good fun I |
| CU – C looks | 65 | | think (.) and I wish them luck er and I'll watch |
| embarrassed, covers | 66 | | them with interest (.) I'm speaking with my |
| mouth with left hand. | 67 | | mouth full on tele (.) |
| LS – G alone in party | 68 | N (vo) | sadly (.) Gordon didn't get selected to run in the |
| room eating cake. | 69 | | four by four hundred metre relay in the |
| | 70 | | Olympics (.) his team mates didn't make the |
| CU – flight cage being | 71 | | final (.) the next day Finn was well enough to |
| loaded into airplane. | 72 | | travel (.) he's now living happily in Winnipeg |
| MS – Finn in flight | 73 | | Canada (.) none the worse for his traumatic |
| cage. | 74 | | experience |
| Closing credits. | 75 | | (10.0) |

he's lost his passport . . . but they were good fun I think' (lines 63–65). He also performs his character as though there were no camera. Note, for instance, his 'embarrassment' in lines 66–67 as he realises that he has been speaking with his mouth full on television. This gives the impression that viewers are directly accessing not only the documentary taleworld but also its storyrealm – an impression which is constructed in these closing sequences by having King and Cullen look at the camera directly as they speak (lines 53 and 63–67). In addition, King and Cullen give future predictions for several of the story characters: Finn will 'hopefully' leave the airport the next day (line 53), Gordon will be 'sent up' (lines 63–64) and Cullen will watch the performance of the Irish Olympic team with interest (lines 65–66).

The narrator, too, connects the resolution of the two stories to the world beyond in time and outside the documentary. In lines 68–71, he announces an unhappy ending to the story for Gordon and his team, and in lines 71–74 a happy ending to that of Finn and his owner. By referring to a specific real-life event (i.e., the forthcoming Olympics) that is chronologically subsequent to events in the documentary taleworld, the narrator seeks to strengthen the

### Airport (BBC, 2000)

[K: Stuart King; N: narrator; Russell, Steve and Shaker: Heathrow airport employees.]

| | | | |
|---|---|---|---|
| MS – boxer holds up medal. | 01 | N | next week on Airport (.) Steve and Russell sprint |
| | 02 | (vo) | after an <Olympic scoop> (.) |
| LS – car on trailer. | 03 | | Gulf Air's Shaker battles to get an exclusive car |
| CU – K looks shocked. | 04 | | on board (.) a::nd Stuart's dealing with some |
| CU – large, furry spider | 05 | | <cree::py> cargo that's been detained in terminal |
| in box. | 06 | | one [. . .] |

relationship between the documentary and the world out there. This narrative device, which is common across serial programming, contributes to the referentiality of docusoaps, which are generally broadcast in their original scheduling slots rather than as repeats over time.[3]

The two stories examined in this episode of *Airport*, then, end with a return to a state of equilibrium which, as in Todorov's model, is slightly different from the initial state of equilibrium. However, the serial nature of docusoaps means that these stories are never fully closed. Following the end credits of the episode of *Airport* from which Extracts 3.1–3.3 come, for example, the sequence reproduced in Extract 3.4 above is shown.

Docusoaps treat stories within a single episode as sequences within a larger story – the docusoap in its entirety. To maintain coherence, they keep locations and some characters constant. In the extract above, three new characters – Steve, Russell and Shaker – are introduced (lines 01–03) but an 'old' character, Stuart King, is retained (lines 04–06). For all four, new disequilibrium states await: sprinting after an Olympic scoop (lines 01–02), 'batt[ling] to get an exclusive car on board' (lines 03–04) and 'dealing with some <cree::py> cargo' (lines 04–05). These are presented as journalistic teases: incomplete but high in dramatic potential. Note, for instance, the narrator's use of expressions that connote drama and/or suspense, namely 'sprint after an <Olympic scoop>' (lines 01–02), 'battles' (line 03) and 'dealing with some <cree::py> cargo' (lines 04–05). Note, too, the two consecutive close-up camera angles of King looking shocked and of a large, furry spider in a box (lines 04–06). Unlike classic realist fiction narratives, therefore, the stories told in docusoaps lack closure. Instead, they open up avenues for further stories and build anticipation for the next episode. Even the closing of the last episode of a docusoap generally leaves a narrative door ajar for a further series.[4]

## 3.2   Attractive personalities and documentary storytelling

As important as narrative structure is to documentaries, it is nothing without the 'right' commentary by the 'right' narrator. Commentary is the primary organiser of meaning in documentaries. Because of its salience, great care goes into choosing who is responsible for it. We noted in Chapter 2 that two types of narrator can generally be found in documentaries: heterodiegetic and homodiegetic. The former are situated outside of the documentary taleworld and remain generally unseen (off-screen). Homodiegetic narrators double as characters within the stories that they tell and are often seen (on-screen) during the documentary. Whilst too sweeping and clear-cut a distinction to fit all documentaries, these two modes of narration provide a useful starting point to explore how the narrator's discourse (commentary) contributes to documentary realism.

The documentary variety selected for analysis in this section of the chapter is known as expository. Public service broadcasters especially have adopted this format, which originally developed in the 1930s as a socially responsible cinematic record that contrasted with Hollywood's focus on fantasy and individual desire (Corner 1995; Kilborn and Izod 1997). Expository documentaries claim to offer a truthful view of the socio-historical world that they show. To do so, they seek to create a sense of realism about the stories that they tell. Typically, this documentary variety uses a script (the commentary) to offer viewers selected information on a given topic. This narrative commentary is nevertheless generally offered as objective and it is verified by the accompanying visual footage.

Whilst 'pure' expository documentaries are still broadcast nowadays, since the mid-1990s an increasing number of programmes combine observational and expository modes (Born 2004; Nichols 2001). The resulting 'hybrid' variety mixes sequences in which viewers witness others' experiences and direct testimonies to camera, with sequences in which a generally off-screen narrator tells them about such experiences. Examples of the pure and hybrid formats of expository documentaries have been selected in the remainder of this chapter to illustrate and discuss the role of the narrator in documentary storytelling.

### 3.2.1   Narrative commentary and ' the voice of God' in documentaries

Three interrelated reasons are normally given for the effectiveness of off-screen, heterodiegetic narration (or 'the voice of God') in constructing documentary realism. First, viewers seem to be psychologically predisposed to believing incorporeal voices addressing them directly on television (Kilborn and Izod 1997; Nichols 1991, 2001). As a disembodied voice talks to us in documentaries and news reports, for example, our attention is seemingly seized by a concatenation of images that have a very close connection with our phenomenological world and thus a strong ability to trigger reality-like experiences (Messaris 1997).

Secondly, and connected to the above, off-screen narration has become so conventionalised in documentary and other forms of non-fiction television that it apparently goes unnoticed. When we watch a documentary that uses narrative voice-over, we do not tend to ask ourselves 'who is telling me all this?'. Instead, our reaction seems to go along the lines of 'Ah, ok, this is a documentary and it is being explained to me what happens on the screen.' In fact, it is only when we recognise the person behind the voice that this mode of narration becomes marked. The BBC documentary series *Planet Earth* (2005–06), for instance, was narrated by David Attenborough, who has over the years become *the* trusted voice of British natural history documentaries. Viewers in Britain were likely to notice him straightaway. For those who might not, the opening credits of each *Planet Earth* episode included the large font-size caption 'Narrated by David Attenborough'. This is quite rare in expository documentaries. With the exception of documentaries narrated by celebrities, the names of narrators tend to appear in the closing credits and as part of a longer list of names, including producers, camera crew, and so forth. The deanonymising of the *Planet Earth* narrator may be seen as an attempt to achieve credibility by capitalising on the reputation of the broadcaster, whilst maintaining the authority of, and trust in, the voice of God mode of narration.

The third, also related, reason why heterodiegetic narrators have been seen to help documentary realism is their outsider stance. These narrators tend to comment on the documentary taleworld not only authoritatively but also at arm's length, which is often discursively realised through a detached, third-person narration style.

In a televisual climate of 'closeness' (Part II), however, heterodiegetic narration does not always seem to be concerned with maintaining an outsider stance. It becomes involved when there is perceived to be an advantage in doing so. This is not necessarily a case of narrators giving their opinion on, and sharing their experience of, the topic of a given documentary – although that also happens, especially in hybrid documentary varieties (see Section 3.2.2). It can also be a matter of full-hearted commitment to the act of narrating. Consider in this respect Extract 3.5 (see p. 32) from *Planet Earth*. The extract comes from the first ten minutes of an episode thematically focused on the jungles of our planet. Attenborough is describing the courting ritual of a rare species of bird of paradise in the Amazon jungle.

The photography in *Planet Earth* was exceptional – it was one of the main reasons indeed behind the series' success. 'The Planet Earth Diaries' part of the episode from which Extract 3.5 was taken, for example, was entirely devoted to describing the incredible patience of the cameraman in filming the images of the birds of paradise. He waited over one hundred hours in a small and uncomfortable hide to shoot approximately thirty seconds of footage time on the courtship displays of these birds – something which, viewers were reminded in 'The Planet Earth Diaries', was remarkable even by natural history documentary standards.

As exceptional as the photography was, the relationship between the images and the narrative commentary in *Planet Earth* largely corresponded to that traditionally established in expository documentaries: the former supported the latter, often verifying it at the same time. This is largely the case in Extract 3.5, where footage of the two birds of paradise complements, confirms or announces Attenborough's script. In line 03, for instance, Attenborough's reference to modest dress is offered in sync with footage of a brown female bird and in contrast to the prior close-up of the brightly coloured male bird (lines 01–03). In lines 06–08, he informs viewers that male birds' courtship rituals are rounded performances, not

**Planet Earth (BBC, 2006)**

[ A: Attenborough.]

| | | |
|---|---|---|
| CU – male bird on branch | 01 A | the ma<u>gnific</u>ent bird of paradise favours |
| fluttering its brightly coloured | 02 (vo) | the low branches of bushes (3.0) |
| wings. CU – female bird (brown). | 03 | its female (.) is modestly dressed |
| CU – male bird tweeting loudly. | 04 | (4.0) |
| MS – male and female bird on | 05 | the male has a <u>good</u> set of lungs (.) |
| two close branches of same bush. | 06 | but it'll have to do better than flutter |
| CU – male bird twittering loudly, | 07 | his eyelids if he wants to im<u>press</u> her (.) |
| fluttering wings and swivelling | 08 | it <u>all</u> depends on his performance (2.0) |
| head. | 09 | the females may be <u>dull</u>-looking but |
| MS – male and female bird. | 10 | they're <<u>very</u>> picky (2.0) and it's time |
| | 11 | for a <u>really</u> close inspection |
| CU – male and female bird now | 12 | (5.0) |
| closer, female bird looking in the | 13 | this side looks <u>fine</u> |
| direction of male bird's right side | 14 | (2.0) |
| then left side. | 15 | but what about his left? |
| | 16 | (3.0) |
| CU – female bird. | 17 | <pretty> im<u>press</u>ive (.) |
| CU – male and female bird | 18 | but is he <<u>magnificent</u>> <<u>enough</u>>? |
| together. MS – female bird flies | 19 | (2.0) |
| away. | 20 | o::<u>h dear</u> (.) her departure says it all |
| CU – different, colourful bird of | 21 | (2.0) generations of choosy females |
| paradise species on tree branch. | 22 | have driven the evolution of these |
| | 23 | remarkable displays [. . .] |

just eyelid-fluttering exercises. This piece of commentary is next confirmed by footage of the male bird twittering loudly, vigorously fluttering its wings and swivelling its head from side to side (lines 07–09) – all undeniable visual 'proof', too, of Attenborough's overall evaluation a few seconds later (lines 21–23).

Whilst ascribing to the traditional primacy of commentary over images, part of Attenborough's narration in Extract 3.5 departs from the narrative detachment traditionally associated with the voice of God. Up until line 12, Attenborough offers viewers factual information about birds of paradise. His only poetic licence, as it were, is his use of the human, gendered pronominal forms ('his'/'he' and 'her' in line 07) to refer to the two birds being filmed. Yet, this is quite a moderate example of animal anthropomorphising, a practice which is in any case quite common on television.[5] More is needed to entice viewers into what might otherwise be received as a dull recording of animal-mating habits, and Attenborough skilfully delivers this in lines 13–18.

Following the information on the birds' courting ritual and the setting up of a forthcoming 'close inspection' scene, a five-second pause ensues (line 12). This takes viewers from narrative commentary about two birds by a one-step-removed Attenborough to narrative commentary about the birds' courting ritual by the female bird. The latter cannot, of course, use human language. But

Attenborough can, and does precisely this. In lines 13–18, Attenborough performs an act of what Goffman (1974) calls 'say-foring' or 'ventriloquising'. Ventriloquising is a mock representation, a form of verbal self-display, which occurs when: 'a speaking adult acts out a response that a nonspeaking child might make if he [sic] could (or would) talk. A similar form of ventriloquism is used to animate pussy cats, teddy bears, and other lovable objects' (1974: 536).

The ventriloquiser allegedly gets inside the ventriloquisee and speaks for the latter, making public his/her personal intentions, feelings and views. In doing so, the ventriloquiser also livens up his/her own talk. The mock dimension of the device in particular makes it an apt vehicle for the verbalisation of the ventriloquiser's witty self. This mock dimension, moreover, often entails a colloquial registry, which contributes to a sense of informality and, crucially for our discussion of narrative commentary styles, of ventriloquiser–ventriloquisee involvement.[6]

Attenborough's ventriloquising in Extract 3.5 is a fine act of verbal self-display. His choice of the superlative adjectives 'impressive' and 'magnificent' portrays the female bird as a choosy female who will not settle for anything other than the best. His pretend, question–answer dialogue (lines 15, 17–18) creates anticipation regarding her decision to mate or otherwise, especially because each part of this pretend dialogue is punctuated with pregnant pauses (lines 12, 14, 16 and 19). But it is Attenborough's paralanguage that most enlivens his mock representation.

Generally, Attenborough's narration is delivered in a rather grave voice. In lines 13–18, though, he raises the pitch of his voice considerably, to the point that his utterances sound stereotypically 'feminine'. The intonation contours of his questions, with marked final rises, also resemble those identified as characteristic of women's 'unassertive speech' (Lakoff 1975). Clearly, not all women use such a high-pitched voice and such high-rise final intonation contours when they speak. Yet Attenborough's mock-representation of the female bird's paralanguage wittingly plays with the stereotype of the unassertive, fickle female. This stereotype is immediately confirmed by the video footage. In line 19, a medium-range angle captures the female bird starting to fly away in spite of what – by the standards of the patient cameraman and the narrator – has been a truly remarkable male performance.

Attenborough's departure from the detachment typically ascribed to heterodiegetic narration is further illustrated in line 20. His utterance 'o::h dear (.) her departure says it all' is delivered as the voice of Attenborough, not of his narrator self. The inflection of his voice differs noticeably from that in the subsequent lines. In line 20, it is emphatic and carries resigned yet perceptive 'I told you so' undertones. But in lines 21–23, it is authoritative and grave and places Attenborough back in the familiar role for the viewers of the one-step-removed narrator. Line 20 therefore provides a kind of bridge between two different styles of narration: involved (playful ventriloquist) and detached (authoritative voice of God). In doing so, it connects the taleworld of the birds of paradise (which Attenborough has personally accessed to give them a 'public voice') and the storyrealm of the documentary (in which he is guiding viewers through the 'reality' of jungle life).

### Michael Palin around the World (BBC, 1989)

[After eight days of travel, Michael Palin enters the bustling city of Bombay on foot, ready for a shave, a wash and some rest. The barber and the local in the excerpt below speak mainly in their native language. This has been arbitrarily transcribed with four consecutive capital 'X's to distinguish it from talk that, due to loud traffic noise throughout most of the excerpt, is indecipherable (xxxx). P: Michael Palin; B: Barber; L: Local.]

| | | | |
|---|---|---|---|
| LS – busy street of | 01 | P | h<u>e</u>llo (.) excuse me |
| Bombay. MS – P | 02 | | (2.0) |
| approaches B. | 03 | | excuse [me |
| MS – B in front of | 04 | B |       [XXXX |
| shaving stool on | 05 | P | you're a barber (.) do y- do you shave? |
| the street. | 06 | B | yes |
| MS – P and B. | 07 | P | would you do (xxxx) would you shave on- take this |
| | 08 | | beard off? (.) [will you? |
| | 09 | B |           [XXXX |
| CU – P, to camera. | 10 | P | o:::ka::<u>y</u> (.) |
| MS – P, to B. | 11 | | what do I do? |
| MS – B and P. P | 12 | B | yes (.) sit here |
| looks around. To L, | 13 | P | barber's seat is it? |
| next to them, iro- | 14 | L | XXXX |
| nically. P sits. To L. | 15 | P | I face him? |
| LS – P being shaved. | 16 | L | yes |
| Group of curious | 17 | P | he can- er (xxxx) O:::H (xxxx) |
| locals gather around | 18 | | |
| P. To B, points at L. | 19 | | he's your agent is he? (2.0) |

→

### 3.2.2   Narrative commentary and celebrity in documentary

Having illustrated how heterodiegetic narration is sometimes performed from within positions of involvement rather than detachment, what follows further explores narrator involvement in relation to documentaries fronted by media personalities.

Use of media personalities as narrators is driven at least in part by the current fascination with celebrity (Evans and Hesmondhalgh 2005; Rojek 2001). In New Zealand, for instance, an increasing number of documentaries have been fronted by well-known personalities since the late 1990s. Debrett (2004) esti-mated the number at ten in 1998, of which seven were presented by comedians. Smith (2005) gives the further examples of *Heartland*, narrated by New Zealand comedian Gary MacCormick, and the eight episodes of the 2005 documentary series *Billy Connolly's World Tour of New Zealand*. Billy Connolly has presented similar travel documentary series filmed in the UK. He has in fact joined the rather long list of television personalities to front (natural) history and travel documentaries in that country, including celebrity chef Ainsley Harriott, former footballer and current sport pundit Ian Wright and, as Extract 3.6 (see above and p. 35) shows, comedian and actor Michael Palin.[7]

| | | | |
|---|---|---|---|
| MS – P on seat. CU – | 20 | | right (xxxx) eight days' growth here (.) so go easy |
| P's smiley face. To B. | 21 | | (xxxx) er::: (.) this is <u>great</u> (.) |
| MS – B and P. CU – | 22 | | are you one of the best? (3.0) |
| P looks uneasy. | 23 | | <you (.) <u>good</u> barber?> |
| CU – P mock-smile | 24 | | quiet man see? (2.0) |
| to camera. | 25 | | Sheffield United won last Saturday (4.0) lucky |
| LS – P and B. | 26 | | really (3.0) they've got a good team this season |
| CU – P, panicked | 27 | | (4.0) oh <u>o:::h</u> <u>WOW</u>(.) <u>right</u> Michael (.) stay still (.) |
| expression. LS – | 28 | | still as you can (.) <u>oh oh</u> leave the nose (.) I know |
| amused locals. | 29 | | it's big (.) oh <u>a:::h</u> (2.0) |
| LS – B, P and crowd | 30 | P | suddenly I realise what it is about the barber's |
| of locals. | 31 | (vo) | manner that worries me (.) the way he handles me |
| | 32 | | and stares past me (.) I form the distinct impression |
| | 33 | | that he's blind |
| MS – B shaving P. | 34 | | (4.0) |
| CU – to camera | 35 | P | I'm <u>not</u> going to talk because if I <u>do</u> he might get the |
| above, whispering. | 36 | | jugular (3.0) |
| LS – B, P and locals. | 37 | | <u>this</u> is why the crowds are here (.) they haven't |
| CU – P looking up. | 38 | | come to watch a shave (.) they've come to watch an |
| MLS – P looks at | 39 | | <exe<u>cution</u>> (.) I <u>never</u> thought I'd have a shave |
| cameraman amongst | 40 | | here (2.0) see in the trees above? vultures gathering |
| locals. LS from below | 41 | | |
| – trees above. MS – B | 42 | | (4.0) |
| and P, panning to LS | 43 | | |
| – different street in | 44 | P | shaved and washed |
| Bombay. LS – P walks | 45 | (vo) | and (.) briefly rested (.) |
| along the street, away | 46 | | it's time to move on around the world again |
| from the camera. | 47 | | [. . .] |

All these celebrity narrators possess an 'attractive personality'. According to Fairclough (1995: 137–8), this is nowadays assessed in relation to the use by media personalities of an informal, personable and, on the whole, conversational communication style.[8] These celebrity narrators also adopt on-screen, personally involved (homodiegetic) narration styles. Let us take a look in this respect at an excerpt from an episode of *Michael Palin around the World in Eighty Days*, in which Palin replicates the fictional journey of Phileas Fogg in Jules Verne's novel of the same title.

In Extract 3.6, Palin uses off-screen narration briefly. In lines 30–33 and 44–46, his narrative voice-over guides viewers along the documentary's tale-world as various pieces of complementary visual evidence are shown. In both cases, his narrative commentary refers to his own experiences in that taleworld, thereby connecting the latter with the documentary as a storyrealm through his own involvement in both. In lines 30–33, a long-range shot of a crowd of locals is offered over Palin's statement of his realising that the barber is blind. And in lines 44–46, footage of a clean-shaven and groomed Palin walking along a street in Bombay is synced with his remark that 'shaved and washed and (.) briefly rested (.) it's time to move on around the world again'. In both cases, too, Palin's commentary is coded as contemporaneous with the witnessed events, as indicated by his use of present tense verbs in lines 30–34 (e.g. 'suddenly I realise . . . I form the distinct impression') and line 46 ('it's time to move on').

Aside from these two brief, off-screen narrative incursions, the rest of the extract – and a good proportion of the episode and the documentary series – is narrated by an on-screen Palin, who doubles as a character in the documentary taleworld (lines 01–23, 25–29) and, at times, talks directly to camera about his experiences and feelings in that taleworld as the viewers witness these very experiences (lines 24, 35–40). Let us begin with the former. It entails Palin playing the part of a scruffy-looking Englishman arriving in an unfamiliar city, helplessly trying to communicate in English with locals who do not share his language, and unknowingly being shaved by a blind man. This part could be constructed as argument-building narrative evidence of the risks of travelling abroad without speaking the languages of the countries visited. It is instead constructed as a safe, humorous travelling experience in the documentary. Two factors make it so.

First, as (media-)literate people, we know that the protagonist of a story/documentary series does not usually die half-way through the story/series. So, despite the apparent risk involved on Palin's part, we know that he will survive to tell his Bombay shaving tale. We know, too, that Palin is not alone on this trip but has a camera team along with him. Note, in this respect, his remark to a member of his film crew amongst the group of locals: 'see in the trees above? vultures gathering' (line 40). Although Palin is clearly building a comic (not a tragic) narrative, his version of the travel documentary is performed here more 'honestly' than in those other cases in which an on-screen, homodiegetic narrator continues with the pretence of, for example, the solitary walker, mountaineer or rower who 'communes' with nature. Palin's approach is, in contrast, based on the premise that viewers know better.

Secondly, Palin's choice as the main character for this documentary invests narrative developments therein with his 'pre-speech ethos', or image, as a well-known comedian, which he clearly brings about during Extract 3.6. For instance, having gone through the initial attempts at negotiating a shave by a local barber (lines 02–12); having sat properly (line 15) on what he ironically questions to be a 'barber's seat' (line 13); and having unsuccessfully tried to communicate by using foreigner talk (grammatical simplification and careful, slow enunciation in line 23), Palin engages in typical 'small talk' with the barber,[9] typical, that is, in the context of going to a barber in Palin's home country and overlooking the fact that most men in the UK nowadays shave at home and only go to the barber's to have their hair cut.

Palin's performance at this juncture may be interpreted as an innocent parody of Phileas Fogg and his journey. It resonates, in fact, with the kind of parody of Englishness that ran through the successful acts in *Monty Python's Flying Circus* and the subsequent *Ripping Yarns*. Specifically, his performance in Extract 3.6 may be interpreted as a tongue-in-cheek parody of the English male abroad.[10] Palin's attempt at stereotypically male small talk, namely football, in lines 25–26 is a good case in point. It is met with uncomfortably long pauses which stand in contrast to the continuous flow of exchanges that characterises small talk and thus highlights the fact that things are not going according to Palin's plan. A four-, a three- and a four-second pause punctuate Palin's three respective attempts at friendly small talk with the barber via highly specific cultural references. The team about which Palin wants to chat is, for example, a regional one – possibly his team, as Palin was born in Sheffield. In lines 25–26, then, Palin is not transferring a visit to *any* barber in the UK to the context of Bombay, but a visit to a local barber, possibly *his* local barber, to a foreign country and to a native of that country. In such circumstances, and given the absence of a fully shared linguistic code, Palin's small talk is clearly doomed to fail. The potential for humour stems, partly at least, from his knowing enactment of such an obvious case of cross-cultural unawareness.

Another instance of Palin bringing about his pre-speech ethos as a comedian in the above extract occurs in lines 27–29. Confronted with the barber's silences, Palin eventually gives up trying to communicate. This, however, does not mean that Palin goes quiet. On the contrary, he becomes a lively *solo* performer. First, he enacts a dialogue with himself, in which he instructs himself as to the sensible course of action in a 'risky' situation: 'oh o:::h WOW(.) right Michael (.) stay still (.) still as you can' (lines 27–28). Next, in lines 28–29, he performs his part in a pretend dialogue with the barber (e.g. 'I know it's big', referring to Palin's nose), using expressive paralanguage (e.g. various 'oh's and 'ah's) to enliven it. A combination of close-ups of an uneasy-looking (line 23), panicked (line 27) Palin and of long-range shots of a gathering of initially curious (lines 16–19) and then visibly amused (lines 27–29) locals maximises the comic value of Palin's parody of the helpless English male abroad.

Last but by no means least in Palin's on-screen narration are his two asides to camera in Extract 3.6. In the first one, he gives a mock smile to camera as he delivers his evaluation of the barber's character: 'quiet man see?' (line 24). This evaluation is an intentional misreading of the situation and of the barber's personality, who may well be a loquacious man were he to be addressed in his native language. Such a misreading carries along the humorous potential of equivocation, upon which comedy is often built. In the second one, Palin whispers to camera his intention to remain quiet for a while, which he justifies through the expression 'if I do [talk] he might get the jugular' (lines 35–36). This is a literal expression, inasmuch as were the barber to err from his course, it would most likely be Palin's throat that would bear the brunt of the damage. But it is also a colourful, colloquial expression, which contributes to Palin's attractive personality.

Whilst brief, Palin's two asides to camera are important to the construction of a sense of narrator–viewer involvement. Particularly effective in this respect is the fact that Palin's mock smile (line 24) and whispering tone (lines 35–36) are filmed in close-up. In the case of the second aside, furthermore, the close-up is offered from above – a camera angle that positions subjects (here Palin) as powerless vis-à-vis the viewer (Lury 2005). This is intended to enhance the image of the helpless Englishman abroad, around which the comic effect of Palin's performance revolves.

All in all, Palin delivers involved, and primarily on-screen, storytelling. It is worth noting that the different parts played by Palin in Extract 3.6 (helpful narrative guide, helpless Englishman abroad, viewer confidant) are potentially contradictory, for they pursue rather different goals: to record travelling experiences, to entertain viewers, to construct English vis-à-vis Asian identities, to create a rapport with viewers, and so forth. Yet they do not seem to create a credibility problem for him. This is mainly because they are subsumed beneath an overarching attractive personality, which he not only brings along to but also constantly brings into play during the documentary: Palin the comedian. We are reminded here of Goffman's (1967) work on self-presentation, and specifically of his views that successful self-presentation requires the performance of a consistent self, which is not to say that a degree of variability is altogether discouraged. Within Goffman's (1961, 1967, 1969) metaphor of social life as a game, in fact, individuals are constantly engaged in trying to maintain composure and self-sameness whilst taking certain 'character risks' in the hope that, by doing so, they 'will make a good showing' (1967: 237). The multi-part performance of celebrity narrators such as Palin is a good illustration of this.

## 3.3   Conclusion

The term documentary conjures up ideas of realism and truth. To document, after all, means to record some aspect of reality. The reality of documentary discourse is not so straightforward. Even in programmes that endorse the genre's so-called assertive stance to reality, a range of semiotic resources that 'tamper with' the world out there is drawn upon as supporting evidence of, paradoxically, direct access to that world.

The fictional realism of documentaries has been seen to follow established narrative structures and types of commentary. Popular classic fiction narrative structures, for instance, are used in order to transform the banal taleworld of docusoaps into an exciting one. That said, one needs to resist the temptation to make docusoap storytelling fit into structures originally proposed for fictional texts. There are some important differences. For example, in their effort to maximise entertainment, docusoaps tend to compress the initial state of equilibrium and to extend maximally the recognition and restoration parts of their narratives. Also, docusoap stories defer as long as possible their resolution states, both within a single episode and along the various episodes that comprise a given series. What is more, the ratio of narrative meanwhiles, climaxes, delays and plot twists per episode is far higher in docusoaps than, say, in the narratives examined by Todorov. Crucially, though, this is not because the stories told are action-packed but because the banality of everyday talk and the routine of work at certain public service institutions is maximally dramatised in docusoaps.

Despite these differences, the cognitively simple conflict–resolution structure of classic realist fiction narratives offers a particularly attractive storytelling option for docusoaps. First, the linear, cause–effect plot of classic fiction narratives creates a sense of consistency in time and place which facilitates the incorporation of new elements, for these are embedded in familiar surroundings. This is particularly useful to multi-story docusoaps, which also draw upon consistent surroundings (e.g. an airport building) and set chronologies (e.g. a working day/week). Secondly, characters in classic fiction narratives are psychologically rounded and fit our sense of motivation and/or consistency. Once again, this is particularly useful in docusoaps, where characters are selected from a constant, ordinary-people collective (e.g. employees at a London airport) and behave according to certain expectations and stereotypes. Thus, although entertainment demands mean that docusoaps' characters are also selected on account of their being somehow different, they are never that different from our expectations of the discursive and social category which they represent (e.g. young male with a middle-range job). Thirdly, as in classic realist fiction narratives, storytelling in docusoaps revolves around a narrator who is often unseen and who, from an omniscient position, signals the potential for drama in past, present and future story developments. This narrator also makes explicit the connections between sequences within and across stories.

Storytelling in documentaries has been examined in this chapter also in relation to the use of professional and celebrity narrators and their particular styles of commentary. Professional narrators generally operate off-screen. But even then, and as the analysis of Extract 3.5 illustrated, off-screen, voice of God narration need not always be articulated from a position of detached authority. It can also be realised through a style of narration that sounds fresh, enthused and surprised to see the recorded world anew. As for celebrity narrators, these often appear before the cameras and draw upon their attractive personalities to lend 'affective' credibility to the documentary taleworld. For instance, as Extract 3.6 showed, Palin skilfully played the part of the stereotypical English male abroad for comic effect. He also used colloquial asides to camera to get interactionally close to viewers. It was from such positions of comic character in the documentary taleworld and viewer confidant that he sought to authenticate, as it were, his narration. Regardless of whether it is left in the hands of professional broadcasters or celebrities and whether it takes place on- or off-screen, then, a number of documentaries assign primacy to the projection of narrator–narrative involvement. They seem to be using such involvement, in fact, to claim the kind of direct access to the socio-historical world that was traditionally sought through positions of narrator–narrative detachment.

# Once Upon a Time in a Talk Show

4

This chapter continues to examine storytelling in television formats that claim to provide direct access to the socio-historical world and, hence, to tell viewers 'true' stories about 'real' people. The specific television format selected on this occasion is the talk show. Because these shows differ considerably amongst themselves, the chapter focuses on the daytime variety. Even here, different formats have developed, especially since the 1990s, including talk shows with overriding therapeutic intentions, like *Oprah* (US); 'tabloid' talk shows, like *Ricki Lake* (US); and audience discussion shows, like *Kilroy* (UK). Across talk show varieties, storytelling remains the chief means through which particular aspects of reality and specific facets of one's identity and the identities of others are constructed in these programmes. The main tellers are ordinary men and women – the lay participants – invited to the shows to share their views and experiences. Yet their storytelling is often controlled by the hosts, who also relay their own experiences and viewpoints from time to time.

The chapter is divided into two sections. The first one examines the kind of personal-experience stories that lay participants and hosts provide in talk shows. Data for this section comes from *Kilroy*. The second one looks at how these personal-experience stories are transformed into public narratives in the talk show studios by analysing lay participant–host co-narration and the effects that this has for the construction of particular individual and social identities as contextually appropriate or otherwise. Illustrative extracts from *Ricki Lake* are used in this section. Throughout the chapter, both the role of personal experience in 'authenticating' one's storytelling and the performed nature of such telling are foregrounded.

## 4.1  Personal experience stories and 'authentic talk'

Storytelling is the staple diet of daytime talk shows. The stories told in these programmes have been seen to fulfil a number of mutually inclusive functions, including the articulation of debate (Thornborrow 1997), the display of lay experience as a counterbalance to expert systems of knowledge (Carpignano et al. 1990; Livingstone and Lunt 1994), the construction of a sense of intimacy conducive to the public baring of participants' souls (Joyner Priest 1995; Shattuc 1997), the performance of enjoyable talk (Tolson 2006) and, importantly for us here, the creation of the impression that certain aspects of the socio-historical world are being directly accessed.

The latter function seems to persist in spite of known cases of hoaxes and 'fake' stories in these shows. In their search for spectacle, some talk shows have been accused of populating their studios with 'freaks' rather than 'ordinary folk'. In the US, for instance, this has led to viewers progressively 'com[ing] to look askance at the "truth" of talk' in these programmes. Already in 1995 the situation was such that questions about the shows shifted from '"where do they get these people?" to "are those people real"' (Shattuc 1997: 161).

Regardless of how 'real' daytime talk show participants may be, they are consistently encouraged to interact in ways that appear to be so: to generate 'authentic talk'. What does the latter consist of, though? To answer this question, let us first remind ourselves of the double articulation of broadcast talk – of its being locally triggered yet designed and produced for audiences situated elsewhere (see Chapter 1). This being the case, authentic talk in talk shows – and in broadcasting in general – cannot be other than its performance: the adoption of certain markers and production formats that may be validated as authentic by their intended audiences (Montgomery 2001). What these markers and production formats are depends, of course, on the particular broadcast context, the specific participants involved, the actual issues being talked about, and so forth.

There are three criteria for the performance of authentic talk, however, that seem to apply to a number of broadcast contexts (Montgomery 2001: 404–5). First, authentic talk designates the performance of 'talk that is true to the event/experience'. Secondly, it describes the performance of 'true to itself talk': 'talk that projects itself as nothing more or less than talk itself'. This refers to the performance of talk in ways that do not sound simulated or contrived. Thirdly, authentic talk is 'talk that is true to the self/person'. I agree with Montgomery that the third criterion has the least currency nowadays. Although, as we shall see in Part II in particular, many public figures and lay people currently engage in self-disclosing and/or confessional discourse in their television appearances, 'in a world of mass-mediated experiences, it is not clear that a strong public sense of the existential self can survive' (2001: 404). Instead, and paradoxically, it is seemingly only in fictional contexts that existential selves may be developed.

As for the other two criteria, they certainly apply to talk show talk and, in particular, to talk show storytelling. True-to-experience talk is usually performed through what Goffman (1981) calls 'fresh talk': a certain 'production format' in which all three speaker positions of 'animator', 'author' and 'principal' coincide. When speakers use fresh talk, they talk about their own experiences, beliefs, opinions, and so on. Personal-experience stories – the kind of stories that lay participants generally provide in talk shows – therefore meet the first criterion stipulated by Montgomery (2001). True-to-itself talk, in turn, is the kind of talk that lay participants' personal experience stories often yield. Although closely monitored by talk show hosts, these stories are usually performed as naturally occurring, spontaneous talk. Their 'authenticity' also owes to the fact that they reflect 'naturally' their tellers' lay (rather than expert) discursive category, as is next discussed.

### 4.1.1   Extraordinary tales of the ordinary

In a study of Jewish-American families' talk at dinnertime, Blum-Kulka (1997) found that parents generally directed their children's storytelling through practices of 'scaffolding', namely test questions and prompting combined with specifications and check questions. This was the case because at least one parent was generally privy to the events in their children's stories. Blum-Kulka's study also revealed that category membership – specifically, being a member of the category 'children' – was the only criterion against which parents assessed the tellability of their children's stories. In other words, even the hardly exceptional stories of the very young children were allowed to be told at dinnertime.

Blum-Kulka observes that there are similarities and differences between children's dinner-time stories and lay participants' talk show stories, especially in the audience discussion variety. Telling rights in the latter, for instance, are not automatically granted by virtue of category membership. Instead, the thematic world of these shows uses exceptionality as its main criterion to assess lay participants' entitlement to enter the realm of telling. Everyday, run-of-the-mill stories do not go far in the studio talk, even though tellers are invited to the programmes precisely because of their being ordinary folk. Instead, unexceptional-teller–exceptional-tale stories are favoured, which results in a plethora of personal-experience narratives that, by and large, fit Yatziv's (2000) categories for television's storytelling. They are stories that present deviations from either normality (e.g. 'man bites dog') or the normative order (e.g. 'homeless person found dead on the street').

Because the exceptionality criterion works by contrast, it also results in the performance of tellers' identities within these stories being monitored in different ways. In 'tabloid' talk shows, for example, lay participants' identities fall within three overarching categories: villains, victims and heroes (Gregori-Signes 2001). This is determined by the perceived needs of the shows' taleworld, their high confrontation levels (Hutchby 2001; Munson 1993) and their distinctly polarised moralising ethos. Storytelling here is reminiscent of pantomimes, with tellers' identities conforming to predictable types. It also bears resemblance to the gallery of (stereo-)typical characters that populate the taleworld of soap operas, such as the weak husband, the vindictive wife, and so forth.

Whilst retaining some of the black-and-white moralising ethos of 'tabloid' talk shows, other talk show varieties allow lay participants to perform less polarised, more diverse identities. As discussed in Chapter 2, for instance, in shows like *Kilroy* (and in *Oprah*) these participants have been likened to fairy-tale heroes who manage to achieve their goals partly thanks to the host's support, be it pragmatic (e.g. funding and celebrating in the studio a luxurious wedding, *Oprah* 2003) or emotional (e.g. counselling participants on a variety of problems), or both. A range of locally relevant identities within the overarching one of the fairytale hero are also available to lay participants, depending on the episode, the story and the particular ethos of the shows.

In a study of identity construction in *Kilroy*, for example, it was found that personal-experience stories of coping with distress often allowed for three main lay participant identities to be performed. One of them in particular, 'the ordinary self', met the terms of the unexceptional-teller–exceptional-tale criterion. Discursively, it was performed through what Sacks (1984: 417) refers to as 'the ordinary cast of mind', which includes the use of mitigating expressions (hedges) when referring to one's actions, such as 'nothing much' and 'just'. It was also frequently achieved by framing one's story within commonplace societal standards and by accompanying it with suitable non-verbal behaviour – such as using a soft, unassuming voice and looking down humbly at strategic moments, which was often captured by close-up shots. The other two identities were 'the fighter-cum-survivor self' and 'the humanitarian self'. These were chiefly performed through lexis that emphasised proactiveness and care for others, respectively, and through pronominal choices that combined sole-agency and other-sensitivity (Lorenzo-Dus 2001a).

Extract 4.1 (see p. 44) offers a typical example of the performance of these locally relevant identities within the context of a story about coping with bereavement in the family. Here, John presents himself as someone capable of making decisions in difficult moments. When his wife's nose bleed began, for example, he displayed a proactive disposition, first trying to stop the haemorrhage (lines 04–06) and then contacting, and taking her to, a hospital (lines 06–09). Note that in lines 04–09 he uses the first-person plural pronoun 'we' to refer to what most likely were sole-agency actions. Apart from allowing him to deflect extraordinariness, this enables John to present an image of marital togetherness and care for his wife. His performance of 'the fighter-cum-survivor self' is further realised through presenting himself in the internal evaluation of the story as a man who remained optimistic throughout clearly negative events (lines 12–15).

John's performance of 'the ordinary self' comes mainly from his plain telling style. In terms of paralinguistic and non-verbal behaviour, for instance, John uses only minimal voice inflection and gesturing (note the absence of relevant transcription symbols in the extract). Verbally, his is a clearly structured story, in which the complicating action is presented as a list of chronologically ordered facts (Labov 1972a): (1) 'we woke up and we tried to (.) stop . . .'; (2) 'all of a sudden we realised . . .'; (3) ' we phoned the hospital'; (4) 'and then we went off to the: hospital'; (5) ' they stopped the nose bleed . . .'; (6) 'so we did that'; (7) 'and they couldn't stop . . .'; (8) 'they kept her in hospital'; (9) 'they tried . . .'; (10) 'the wait went on'; and (11) 'a week went by . . .'. It is, nevertheless, a story that, within talk shows' reported preference for emotional self-disclosure, focuses on 'less storyable' events (Sacks 1984), such as a telephone call (lines 07–08) or the specific hospital to which its characters were referred (line 10).

### Kilroy (BBC, 1999)

The host, Robert Kilroy-Silk, has just asked a lay participant, John, whether it is actually possible to cope with the death of one's spouse. John's opinion comes in the form of a five-minute personal-experience narrative. Part of the 'orientation' (lasting approximately thirty seconds) and the 'result' (lasting approximately one minute) of this narrative has been omitted in the extract below. The former provides background information about John, his wife Donna and their three children. The latter, immediately after line 19 below, relays Donna's sad death in the final month of her pregnancy, her baby's arrival, and John's raising their four children on his own. Line 04 is the first event within the 'complicating action' of this story.[1] J: John; K: Robert Kilroy-Silk.

| | | | |
|---|---|---|---|
| *MS – K and J.* | 01 | J | [. . .] in er:: ninety eighty-three she developed a nose [ bleed |
| *CU – K leans* | 02 | K | [ how old |
| *forward closer* | 03 | K | were you then? |
| *to J. CU – J, to* | 04 | J | I was: we were both twenty nine and I::: (.) the nosebleed is like |
| *K.* | 05 | | six thirty on a Sunday morning so we woke up and we tried to |
| | 06 | | (.) stop the nose bleeding in all ways (.) and then all of a sudden |
| | 07 | | we realised this was too much >it wouldn't stop< (.) we phoned |
| | 08 | | the hospital and then we went off to the: hospital to have it |
| | 09 | | treated (.) they stopped the nose bleed and said if it if it star- |
| | 10 | | starts again to:: go to the: hospital that she was treated for (.) for |
| | 11 | | the: baby so we did that (.) and they couldn't stop the nose bleed |
| *LS – J, K and* | 12 | | to begin with (.) they kept her in hospital (.) and um (2.0) at this |
| *studio audience,* | 13 | | point I just thought everything was gonna be fine (.) and they'd |
| *around them.* | 14 | | fix the nose bleed quite shortly and we'd be going home with the |
| | 15 | | rest of the family on that day (.) but two days went by and they |
| | 16 | | tried three variations to stop it and she was given a blood |
| *CU – K, nods* | 17 | | transfusion (.) the wait went on to the fourth and fifth day and |
| *sympathetically* | 18 | | then a week went by and they still hadn't been able to stop the |
| *at John.* | 19 | | nose bleed [. . .] |

Why, then, is this lay participant allowed such extensive telling rights, with minimal host direction? Two reasons. First, the local identities that he performs in and through his narrative tally with the overarching lay participant identity of the fairytale hero (Chapter 2). John 'was there for' his wife and, since her tragic death, he has raised their children on his own through a great deal of determination. Secondly, these local identities sanction values of marital togetherness and of being able to cope with distress, both of which fit squarely within the show's underlying 'emotional DIY' ethos (Lorenzo-Dus 2003, 2005). The latter subsumes two beliefs: (1) one needs to work at improving one's life and (2) one benefits from advice-giving and advice-receiving in doing so. The first belief is characteristic of the enterprise culture (Fairclough 1991; Russell and Abercrombie 1991) and places a strong emphasis on developing, not necessarily within a business environment, 'a set of attributes, values and behaviours – such as resourcefulness, self-discipline, openness to risk and change – that enable people to succeed in bold and difficult undertakings' (Cameron 2000:

7). John's tale of coping in the face of adversity is a case in point, especially since he presents his 'difficult undertaking' from a position of humbleness (the ordinary self) and kindness (the humanitarian self).

The second belief is deeply rooted in British DIY society, where the enterprising individual is encouraged to solve his/her own problems but to do so by seeking advice about how to succeed, both from established sources – for example, manuals and experts such as psychologists and personal trainers – and from others in similar situations. This complements the therapeutic value attached to verbal sharing, the so-called 'talking cure' (Shattuc 1997), which is characteristic of many daytime talk shows. Thus, John's coming to the programme to talk about Donna's illness and death is not only positively appraised in the show as his implementing this talking cure but also as a case of advice-giving to others in the studio and at home, who may wish to become emotional DIYers, too.

Given the far from idiosyncratic nature of 'the ordinary self', 'the fighter-cum-survivor self' and 'the humanitarian self' in the context of lay participants' personal-experience stories in *Kilroy,* these locally instantiated identities and the versions of reality (e.g. the reality of coping with family bereavement) that they project are seen as natural in *Kilroy.* Through a concatenation of stories and storytellers like John, emotional DIY becomes *the* prism through which the world out there is viewed in the show.

### 4.1.2    Ordinary tales of the extraordinary

Lay participants are not the only people in talk shows who provide personal-experience stories. Talk show hosts do this, too. When playing the storyteller part, they temporarily step out of their main institutional role of 'talk monitor' (Illie 1999) to become involved in the taleworld of the talk show. But what kind of personal experiences do talk show hosts share with guests, studio audiences and viewers? Two factors play a salient part in deciding upon their precise content and form. First, talk show hosts are well-known, some of them are (inter)national celebrities. Their public status, not to mention their financial means, distances them from the average lay participant in their shows. Yet, and secondly, host–participant rapport is strongly promoted in many daytime talk shows, especially in those with therapeutic goals. This means that the hosts' personal-experience storytelling needs to find ways to connect at some level with the personal-experience storytelling offered by the lay participants.

Faced with such a conundrum, daytime talk show hosts have often opted for disclosing ordinary experiences within their otherwise extraordinary identities. Possibly the best-known case of this practice is Oprah Winfrey, who in her shows and other public appearances has frequently spoken about her working-class background, the abuse she suffered as a child and her weight problems. These experiences are not ordinary *per se* – child abuse, for instance, is fortunately not something that most ordinary men and women experience in their lives. But they are ordinary within the microcosm of the talk show and, especially, of episodes on weight problems, child abuse, poverty, and so forth. Talking about such experiences thus seeks to create a rapport – even to promote

### Kilroy (1999)

[Jane is a young female with a broad Liverpool accent. She is talking about her experience of sexual harassment at work. J: Jane; K: Robert Kilroy-Silk; A: studio audience.]

| | | | |
|---|---|---|---|
| MS – J and K sitting | 01 | J | [. . .] but then it started to get into (.) getting weird (.) it's |
| side by side in the | 02 | | not a joke anymore (.) it's like when I was bending over |
| studio. | 03 | | he would smack my arse (.) [ and it went on |
| CU – K, offended tone | 04 | K | [YOU MIGHT HAVE |
| of voice. MS – J and | 05 | | SAID BOTTOM (.) |
| K. CU – K smiling | 06 | | oh THANK YOU very much (.) thank you (2.0) |
| broadly at J. LS – J | 07 | A | [laughter |
| and A. CU – K covers | 08 | K | [o:::h dear |
| face with hands as if | 09 | | I am going to get ten thousand letters now and you know |
| in despair. MS – K | 10 | | what? (.) I'm the one who has to reply to them and put |
| looks around him at A. | 11 | | the stamps on them |
| CU – J. | 12 | | [ and you'll be off back to Liverpool (3.0) |
| | 13 | J | [laughing heartily |
| LS – A. | 14 | A | [laughter |
| MS – K and J. | 15 | K | right well (.) what did you do then? [. . .] |

an identification – between host and lay participants. It also contributes to a 'rhetoric of authenticity' (Dyer 1991; Tolson 1991) that relies on subscribing to down-to-earth, ordinary self-constructions.

Not all talk show hosts, however, take their 'ordinary' selves seriously, as Extract 4.2 above, from a *Kilroy* episode on sexual harassment in work, shows. In this extract, Kilroy is performing his role of talk monitor. He is specifically concerned with ensuring that the participants in his show use the appropriate register for BBC daytime television, which explains why, as soon as Jane uses the term 'arse' in line 03, Kilroy interrupts her. Raising his voice over Jane's, in lines 04–05 he self-apportions – and succeeds in retaining – the speaking floor. What follows continues to be a performance of his talk monitor role, but one which seeks to establish a rapport with Jane and, simultaneously, to project a particular self-identity.

Participant–host rapport is built through references to common ground and ironic banter. At first sight, Kilroy's interruption in lines 04–06 of Jane's self-disclosing talk may appear anything but an attempt to build rapport, especially given the loud and offended tone of his voice. Yet, the latter is overtly exaggerated and coincides with a close-up of the host smiling broadly in Jane's direction. The contrast between his language and his body language, skilfully captured by the camera in lines 04–07, promotes the interpretation of his turn as ironic banter, that is, as a rapport-building strategy. It is easy for Jane, and the studio and home audience likewise, to interpret Kilroy's turn as playful irony.

Consider line 06 in particular. There is a clash between the item chosen by Kilroy to fill this part of his turn (the speech act of thanking) and the preceding part of the turn in which it appears (a loud reprimand, in lines 04–05). The message thereby conveyed is that Jane may have committed a register *faux pas* but that she can nevertheless still count on the host's support in telling her story. The studio audience also recognises the ironic force behind Kilroy's turn, as their outburst of laughter in line 07 indicates. Kilroy's irony may signal, too, his desire not to approach directly what is really a sensitive topic at a difficult point in Jane's story, namely her becoming aware of her boss's inappropriate conduct (lines 02–03). Moreover, as is generally known in the UK, Kilroy comes from Liverpool. His reference in line 12 to Jane returning to that city untroubled by the 'chaos' that her contribution to the show has brought to her famous regional 'equal' is therefore an attempt to construct a common geographical ground despite the social and dialectal distance between them. After all, Kilroy is neither a subordinate in his workplace nor does he have a noticeable Liverpool accent.

Regarding Kilroy's self-presentation in Extract 4.2, this revolves around his telling a brief personal-experience story. In lines 08–12, Kilroy elaborates on his previous ironic thanking. His talk sounds 'true to itself' at this stage. It includes expressive, emphatic (para)language ('o:::h dear') and body language (covering his face with his hands). It also sounds 'true to experience': it describes a scene in which he is engrossed in the task of answering letters. Kilroy's talk in lines 08–12, then, provides an instance of a media personality performing authentic talk on television through the seemingly unscripted relaying of personal experience.

At the same time, Kilroy's personal experience is plainly fictitious. Kilroy may well be answering letters in his story but these are letters in which he, as a media personality, replies to displeased viewers. They are far from ordinary letters. In 'real life', such letters are likely to be written by the show's administrative staff, perhaps by Kilroy's personal assistant. Furthermore, the audience knows that it is unlikely that a media personality would stick the stamps on the letters to be sent to viewers. Kilroy's story is thus neither one to which lay participants in the studio can relate easily nor one meant to be taken as literally true. Instead, it is a means to an end: to make his audience laugh. Note, in this respect, the orientation of his body language towards, and his direct gaze at, the studio audience in lines 10–11, as well as his three-second pause in line 12 to allow for the audience's, and Jane's, supportive laughter to be heard.

Kilroy's brief story is, too, an attempt to authenticate his media persona both by explicitly acknowledging his extraordinary self and by ironising the image of the ordinary talk show host. Whilst not always ironic, this combining of ordinary (layman) and extraordinary (media personality) aspects of Kilroy's identity was a recurring feature of his performance. He would refer, for example, to his having similar health problems to those relayed by participants in the studio but then reveal his being examined by the best consultants in the world. He would, too, openly side with laity and against the political system whilst also overtly admitting to using his position as a Labour Party Member of Parliament in the past to favour certain citizens over others (Lorenzo-Dus 2005). In short, then, Kilroy's presentation of self through an imaginary personal-experience anecdote in Extract 4.2 uses performativity (the overt, reflexive performance of self) to project, paradoxically, a rhetoric of authenticity about himself.

## 4.2    Co-performing narratives

Daytime talk show storytelling shares with other forms of television discourse the fact that it is primarily oriented towards an unheard and unseen viewing audience. It is this characteristic that determines the principal style of narration used in these shows, namely 'heavily scaffolded pseudo-dialog' (Blum-Kulka 2001:104), in which host and participant deliver a story through question–answer sequences.

Although relayed to a host in a television studio, talk show stories are not conversationally new to him/her. Instead, and similarly to the children–parents dinnertime stories in Blum-Kulka's (1997) study (see Section 4.1), they comprise 'A–B events' (Labov, 1972b): events that are known to teller and recipient and that therefore give authorship rights to both. What is more, given the host's interactionally powerful position as the studio's talk monitor, it is often he/she who decides who does what during the telling.

To illustrate this feature of daytime talk show storytelling, and its potential impact on the construction of particular versions of reality in these shows, let us next analyse an extract from a *Ricki Lake* episode broadcast on the US National Day to Prevent Teen Pregnancy.

Extract 4.3 below eproduces the orientation stage of a narrative that continues

---

**EXTRACT 4.3**

### *Ricki Lake* (Sony Pictures Television, 2003)

[Ricki Lake is sitting among a group of approximately twenty female teenagers on the studio stage. One of them, Latoya, has just told the story of her becoming pregnant at the age of fifteen. Another one, Christine, is identified by the caption at the bottom of the screen during most of her contribution as being nineteen years of age and a single mother. RL: Ricki Lake; C: Christine; L: Latoya; Ts: Teenagers.]

| | | | |
|---|---|---|---|
| *MS – RL and C. To* | 01 | RL | you can relate to that can't [you? you got pregnant at |
| *C.* | 02 | C | [°yeah° |
| | 03 | RL | sixteen <u>AND</u> seventeen |
| *CU – C, nods.* | 04 | C | yes (.) °correct° |
| *CU – RL.* | 05 | RL | and um er::: your children are no::w <u>how</u> <u>old</u>? |
| *MS – RL and C. RL* | 06 | C | my oldest is gonna be three and my baby's just turned |
| *nods.* | 07 | | one = |
| *CU – RL.* | 08 | RL | = and <<u>both the fathers</u>> are no longer in the picture |
| *MS – RL and C.* | 09 | C | °correct° |
| | 10 | RL | you are raising two ba[bies |
| *CU – C, nods.* | 11 | C | [on my own = |
| | 12 | RL | = and you're <u>STILL</u> a baby [yourself |
| *LS – studio stage.* | 13 | C | [correct = |
| *LS – some Ts talking.* | 14 | L | = she's <u>far</u> too [young |
| *MS – L.* | 15 | Ts | [yeah too y- (xxxx) too young (xxxx) |
| *CU – RL, to camera.* | 16 | RL | <u>OK</u> (2.0) let's hear more [. . .] |

for approximately five more minutes. Being a personal-experience story, its principal would be expected to be also its author and animator. As Goffman (1981) and other commentators (Clayman 1992; Clayman and Heritage 2002) note, however, production roles in broadcast talk are often shared. In Extract 4.3, Christine occupies the production role of principal but those of animator and author are mainly realised by Ricki Lake. It is the host who physically provides the background to Christine's story, namely that: (1) she twice became pregnant as a teenager (lines 01–03); (2) her partners left (line 08); and (3) she is raising her children by herself (line 10). Christine only confirms the host's orientation through minimal responses in lines 02, 04 and 09, and through turn completion in line 11.

It is also the host who, at this orientation stage, filters the story through a particular perspective, selecting the specific words that will make it retrievable to its audience in a certain fashion. Within her production role of author, for instance, Ricki Lake uses the idiom 'no longer in the picture' (line 08), which evaluates and adds colour to the fact that Christine's partners have left her. She also chooses the word 'baby' (line 12), thereby making Christine's youth a salient aspect of the story. Note, too, Ricki Lake's loudness and marked stress in 'AND' (line 03) and 'STILL' (line 12), which emphasise Christine's teen pregnan*cies* and her being too young to be a mother, respectively.

The host's animation and authoring of the orientation of the personal-experience story, which Christine endorses, have the effect of projecting an 'agreed' identity for this participant in the studio right from the outset. This can be seen, for example, when in line 14 Latoya latches on to Christine's confirmation turn (line 13) to support emphatically the host's evaluative remark regarding Christine's youth (line 12) thus: 'she's far too [young'. Latoya's remark is immediately validated by the group of teenagers in the studio who, in line 15, interrupt her to show their support: '[yeah too y- (xxxx) too young (xxxx)'. The host's seemingly neutral observation regarding Christine's age in line 12 therefore triggers an evaluative snowball, which brings to the fore of the studio talk the negative consequences for female teenagers of having unprotected sex.

If 'fresh talk' is important to the performance of authentic talk in shows such as *Ricki Lake*, and since these shows claim to give a voice to ordinary men and women, why, then, do their hosts appropriate the authorship and animation of their lay participants' stories? The answer rests, once more, in the double articulation of broadcast talk, as we next discuss.

The storyrealm of talk shows is designed and articulated for multiple 'hearers'. First, there is the host, to whom the stories are generally recounted in the talk show studio, even though more often than not he/she is also actively involved in their telling and is privy to most of their facts. Then there are the other participants in the studio. For instance, in 'tabloid' talk shows, villain and victim are often brought together on the stage and, once there, they tell each other their own, usually contradictory, versions of the same story. In audience discussion shows, participants gather on a studio set to have their say and this means that their stories are sometimes directly addressed to other participants (Thornborrow 1997). In addition to host and participant(s), there are also the members of the studio audience, who evaluate the participants' stories in various ways. And then, of course, there are the viewers. Although each of the above 'hearers' is a ratified recipient of the stories being told in the talk show studios, it is vital that demands for 'freshness' be made compatible with those for comprehensibility, entertainment and the construction of particular versions of reality and the promotion of specific facets of identity. Host intervention in lay participants' storytelling is mainly geared to ensure that such compatibility exists, especially for the benefit of the viewers.

Ricki Lake's input in Extract 4.3 is thus oriented towards producing a story that the programme's viewers may be able to enjoy, to retrieve easily and to evaluate 'appropriately'. This is achieved, for instance, by dramatically introducing certain details in the orientation, such as the ages at which Christine became pregnant (lines 01–04) and her children's ages at the time of the show's broadcast (lines 05–07). From within her author and animator roles, Ricki Lake highlights the negative consequences that having unprotected sex may have, rather than allowing the show's audience to draw that same conclusion – or not, as the case may be – by themselves. The programme's stance on the day's topic is succinctly but effectively captured in its title 'Stop Teen Pregnancy!' and evaluated by Ricki Lake at the onset of the episode as 'the endemic disease of teen pregnancy'. A number of heavily scaffolded pseudo-dialogues between the host and the participant, such as the one involving the orientation to Christine's personal-experience story in Extract 4.3, contribute to the construction of an 'agreed' stance on the reality of teen pregnancy and the identity of teenage mothers.

Talk show hosts influence strongly who tells what part of a lay participant's story, selecting its tellable events and foregrounding specific evaluations of these events and of their protagonists. Lay participants' personal-experience stories in daytime talk shows are, consequently, interactionally mediated or 'narrativised' through a set of semiotic resources which we explore in the final section of this chapter.

### 4.2.1   The narrativisation of lay experience in talk shows

In one of the pioneering studies of broadcast talk, Montgomery (1991) found that the retelling of personal-experience stories by a radio disc jockey (DJ) in the Simon Bates' show *Our Tune* (Radio 1, UK) deftly combined the styles of private confessional letter and public narrative. The former entailed the DJ's performing empathetic orientations towards the principals of those personal-experience stories. The latter involved his presenting the stories at a 'discursive arm's length' (1991: 174), that is, framing them as authentic but withholding sufficient information to preserve anonymity.

Within daytime television talk shows, the transition from private experience to public narrative goes beyond hosts enabling the telling of lay participants' stories. When it comes to talk show storytelling, lay experience is jointly narrativised by hosts and participants. This involves, amongst other things, making and implementing decisions regarding when and how to embed participants' experiences into the talk show talk, how to go about constructing participants' identities in the studio, and how to ensure that viewers get the 'right' message and are sufficiently entertained to remain loyal.

Different narrative roles are used to achieve the above, some of which intersect with those found in conversational storytelling, namely story introducer, narrator, co-narrator, protagonist, primary recipient, problematiser and problematisee (Ochs and Taylor 1992). In daytime talk shows, lay participants' stories are often host-introduced (Extracts 4.1–4.3). Lay participants generally retain the role of protagonists (principals), whilst hosts often act as co-narrators, which may involve appropriation of the production roles of animator and author (Extract 4.3). The role of primary recipient is invariably assumed by the viewers, with co-present others (the studio audience) occupying the role of also ratified, yet secondary, recipients. As for the roles of problematiser and problematisee, these respectively describe the critical evaluation of the story and the target of such evaluation. Lay participants are normally the problematisees, and the host and, less frequently, the studio audience the problematisers.

To these roles Thornborrow (2001) adds that of the 'dramatiser', which entails the explicit production of the stories as public performances. This role is realised mainly by talk show hosts, often through the use of a number of interactional devices such as marked stress on, and/or repetition of, specific words, 'haranguing' the studio audience at key moments to elicit their booing, cheering and other forms of evaluation, strategically pausing prior to and/or following dramatic revelations from the participants, and so forth.

All the above narrative roles are fluid; in other words, they are all open to some negotiation during the telling. For example, the role of problematiser may first be realised by a member of the studio audience asking the participant a question and then immediately followed up, and further problematised and/or dramatised, by the host.

Extract 4.4 (see p. 52), from the third segment of the *Ricki Lake* episode 'Stop Teen Pregnancy!', illustrates the narrativisation of personal experience in talk shows. Ricki Lake's first turn brings Reinaldo into the talk show storyrealm. In line 01, and looking at her cue card, she alerts viewers of a coming teen-pregnancy story and introduces its protagonist: 'now I wanna talk to Reinaldo'. She next animates and authors the story's orientation (lines 02–04), providing information that already sets the moral background against which Reinaldo's identity will subsequently be evaluated, namely that having unprotected sex and becoming a father at the age of fourteen have negative consequences. As with Christine in Extract 4.3, Reinaldo's narrative and production roles at this initial stage are only those of, respectively, protagonist and principal.

Throughout the extract, the host problematises and dramatises specific aspects of Reinaldo's story. The first instance occurs in line 03. Here she uses marked stress on, and slowly utters, the phrase '<the first time>', at the same time as stopping reading from her cue card to look directly to camera. Her strategic combination of language, paralanguage and body language at this point not only increases the dramatic potential of the fact recounted but also

### *Ricki Lake* (Sony Pictures Television, 2003)

[The extract follows a brief prerecorded video of 'bad teenage boys' speaking individually to camera of their lack of qualms about getting teenage girls pregnant and then 'ditching' them afterwards. Immediately after the commercial break that follows the video, there is a long-range, establishing shot of the studio stage. The host is now sitting amongst a group of approximately twenty male teenagers that includes the bad teenage boys. RL: Ricki Lake; R: Reinaldo. He is identified by a caption as nineteen and a father.]

| | | | |
|---|---|---|---|
| CU – RL, *looking at her cue card.* | 01 | RL | well (.) now I wanna talk to Reinaldo (2.0) |
| MS – RL and R. | 02 | | you got a girl pregnant |
| CU – RL, *looks up from cue card,* | 03 | | <u>the first time</u> that you had sex at |
| *to camera.* | 04 | | fourteen (2.0) |
| CU – R, *looking down as though* | 05 | R | °yeah° = |
| *embarrassed.* | 06 | | |
| CU – RL, *looks at 'bad boys',* | 07 | RL | = (3.0) |
| *at camera, and then at R,* | 08 | | |
| *who is looking at the floor as she* | 09 | | <u>rotten luck huh?</u> |
| *speaks.* | 10 | | |
| CU – R, *looks up at RL and nods* | 11 | R | °yeah° |
| *with embarrassment, then quickly* | 12 | | |
| *to MS of several 'bad boys' in* | 13 | | (4.0) |
| *studio also looking down as* | 14 | | |
| *though embarrassed.* | 15 | RL | did you know about the consequences of |
| CU – RL. | 16 | | having unprotected sex? |
| CU – R. | 17 | R | I mean (.) I wasn't even thinking about the |
| | 18 | | consequences (.) I was just (.) thinking |
| CU – RL *nodding.* | 19 | | about the present er (.) it happened (.) >I'm |
| | 20 | | not saying I regret it< (.) er it's (.) it's just |
| CU – R. | 21 | | (.) it took my childhood from me (.) er (2.0) |
| | 22 | | er (.) my son's growing up (xxxx) you see |
| MS – RL and R. | 23 | | (.) I took a lot from <u>him</u> too (.) you know (.) |
| | 24 | | things could've been <u>a lot better</u> (.) I'm not |
| | 25 | | saying things were the worst for him but (.) |
| | 26 | | it could've been a whole (.) <u>lot better</u> for me |
| | 27 | | as well [. . .] |

invites viewers to problematise (i.e., here, to condemn), as she is doing, Reinaldo's behaviour.

For his part, Reinaldo takes up the roles of problematisee and co-dramatiser. During the whole extract, in fact, Reinaldo appears at ease with his role of problematisee. With the exception of two challenges to the show's 'Stop teen pregnancy!' lesson ('>I'm not saying I regret it<', lines 19–20; and 'I'm not saying things were the worst for him', lines 24–25), he co-constructs his identity as that of a young man who has learnt his lesson and now knows that 'things could've been a whole (.) lot better' for him and for his son (line 24–27).

Host/participant co-dramatisation is particularly evident in lines 01–15. Ricki Lake's ironic question '<u>rotten</u> luck <u>huh</u>?' (line 09), the three-second pause that precedes it (line 07–08), and the marked stress with which the question is partly uttered are all intended to trigger a reaction from the story's addressed recipients at this moment in time: the bad teenage boys, including Reinaldo. This comes in the form of embarrassment both from Reinaldo, who lowers his gaze and head, nods and quietly agrees with the host (lines 11–12), and from the bad teenage boys, who also look down discomfitedly (lines 14–15). The host's ironic question is, too, intended to elicit agreement from the viewers, who in line 08 are once more, through Ricki Lake's direct gaze to camera, invited to problematise – and evaluate – Reinaldo's story.

Crucially, the dramatisation and problematisation in Extract 4.4 by Riki Lake and Reinaldo are made salient through a clever selection of camera angles. Within the space of a few seconds, viewers are offered consecutive host and participant close-ups and, next, shots of the other teenagers in the studio engaged in 'appropriate' narrative evaluation. Following the host's ironic question in line 09, for example, there is a brief close-up of Reinaldo's (non-)verbal acknowledgement of past wrongdoing. The camera then generalises his response through a lengthy (four seconds) medium-range shot of some of the bad teenage boys also nodding and looking embarrassed (lines 11–15). It is this use of verbal and visual resources involving host, participants and talk show teams (camera crew, show producers) that transforms Reinaldo's personal experience of teen parenting into a public narrative. *Ricki Lake*'s viewers may thus still receive this as a private experience but in an entertaining and moralising format.

## 4.3 Conclusion

This chapter has examined the 'depiction' of the socio-historical world in daytime talk show storytelling. In the case of ordinary people's experiences, and within the context of narratives of considerable emotional distress in *Kilroy*, the chapter has illustrated the value of performing local identities of ordinariness, resilience and solidarity. Even when storytelling is performed through talk that is neither particularly 'true to itself' nor focused on remarkable events, as was the case in Extract 4.1, its projection of local identities that are seen to be congruent with the underlying 'emotional DIY' ethos of this show secures extended telling rights.

As for extraordinary tellers, specifically talk show hosts, the benefits of performing first-hand experience stories have been seen to lie in the building of a participant–host rapport. They have also been seen to reside in the construction of media personalities that may be validated as authentic. Traditionally it was believed that small-screen personalities needed to subscribe to images of ordinariness to achieve this. However, and as the analysis of Extract 4.2 showed, some of these personalities are actually choosing to ironise their public selves in order to come across as authentic – an issue that is further explored throughout the book and discussed in detail in Chapter 14.

Talk shows' claim to provide true stories by real people goes hand in hand with their need to provide entertainment and to monitor the particular versions of reality and the specific ordinary people identities to be projected through storytelling. Because of this, talk show storytelling is often produced through host–participant co-narration, whereby hosts play a leading part in the participants' verbal sharing. Through narrative practices such as heavily scaffolded pseudo-dialogues, the hosts of these shows ensure that the participants' personal experiences and emotions become public accounts that fit the shows' claims and needs. Aided by the strategic use of camera work, for instance, the hosts dramatise and problematise certain narrative facts for the viewers.

Talk show storytelling, then, offers a clear instance of the ideological, bardic role of television (see Chapter 2). Even though the shows claim to give a public voice to a gallery of ordinary men and women whose opinions and experiences would otherwise remain unheard, the narrative practices in place in these shows mean that the opportunities for these ordinary folk to express their views and relay their experiences are carefully mediated. In the next part of the book, specifically in Chapters 6 and 7, we explore further how different discursive categories (ordinary people, professional broadcasters, celebrities) disclose their feelings and relay their experiences before the cameras. First, though, Chapter 5 examines at a conceptual level the television climate of 'closeness' in which such verbal sharing takes place.

# Part II

## Closeness

# Closeness . . . or How Television Gets Up Close and Personal

5

Broadcasting could not speak to its audience as a crowd.
It had to learn to speak to them as individuals. (Scannell 1991: 3)

In the above quote, Scannell is commenting on the BBC's realisation in the early 1930s that radio and television might well be mass media but that their ways of communicating could not be so. As the then BBC Head of Talks, Hilda Matheson, reportedly argued at the time: 'The person sitting at the other end expected the speaker to address him personally, simply, almost familiarly, as man to man.' (Matheson (1933: 75–76) in Scannell 1991: 3). This was believed to attune radio and television to the spheres of domesticity and leisure, in which the activities of listening to the radio and watching television were understood to take place. Broadcasting, it soon became apparent, had to talk to millions as though it were talking to one. It had to use 'for-anyone-as-someone structures': each viewer had to feel that what he/she was seeing and hearing was addressed to him/her directly and individually, even though it was clearly intended for anyone who happened to be tuned in (Scannell 2000). Broadcasting had, in short, to get up close and personal with audiences for its survival.

In principle, viewers should listen to what is being said on television, rather than simply hear it. They should watch what they are being shown, rather than merely see a flow of moving images on their screens. Yet television producers can neither force viewers to watch specific programmes nor to behave as ideal viewers, for example by watching programmes from beginning to end. They have therefore had to devise ways first to secure viewer interest and then to retain viewer loyalty. One favoured means of doing so is to create the impression of television–viewer interactivity.

When one first thinks of interactivity in relation to contemporary television, one tends to associate it with technological innovation. Phone-ins, for example, are not just revenue-raising schemes but are also amongst the earliest vehicles to enable viewers to participate in – or interact with – television. These have now become common across television formats ranging from morning television through to quiz and talent shows. More lately, especially with the development of digital television and the web, new vistas of interactivity opportunities have opened up, such as podcasting, on-demand programming and interactive features accessed through one's remote control.

However, and as mentioned in Chapter 1, one should appreciate but not get carried away by what technology may contribute to the future of television (discourse), the communicative ethos of which – and of radio – remains one of interactivity or, in Scannell's (1989: 156; see also 1996) term, 'sociability'. Television talk appears 'relaxed and sociable, shareable and accessible, non-exclusive, equally talkable about in principle and in practice by everyone'.

At a basic level, attempts at creating a sense of television–viewer sociable interactivity are demonstrated in the opening and closing segments of a number of broadcasts. As we noted in Chapter 2, for example, talk show hosts often close their programmes by addressing viewers 'directly' with narrative codas that wrap up the content and moral significance of the preceding talk. In some cases, they also 'summon' viewers for their next 'interaction'. Robert Kilroy-Silk, for instance, regularly ended his show with the following words to camera and always in close-up: 'Take care of yourselves. I'll see you in the morning.'

The news, too, opens and closes with formulae such as, respectively, 'Good evening. This is the News at Ten' and 'From all of us here in the newsroom, good night.' Clearly, there is no expectation that the viewers will reciprocate this 'direct mode of adddress' (Allan 2004; Corner 1995; Tolson 1996) and actually produce the second part of these greeting and leave-taking adjacency pairs. Newsreaders just move on to list the main headlines of the day or break their gaze to camera and look down at their notes to signal that the news is over. Newsreaders' look-to-camera whilst reading from an autocue is intended to convey the impression of interactivity. It directs their talk out of the studio in which it is generated, which implies that there is a unique 'someone some-place to receive [it] who turns out, in each case, to be "me"' (Scannell 2000: 11). Unlike in unmediated conversations, newsreaders' direct verbal address and look out to viewers do not signal any actual interpersonal exchange. Yet because they are produced in real time, and performed as for-anyone-as-someone structures, they signal the potential for interaction and place an anonymous collective of viewing someones in a situation of pseudo, or simu-lated, interactivity.

Television's sociability becomes particularly evident when those on it perform emotional talk. Presenters, ordinary people and celebrities alike often talk about their experiences and feelings before the television cameras. In Chapter 3, for example, we showed how celebrity narrators' personal asides to camera in documentaries seek to create a sense of trust and narrator–viewer involvement from which to construct their realism. These asides reduce the visual (close-up camera angles) and verbal (experiential, confidant-like talk) distance between the world inhabited by the narrator and the world inhabited by the viewers. And in Chapter 4 we discussed the role of personal experience in authenticating talk show storytelling. In this part of the book, we explore the links between the performance of private, emotional talk and the medium's efforts at getting close to viewers in 'serious' (live news, Chapter 6) and 'banal' (celebrity talk shows and reality shows, Chapter 7) forms of television. In some reality shows, for example, ordinary folk are filmed talking in personal, emotionally charged ways to portable video cameras in the privacy of their own homes. Use of amateur filming equipment and domestic settings, on the one hand, and the confessional content of their talk, on the other, mean that such talk seemingly reveals aspects of the inner selves of these people. The impression is thereby created that those ordinary people on the screen are getting up close and personal with the viewers.

Sociability between those on television and those watching it is not the only means by which television fosters a sense of proximity and connection. Interactivity amongst those on television is also a popular means of constructing a sense of interpersonal closeness, which viewers are made to feel part of, albeit vicariously. We saw in Chapter 4, for example, that lay participants' stories in talk shows are often performed as heavily scaffolded pseudo-dialogues: as hosts and participants talked to each other, and guided by the prompts and probes of the former, the experiences and emotions of the latter became 'directly' accessible to viewers. On-screen cross-talk (also known as 'happy talk') has become a common form of news packaging, too. This is not simply a matter of two newsreaders talking about the events that they are about to present or have just presented, although this too happens. It is increasingly also a matter of news stories being delivered as sequences of small talk between newsreaders and news reporters. These interactive sequences place viewers as eavesdroppers upon the small talk of those on the screen, even though it is perfectly clear to viewers that newsreaders' and reporters' talk occurs because of them.

Whether amongst those on television or between them and viewers, moreover, a common thread has emerged over the years: the more casual the style of the interaction, the better. Fairclough (1989, 1995, 1998) has famously noted that television and other public life domains have been colonised by private forms of talk, specifically by those typically found in conversational or dialogic modes. The 'conversationalisation' of public discourse, as this phenomenon has become known, is evident, for example, in the rising use across a number of public domains of colloquial and idiomatic speech, conversational discourse markers and populist stances, such as the use of the inclusive 'we' to identify television and viewers.

Whilst Fairclough's concept of conversationalisation highlights the influence that the realm of the private has progressively exerted on public life domains, reciprocal influence should not be underestimated. Consider the emphasis on the emotional DIY value of verbal sharing in talk shows (see Chapter 4). This emphasis is in fact part of a number of practices which, together, promote emotional expressiveness across a range of private and public contexts. Reading self-help books, attending group therapy meetings, 'talking things through' with one's partner, one's children, one's colleagues and one's boss are all symptomatic of the current fascination with the verbalisation of emotions. As Cameron (2003: 30–1) argues, we may say different things in different contexts (e.g. at a private function and in a talk show), but the way that we present ourselves and relate to our interlocutors often conforms to the same 'ideal', namely to be:

articulate, direct, egalitarian, co-operative, emotionally expressive, honest and sincere. This is presented not just as a linguistic ideal, but implicitly also as a definition of a morally admirable person. Gal (1995) has made the point that judgements on language-use very often have this moral dimension. [. . .] In the case of 'good communication', the moral dimension is very overt. In some texts the author [a communication expert] says in so many words that silence or emotional inexpressiveness indicates a closed, ungenerous person.

The ideal of good communication thus requires the performance of emotional talk, which is itself infused with morality in its therapeutic value. Moreover, it is an ideal that spreads across contexts of communication, private and public, in a number of cultures. Montgomery's (1999) analysis of public tributes in Britain upon the death of Princess Diana, for instance, has shown that informal, emotional and open ways of communicating increasingly apply to public as well as private discourse and that their purchase on society as a whole is reinforced by their being routinely performed on television.

In addition to the performance of emotional expressiveness, television's sociability is also partly reliant on 'liveliness' (Tolson 2006). Liveliness is not a new concept – it is in fact Tolson's pun on a well-trodden notion in media research: 'liveness', which is discussed in detail at the beginning of Chapter 6. For now, however, it is important to note that the performance of liveliness on television takes Fairclough's notion of conversationalisation a step further. It is not only the informality of conversation that is appealing to the television medium but also its unscriptedness. Real-life conversations feel spontaneous because they evolve on a moment-by-moment basis, rather than according to predictable steps. We may expect them to start and finish with a greeting and a leave-taking adjacency pair, respectively. But the actual form and content of these pairs are never entirely foreseeable, which is why they sound 'lively' (natural, spontaneous). Much broadcast output nowadays aspires to appear lively too, including that which has evidently been recorded and scripted to some degree. The importance of liveliness for the construction of a general sense of closeness on television is such that even television output which is technically live and unscripted maximally publicises the naturalness of its here-and-nowness.

Chapter 6 explores this aspect of television discourse in relation to live newscasts. These newscasts, which aim to appear unscripted and live, meet the technical requirement of temporal synchronicity with the real-life events that they broadcast. Yet they regularly draw upon a number of semiotic resources to bolster this impression. Speech often sounds unrehearsed and involves interactions that are associated with naturally occurring contexts of communication, such as personal exchanges between newsreaders and on-location reporters. Images and sound convey at times a 'rough' feel – the visual and sonic equivalent of script concealment. The intended effect of this 'aesthetic of liveness' (Richardson and Meinhof 1999) appears to be the natural (lively) performance of conditions of real time, unmediated viewing. These seek to reduce the distance between what and who appears on the screen and the viewers.

Looking and sounding lively is also important in talk and reality shows, where this not only serves as a chief means of creating the impression of close-ness between those on television and viewers but also of authenticating the former's talk. One favoured means of doing so is for people on television to release their emotions. This is because, generally speaking, we do not plan to feel happy, sad, disappointed, angry, and so forth. We simply feel one or more of these ways depending on a number of factors. By foregrounding emotional talk, then, reality and talk shows try to capture a sense of spontaneity. They package for public consumption, furthermore, a currently much-valued form of enter-tainment, as the analysis in Chapter 7 will show.

An indication of television's success in the various manifestations of sociabil-ity aforementioned is the development of 'para-social interactions' (Horton and Wohl 1956) between some viewers and certain television performers. Based on a pyschological study of the 1950s American programme, *The Johnny Carson Show,* Horton and Wohl (1956: 223) showed that through presenters' (such as Carson's) recurrent use of direct address to their viewers, the latter developed the feeling that they knew the former 'in somewhat the same ways that [they knew] their chosen friends: through direct observation and interpretation of appear-ance, gestures and voice, conversation and conduct in a variety of situations'.

Horton and Wohl, it must be noted, did not substantiate their arguments with empirical evidence. However, a number of subsequent studies on viewers' responses to, for example, talk show hosts' performances have done so. The hosts in these shows are described by some of their viewers as 'real' people, rather than as people playing the part of hosts in a talk show (see Livingstone and Lunt 1994). A number of technical and representational codes in these programmes enhance such an impression. Their studio sets, for instance, are often designed as informal spaces. There are also abundant camera close-ups of the hosts, which allow for viewers' 'direct' observation and interpretation of their (the hosts') appearance, gestures and voice. A marked preponderance of close-ups, too, exposes viewers to the ways in which the hosts interact with others on the screen and conduct themselves in a variety of situations, such as giving advice, smiling sympathetically, disclosing their own feelings and personal experiences, and so forth.

This development of parasocial interactions reflects and further asserts a wider process of 'synthetic personalisation' in a number of contemporary soci-eties – a process whereby non-co-present and/or anonymous relations have progressively moved 'in the direction of equality, solidarity and intimacy' (Fairclough 1989: 217). Synthetic personalisation is by no means restricted to the medium of television. Mediated relationships with absent others are part and parcel of our daily lives. We nowadays conduct many social interactions within a 'mediated social order' (Moores 2000): television, radio, chat rooms, mobile telephone text messages, video-linked conferences, web logs, and so on. Through each and every one of these old and new media, we construct and forge relations with others – often in 'close' ways. Consider, for instance, the relative ease with which we communicate informally by e-mail with people whom we have never met or hardly know. Seen in this light, the synthetic personalisation and 'intimacy at a distance' (Langer 1981: 361) that results from television's performance of interactivity is just one of the many manifestations of today's mediation of interpersonal relations.

Moreover, that television may promote the development of parasocial inter-actions is not to say that viewers are so naïve as to miss altogether their performed status. Nor is it to say that viewers may automatically react in a posi-tive way – as they probably would do in casual conversation – to signs of inter-personal closeness on the part of television performers. They may, for instance, respond to them with varying degrees of cynicism, interpreting them even as Machiavellian: intended only to persuade viewers to stay tuned, to promote their [performers'] public selves and their programmes, and so on.

Television's preoccupation with liveliness, too, may share a similar fate. The several editions of the reality game show *Big Brother*, in which a group of people are placed in a purpose-built house under real-time camera surveillance twenty-four hours a day over ten weeks, is a case in point. On the one hand, the view-ers of this show are able to watch via the internet a constant recording of the day-to-day lives of the housemates. This means that the housemates must some-times forget that they are being watched – that they must at times abandon their scripts. On these occasions, they may orientate their talk to the 'social setting' of the *Big Brother* house – to the interpersonal relations between them. At this level, their talk may be received as lively. *Big Brother* may be seen to provide direct access to the 'real' world of these housemates and consequently an appeal-ing opportunity for viewers to become voyeurs, to eavesdrop upon others' private talk.

On the other hand, the show does not hide the fact that it regularly stages the 'reality' of the *Big Brother* house. To entertain its viewers, the show sets chal-lenges that the housemates need to meet to gain rewards, it generates divisions within the group, it simultaneously broadcasts spin-off shows in which relatives, friends and 'evicted' housemates speculate about the interpersonal relationships developing in the house, and so forth. Also, the evening broadcast of daily high-lights openly preferences slices of the housemates' talk that revolve around romance, sex, conflict, identity crises, friendship betrayals and other melodra-matic ingredients. Furthermore, scenes in which the housemates overtly orien-tate their talk to the competition setting of the show are not necessarily edited out. Viewers are indeed often offered footage of the housemates talking about both their being watched and their participating in a cash-prize competition. On these occasions, their script is far from concealed. This 'double framing' of talk in *Big Brother* (Thornborrow and Morris 2004) partly challenges the liveli-ness seemingly captured by the *Big Brother* cameras. Viewers are shown emotions, revelations, gossip and other forms of naturally occurring close talk. But also revealed are (some of) the ways in which this talk is explicitly designed to be consumed by them. *Big Brother* playfully 'simulates' – in the sense of, for example, the simulation computer game *The Sims* – reality from a construction of places, tasks, characters and images that appear real and close (Dovey 2000).

The issues discussed in this chapter have revolved around the communicative ethos of television – one oriented towards the interpersonal, rather than the ideational. Television's efforts to create a sense of interpersonal closeness with its viewers saw it, as a public medium, driven initially by modes of communication from the private sphere of life. However, the idea that television's sociability is still somehow on loan from the private sphere is not sustainable. Public forms of talk influence private spheres of life, too. And television has appropriated private-sphere communicative practices, such as informality, naturalness and accessibility, so completely that their performance comprises rather than drives its discourse.

Still, though, television's sociability remains a construct: the product of mediation and performance. After all, television is by definition a public medium and interaction therein is, therefore, always designed and produced to be broadcast to viewers. The key question is how this interaction is visually, aurally and verbally constructed on television so as to create the impression of closeness. This is what Chapters 6 and 7 explore.

Chapter 6 examines closeness within the context of live television news. One of the main objectives of this chapter is to analyse how exactly images, sound and words in live news create the impression that viewers are accessing the here-and-now of a given slice of the socio-historical world, rather than a script thereof. The analysis thus builds upon Part I of the book, for it deals with a broadcast format that asserts its direct relation to, if not its direct recording of, the world out there. One of the most revealing arguments in this respect is the reliance of live news on the future and the consequent possibility that television news will/can only construct a direct relation to potential reality or realities.

As Chapter 6 will argue, the presentness of the world around which live news is assumed to revolve is increasingly being sidelined in favour of the 'what's next?' of that world. The result, inevitably, is speculative talk. For some this has led to a 'dumbing down' or 'tabloidisation' of the news (Swain 2003); others argue that as far as news output is concerned there has been no significant change in news agendas (Winston 2002). Montgomery (2007), for instance, has identified changes in news style (delivery, mode of address and discourse structure) since the 1980s but argues that these point towards informationalisation and conversationalisation rather than a tabloidisation of the news.

In the current news environment, the future appears to be treated much like the very recent past used to be treated before the deluge of liveness on television: as a construct open to opinion and evaluation. In yet another attempt to bring viewers and television together, furthermore, viewers are invited to play an active part in the practice of news speculation and close talk. They are, for instance, asked to send to the studio mobile telephone or electronic messages with their opinions on various news items and to confirm or reject with personal, anecdotal evidence the truth value of such items. Viewer polls are started at the beginning of the news regarding a particular story, the results of which become news later in the newscast. The very recent past, the present and the future are thus similarly shaped through various forms of close talk in live news.[1]

Chapter 7 focuses on a different aspect of sociability, namely self-disclosing/confessional talk before the cameras. Reality television and celebrity talk shows are selected here as prime sites in which people reveal their 'true colours'. A gallery of ordinary folk and small- and big-screen celebrities are shown in these programmes talking in personal, often emotional ways. Their talk is treated as a truth sign of these programmes' own promise of closeness and truth (Murdock 2000). Interestingly, and this is indeed the crux of the chapter, their talk is also offered to viewers as a marker against which to assess speakers' claims to moral worthiness. In celebrity chat shows, media personalities disclose private aspects of their lives. Their self-disclosures often become a discursive springboard from which they project their moral worthiness and sometimes develop their motivational 'lessons'. Yet, in some reality shows, ordinary folk's attempts at showing their moral worthiness through emotional expressiveness are trivialised or derided. Their attempts provide, in fact, opportunities for experts (normally the presenters) to perform their own moralistic/motivational talk, frequently through verbal cleverness.

# Live News and Closeness

**6**

Whether audiences are likely to be interested in a particular event or piece of information is determined in reference to a set of 'professional imperatives which act as implicit guides to the construction of news stories' (Chibnall 1977: 167). These imperatives are commonly referred to as news values and are generally understood to be shaped by, amongst other factors, newsmakers, markets, technology and audiences.[1] These factors are, in turn, subject to change over time, which makes news values themselves flexible. Accelerated processes of globalisation and the communications revolution from the last part of the twentieth century onwards, for instance, have brought about a news environment of 'time–space distanciation' (Thompson 1995). This essentially means that it is no longer the case that the further away from a television studio an event occurs, the longer it will take for viewers to receive news of it. As a result, immediacy has become a crucial news value. This is reflected in the competition between news networks to reduce to zero, or near zero, the time elapsing between capturing (reporting), broadcasting and receiving news of an event. In addition, with the immediate present now on news tap, emphasis has also shifted to the immediate future – to imminence – as a particular news imperative. Live news is now often more about newsmakers' construction of what is about to happen than about what has just happened or is happening. And since the future is by definition factless, speculation has become the staple diet of live news.

It is against the above live news context that closeness is examined in this chapter. The analysis reveals how images, sounds and speech seek to bring television, the world out there, viewers, reporters, newsreaders and news actors together in a broadcast nowness (immediacy) and a broadcast nextness (imminence). Before doing so, though, a few words about the concept of television liveness.

## 6.1   Liveness and television

The reference point for the term 'liveness' was initially the ontological here-and-nowness of the television medium: its being broadcast and received in the same moment. As the proportion of programming thus produced declined from the 1960s onwards, the term 'liveness' switched its reference. For Bourdon (2000: 538), for example, it only came to signify the broadcasting of real events in real time – the kind of broadcasting that gives viewers a 'full sense of experiencing a life event'. Such 'fully live' or 'maximum liveness' moments of television, Bourdon further argues, are rare. They are indeed principally confined either to sports coverage or the coverage of major events. The latter has been described as 'holes' in television's 'flow'[2]: the live coverage gives the impression that television is at the mercy of unfolding events, even if television itself may have been part of their becoming so (Dayan and Katz 1992). The relative infrequency of moments of maximum liveness on television, moreover, leads Bourdon to see the medium's liveness as an unfulfilled promise.

Whilst maintaining the importance of real events and real time for liveness, other authors conceptualise television liveness as an ideology and a perform-ance. Thus, for instance, Feuer (1983) has influentially argued that liveness on television is premised on the idea that this mass medium is able to connect us live to significant events – that it allows us to see important things (and people) as they happen (and make things happen). The flip side of the ideology-of-live-ness coin is, of course, that television does not connect us live to *in*significant events and *un*important things and people. Couldry (2003, 2004) is amongst those authors who have developed Feuer's argument. He conceives of television liveness as a form of ritualised practice that normalises wider power relations. Liveness, he therefore argues, 'is a category whose use naturalizes the general idea that, through the media, we achieve a shared attention to the "realities" that matter for us as a society' (2004: 356).

For a number of media discourse analysts, too, liveness is not just a case of real-time broadcasting of real-life material. Montgomery (2006: 238), for instance, sees 'the lack of a precise script' as crucial, much in line with Tolson's (2006) concept of liveliness (Chapter 5). Television liveness designates for these and other scholars a particular performance: a 'distinctive condition under which discourse can be produced' (Montgomery 2006: 238). This condition may not comprise only moments of maximum liveness. Often these days, for example, snippets of fully live material are used in news stories in order to 'thicken out' or elaborate recorded pieces via exemplary material (Thornborrow and Fitzgerald 2004). Live interactions between reporters and newsreaders are also often combined with recorded reports, a popular format being the live, on-location book-ending of taped reports known as 'donut news' in the US (Hoskins and O'Loughlin 2007; Montgomery 2007). But regardless of how 'fully live' live news actually is, there seems to be a need explicitly to mark its liveness. It is the implementation – the performance – of such a perceived need that has actually become the main reference point for the term 'liveness' across a range of television formats.

The distinctive condition under which live discourse is produced on televi-sion is not fixed – either synchronically or diachronically. In live news it is deter-mined by three imperatives, namely: 'to produce the moment, to presence the viewer, [and] yet to deliver the totality of the occasion' (Marriott 2001: 727). To illustrate these imperatives, it is useful to consider a study by Allan Bell (2003), which compared the New Zealand news coverage of two expeditions to the South Pole: one under Captain Scott in 1912 and the other under Peter Hillary in 1998–9. Captain Scott's expedition reached the South Pole but, sadly, all its members perished during their return journey. A search party found their bodies eight months later, together with Captain Scott's detailed travel diary. The *New Zealand Herald* reported the tragic news one year, one month and twenty-five days after the expedition reached the South Pole – hardly a case of live news by today's standards! Captain Scott's wife, travelling by ship to New Zealand from San Francisco to meet her husband, received the news of his death a week after it was first reported. In stark contrast, New Zealanders knew about the success of the expedition led by Peter Hillary within an hour of his party reaching the South Pole. The newscast included a live telephone interview with Hillary from the South Pole. During the interview, Hillary also talked live to his wife at their home in New Zealand.

Hillary's arrival at the South Pole was constructed as a live event, even though the newscast missed the real-time arrival moment. The large-audience television programme *One Network News* covered the story at 6:00 p.m. New Zealand time, which suggests the possibility of this network having arranged the timeliness of this event (Bell 2003). In place of the live arrival moment, the news team considered whatever fully live material they had – the couple's telephone conversation – and produced it as *the* moment. In its acquired momentousness, this live 'event' was produced so as to presence the viewer. The live talk between Hillary and his wife mixed the realms of the public and the private. Hillary used public-speech clichés, such as to be 'delighted to be here', but also personal, emotional talk, such as 'I partially did it for you too darling – I know, I know' (Bell 2003: 15). An intense sense of voyeurism surrounded the broadcast of the conversation, so much so that the news anchor referred to his awkwardness on three separate occasions. Viewers witnessed – rather than simply watched – the 'iconic' moment in which the couple talked live about their feelings; they were given a sense of being in the unfolding of that moment.

Simulating the 'auratic intensity' (Benjamin 1968, cited in Marriott 2001) of an event covered in real time as though one were actually there (i.e. in the unmediated context of its occurrence) has become commonplace within the current aesthetic of liveness. The reason for this may be, as some authors argue, that the impression of being there carries an 'automatic truth value' (Doane 1990: 224). The experience of witnessing an event as it happens appears to be more convincing than that of watching the same event once it has been repacked into a recorded report.[3] Rach (1988) gives the example of the Catholic Church pronouncing those who watched the live broadcast of a papal benediction to be as truly blessed as those people who were in the Pope's presence at the time of the benediction. The idea of live television being able to capture the truth of an event may therefore partly explain its purchase on news and other forms of television that assert a referential relationship with the socio-historical world.

The third imperative behind television's liveness – the ability to deliver the totality of the occasion – is also illustrated by Bell's (2003) study. Simultaneous images of Hillary's wife at home and of Hillary sitting at the Pole were offered in the live coverage of their telephone conversation. Such images positioned viewers as omnipresent: capable of viewing the event in all the locations that mattered – two on this occasion. Live coverage of Hillary and his wife, then, created the impression of viewers being there and being everywhere. Co-presence and omnipresence were concomitantly produced for them.

There is a potential clash, though, between the news creating an impression of being simultaneously there and it being everywhere. Often in the live coverage of major events, for instance, a multiplicity of on-location reporters and live cameras privilege the proximity associated with unmediated viewing – they give viewers the impression of being there. Yet they also offer a ubiquity of vision which is impossible in unmediated conditions, where being physically present at the site of the action generally means being limited to one location and to certain viewing restrictions. Live news coverage places viewers in an unreal (impossible) yet ideal (perfect) state of co-presence, which needs to be managed carefully and in context-sensitive ways (Marriott 2001).

Some viewers may see in the impossible yet perfect co-presence of live news a reason to suspect the truth of that which is being watched. They may see in the mediated liveness of the news an unnecessary distraction from, even an obstacle to, the 'facts' of the moment being captured live. Use of live visuals in political news reports, for instance, has been found to improve neither viewer appreciation nor recall of their content. Viewers have also been found to receive recorded field reports as more immediate than live cross-talk between reporters and newsreaders (Snoeijer et al. 2002). Alternatively, other viewers may be knowing, indeed keen, voyeurs, who find the experience of 'real co-presence' disappointing compared to that of 'mediated co-presence'. Think, for instance, of the dejection that one may feel having spent a considerable amount of money on tickets for a rock concert only to find oneself 'there' but watching the event from the giant screens covering its totality (including live close-up shots of the crowds) because of viewing restrictions from one's seat.

Regardless of its perceived truth and experiential value, some argue that the importance attached to television liveness is largely unwarranted. In his influential book about US broadcasts in the late 1980s, Caldwell (1995: 30), for example, argues that television 'defines itself less by its inherent temporality and present-ness than by pleasure, style and commodity'. Under the term 'televisuality' he describes a presentational manner characterised by 'excessive stylization and visual exhibitionism – a presentational manner of communicative and semiotic over-abundance' (1995: 352). For Caldwell, televisuality is marked by a keenness for stylistic performances, an emphasis on the quality of its authors and signatures, an ability to process images through digital pictures, and a saturation of the present. This last 'televisuality look' suggests – contra Caldwell's own argument – that the ideology of liveness is an integral part of the medium's self-conscious style or aestheticism. Put differently, televisuality is a key signifier of liveness (Hoskins and O'Loughlin 2007).

## 6.2   Live images and closeness

Live news reports, especially of major events, often offer viewers a stream of rapidly succeeding images that are assumed to be occurring in real time. This practice, which corresponds to Caldwell's (1995) identification of a saturation of the present on television, is shared with reality game shows like *Big Brother*. In both, viewers are provided with multiple live images that switch in quick succession between locations and events (or non-events, as the case may be). In the *Big Brother* household, numerous cameras offer viewers a raft of live images moving back and forth from room to room, or from angle to angle within a room. And, in live news, multiple live cameras provide a continuous shift between locations (the studio and the various sites of the action) and events. The impression sought after in both contexts is a witnessing of the unfolding of the moment being broadcast – however factually uneventful that moment may be.

Visual flooding of the present on our television screens is also achieved by presenting viewers simultaneously with live material from different locations. One of the earliest examples of this was CNN's coverage of the 1991 Gulf War. Multiple satellite feeds were simultaneously distributed to different visual frames during the course of live newscasts. The result was television screens frequently being split into windows of different places and present times. Real-time scenes of attacks over Baghdad, for instance, were shown contemporaneously with real-time images of air raid warnings and panic in Israel, of the launching of Iraqi missiles and of responses by citizens in the US and other parts of the globe to the real time war 'news'. Different time zones from around the world, night and day, were simultaneously presented live before viewers' eyes. They created an extremely immediate yet temporally very messy (disordered) present (Hoskins 2001). This windowed look has been seen to characterise television's hypermediacy style of remediation, where 'hypermediacy' designates the marriage of television and computer technologies and 'remediation' designates the 'representation of one medium in another' (Bolter and Grusin 2000).

Figure 6.1 contains a comparatively modest illustration of the above windowed look, which is nevertheless particularly relevant to our discussion of live images and closeness in the news. It comes from *CNN International*, specifically from the seventh news segment of its *CNN 5 to 6* news programme. The segment carried the story of the tenth anniversary ceremony of the Rwandan genocide, which ended in 1994. It started with the newsreader's introductory piece to camera. It then moved on to a five-minute recorded piece on the genocide, which included library pictures of the aftermath of the killings and sound-bites from survivors of the genocide. There was next a brief live telephone report from Rwanda by a news correspondent made over live footage of the anniversary ceremony. Immediately after the report, the news returned to the CNN studio where the news anchor started a live interview with the Rwandan ambassador in the US at the time. Just twenty seconds into this interview, and as Figure 6.1 (see p. 70) shows, the television screen was split into two windows of approximately equal size.

*Figure 6.1*  **CNN 5 to 6 (2004)**

The left-hand window in Figure 6.1 shows live, on-location footage of the commemorative burial ceremony, specifically of the front end of one of the coffins being lowered into the ground. The right-hand window shows a medium-close range (talking-head) shot of the Rwandan ambassador in the US during the live studio interview. The need to split the television screen to offer simultaneous footage of these two live 'events' at this point in the interview is questionable. The left-hand window does not capture any new development in the commemorative ceremony since the previous live telephone report a few minutes earlier. This may explain it occupying the left part of the television screen, where 'old' information is typically placed.[4] It provides, in fact, only a continuation of the images of the ceremony attendees watching an incessant lowering of the coffins of victims of the genocide. Nor does it complement the content of the ambassador's words, who was then talking about Rwandan society. What splitting the television screen into two windows that show two different present moments does is to connect visually and in real time the sanitised reality of the CNN studio (sanitised because it exists away from the location of the massacre and between two people who are not directly affected by it) with the compelling reality of the site of the action (Rwanda and the poignant visual reminder of the sheer atrocity of the genocide as encapsulated by a succession of coffins being lowered into the ground).

The contrast between these two live 'realities' is reinforced by the different picture qualities of the two windows. Though not particularly clear in the video-still reproduction provided by Figure 6.1, the high quality of the studio image in the right-hand window stands in contrast to the intermittent and breaking satellite-fed images provided in the left-hand window. The latter offers a 'rough, unpretentious look' (Caldwell 1995), which creates the impression of naturalness because of the apparent absence of any sophisticated meddling with the reality being recorded.

The live interview, for its part, is visually 'polished', as one may reasonably expect from footage produced in a technologically advanced site (a CNN studio). It projects, moreover, a sense of interactional closeness between the participants. The tone of the interviewer's and the interviewee's talk is amiable, with the interviewer offering several sympathy and empathy tokens to the ambassador's description of the effects of the genocide on Rwandan society. Visually, too, a sense of proximity is created between those on the screen and the viewers. Talking-head shots of the interviewer and, especially, the ambassador (see Figure 6.1) are used much more frequently than medium or long-range ones.

The 'rough' and 'polished' looks in, respectively, the left- and right-hand windows of Figure 6.1 pander to two different televisuality looks. The former reproduces and further asserts the idea that the news 'simply' and 'naturally' records the socio-historical world. The latter reflects and constructs an aesthetic of interpersonal closeness, to which the strategic use of camera angles and seating arrangements contribute. Both televisuality looks are brought to co-exist in a broadcast nowness that, above all, seeks to connect those watching to those in the CNN studio and to those in Rwanda.

There is another reason why Figure 6.1 is relevant to our discussion of live images and closeness in the news: it positions viewers as witnesses of others' suffering. On this occasion, it is the commemoration of a genocide that is poignantly brought to bear by the images of coffins being constantly lowered into the ground. As viewers listen to and watch the interviewer and interviewee in the studio, in the left-hand window of their screens close-ups of coffins are continuously juxtaposed with close-ups of saddened people at the location of the event. Watching others suffer on television has been found to trigger painful witnessing experiences (Peters 2001; Sontag 2003). The mass-mediated witnessing of catastrophes such as terrorist attacks and (natural) disasters has been found to provide a form of vicarious involvement in the pain of others (Rentschler 2004). It can generate viewing conditions conducive to imagined forms of affective participation in the suffering of others (Zelizer 2002).

Finally, and connected to the above, Figure 6.1 provides a snapshot of one of the prototypical moments of television witnessing as participation, namely its live coverage of commemorative events.[5] Such coverage invites viewers to feel part of the commemorative and the commemorated event and thus to feel connected to history in the making. It provides them with the opportunity not only to witness but also to become immersed in the documentation of a salient historical moment in its unfolding.

## 6.3   Live speech and closeness

Visual indices of liveness such as those examined in the previous section of this chapter are not the only way to bring viewers and television together in a salient nowness. Often, the speech that accompanies live news footage is also explicitly marked as live. Specifically, speech in live news tends to emulate the characteristics of speech 'in face-to-face communication contexts, without technological assistance, and constrained by basic conditions of audibility within clearly defined spatio-temporal boundaries' (Richardson and Meinhof 1999: 47). Three properties in particular define this type of speech. First, live speech often displays an orientation to the here-and-now of the situation in which it is generated and which is shared by interlocutors. Linguistically, this is manifest in the frequent use of pure spatio-temporal deictic expressions, such as 'now', today', 'this very moment', 'here', 'on this very spot', and so forth.[6] These anchor one's speech in a present time and in a space inhabited by all the parties concerned. Secondly, when compared to scripted and/or rehearsed speech, live speech contains a considerably higher number of repetitions, reformulations, false starts and fillers. These disfluencies can create the impression of naturalness or liveliness. Thirdly, live speech is often found in conversational exchanges. This is because real-time conversation tends to evolve without participants knowing how specific turns will develop.

The above properties apply to much of the speech generated in live news nowadays, as the analysis of Extract 6.1 (see p. 73) illustrates. The extract reproduces the opening half-minute or so of a live news update on the main story of the day: the BBC's reaction to criticisms made of it in a Government-commissioned, independent inquiry under the direction of Lord Hutton into aspects of British participation in the 2003 Iraq War. Specific to the news story, in March 2003 BBC Radio 4 journalist Andrew Gilligan publicly referred to an anonymous official source having informed him that the British Government had knowingly 'sexed up' its dossier on Iraq's weapons of mass destruction (WMD) to justify its decision to support the US in its military intervention in Iraq. The name of Gilligan's source, Dr Kelly, was somehow leaked to the press. Dr Kelly subsequently committed suicide. Preceded by a frenzy of further leaks and political spin-doctoring, the findings of the inquiry were published in the so-called 'Hutton Report' in late January 2004. This concluded that Gilligan's allegations of a 'sexed-up' dossier were unproven, thereby exonerating the British Government, and it accused the BBC's editorial systems of being defective. A number of apologies, resignations and public statements by members of the BBC ensued, some of which are referred to in Extract 6.1.

The participants' talk in Extract 6.1 is clearly oriented to the here-and-now of the speech situation that they share. Derham and Bradby employ no fewer than five pure deictic expressions (italicised in the extract) within the opening turns of their two-way. These deictics, moreover, are made conspicuous through several linguistic and paralinguistic resources. Derham's temporal '<u>now</u>' in line 02 is pre-modified with the intensifying adjective '<u>right</u>', both of which are delivered emphatically. Likewise, Bradby interrupts his own report to insert a

### ITV News, live update (2004)

[The extract involves two participants: newsreader Katie Derham and reporter Tom Bradby. The two engage in what is known in journalistic circles as a 'live two-way': an interactional exchange between a newsreader in the studio and a news reporter at the scene, which is broadcast in real time. The extract is preceded by Derham reading to camera a scripted piece in which she summarises recent developments in the story, namely the resignation of the BBC Chairman, Gavin Davies, and a public apology issued by the then BBC Director General, Greg Dyke. She also mentions, and it is this which constitutes the reason for the live news update, that Dyke is expected to make a further announcement. BBC HQ: BBC headquarters. D: Katie Derham; B: Tom Bradby.]

| | | | |
|---|---|---|---|
| *MS – D, to camera.* | 01 | D | our UK political editor Tom Bradby is at the BBC's |
| *LS – D turns to* | 02 | | headquarters <u>*right now*</u> (.) |
| *screen on her left,* | 03 | | Tom (.) what's your feeling? |
| *which shows B* | 04 | | what's your gut instinct? |
| *outside entrance of* | 05 | | will Greg Dyke resign? |
| *BBC HQ. MS – B,* | 06 | B | well I- I think he prob- he probably will I think (.) that's |
| *to camera.* | 07 | | <u>certainly</u> the speculation (.) he doesn- I think he'll |
| | 08 | | probably feel tha- (.) er it's <u>clear</u> tha- (.) er (.) he <u>doesn't</u> |
| | 09 | | have much choice (.) we are by the way Katie we're all |
| | 10 | | standing <u>here</u> 'cause we expect (.) er that statement to be |
| | 11 | | delivered to us in one form or another (.) er <<u>*any minute*</u> |
| | 12 | | <u>*now*</u>> (.) I <u>have</u> to say er I never thought I'd say this you |
| | 13 | | know (.) er:: fifteen mo- more or less fifteen years |
| | 14 | | competing against the BBC (.) the idea of <u>beating</u> them |
| | 15 | | every day is what propels me out of <u>bed</u> in the morning |
| *(unseen)* | 16 | D | [*laughter* |
| | 17 | | [but I have to say that there is a degree of <u>sadness</u> really |
| | 18 | | <u>*here today*</u> (.) er about this whole thing I think people feel |
| | 19 | | °you know° in the wider journalistic community <I |
| | 20 | | mean> I mean they're <u>shell-shocked in there</u> (.) but I |
| | 21 | | think in the wider journalistic community there's some |
| | 22 | | anger (.) you know [. . .] |

textual aside – a 'by the way' (line 09) – during which he uses two other deictic expressions: the spatial and temporal adverbs '<u>here</u>' (line 10) and '<u>now</u>' (line 12), respectively. The latter is highlighted through the pre-modifier '<u>any minute</u>', an emphatic slow delivery rate, added stress, and micropause both before and after (lines 11–12). A few seconds later, Bradby provides further deictic references: '<u>here today</u>' (line 18). The frequency and emphatic delivery of Derham's and Bradby's deictic expressions in what is a rather brief exchange foregrounds the nowness of the situation in which their speech is performed and received. In doing so, it connects the news update, the socio-historical world being reported on, and the viewers watching the news update live in a televisually salient present.

Let us consider, next, the various disfluencies in Bradby's speech. These include a number of repetitions ('I- I', line 06; '<I mean> I mean', lines 19–20), speech fillers ('er' 'er::', lines 08, 10, 11, 12, 13, 18; and 'you know', lines 12–13, 19, 22) and self-corrections ('I think he prob- he probably will I think', line 06; 'he doesn- I think', line 07; 'mo- more or less', line 13). Together, they give a spur-of-the-moment feel to his talk, making it sound as though it were occasioned by emergent (unscripted) interactional goals, as is often the case in conversation. This is not to say, of course, that the exchange between Derham and Bradby is a naturally occurring one. On the contrary, it is quite likely that both parties have a fair idea of what the content and structure of their two-way will be prior to their going live with it. On-location reporters are known to feed newsreaders the questions that they want to be asked during the course of their live interactions (Tuggle et al. 2004). Bradby's lively delivery therefore points in the direction of a conscious decision on his (and/or the news producers') part to link live news to an unpolished televisuality look (Caldwell 1995). It is a decision possibly driven by the need to overcome one crucial obstacle to news presentation's liveness: the degree to which it is heard as a script being read out loud.

In addition to illustrating the performance of liveness and naturalness, Extract 6.1 also provides a typical example of on-screen sociability. The sociable, communicative nature of the live two-way has been discussed in detail by Montgomery (2006, 2007), who uses the roles taken up by its participants to describe it as one of four types of broadcast news interview: the affiliated interview (2007: 117–43). The three other types are the accountability interview, the experiential interview and the expert interview. The accountability interview involves journalists and public figures who have some form of responsibility in relation to the news (it is about doing 'accounting'); the experiential interview takes place between journalists and ordinary people who have been affected by or caught up in the news (it is about doing 'witnessing, reacting and expressing opinions'); and the expert interview is between journalists and experts who do 'informing and explaining' (Montgomery 2007: 146–7).

The live two-way interview in Extract 6.1 provides, specifically, an instance of affiliative small talk. This term has its origins in Malinowski's (1923) concept of 'phatic communion' to designate a type of talk orientated towards developing good interpersonal relations and signalling openness to communication. Prototypical examples of phatic communion are greetings, such as 'good morning' and 'how do you do?', and leave-takings, such as 'see you later' and 'have a nice day'. Contextually appropriate variations of these sociable formulae, as we discussed in Chapter 5, are regularly found in the opening and closing sequences of news programmes (from newsreaders to viewers), as well as in reports contained within the main body of the programme (between newsreaders and news reporters).

Small talk was formerly regarded as somewhat trivial – as a form of talk used only to 'defuse the potential hostility of silence in situations where speech is conventionally anticipated' (Laver 1981: 297). In recent years, though, such a dismissive view of the role of small talk has been superseded by a growing awareness that is plays a crucial part in the smooth running of a number of interactional exchanges – including instrumental, transactional and task-oriented ones – and occurs well beyond the fringes of encounters (Coupland 2000). Small talk is nowadays seen to encompass both phatic communion and 'social talk', and not to be 'completely atopical or free from the work context' (Holmes 2000: 38–9).

Extract 6.1 pays testament to the importance of small talk in task-oriented, institutional encounters, namely delivering a news update on television. Bradby's update is referentially poor for it contains not a single new development upon the main news story. It is nevertheless affectively rich. In it, for example, he garners a sense of the emotions felt by others in relation to recent events. Thus he refers to 'people' feeling a certain 'degree of <u>sadness</u>' (line 17), to BBC journalists at their headquarters feeling '<u>shell-shocked</u>' (line 20), and to 'some anger' in 'the wider journalistic community' (lines 21–22). In doing so, he invites viewers to engage at a primarily emotional (not cognitive) level with the news update and the person(s) responsible for the updating.

Bradby's 'mood reporting' (Marriott 1996, 2000) is inevitably subjective. He is unlikely to be privy to BBC journalists' experiences of the event being covered. If he were, his report would probably explicitly acknowledge this and/or include relevant sound-bites. Nor is it literally possible for him to know the mood of such an abstract entity as 'the wider journalistic community'. In offering his own reactions and impressions as being representative of a broader discourse (in this case what journalists are saying and/or feeling), Bradby performs an act of 'propositional ventriloquism' (Montgomery 2006). He positions himself as the animator of a collectively authored position, even though there is no evidence to suggest that this collective agrees with his views. His interpretation of the feelings of others partly fuels his live speech, as is also the case in gossip – a type of small talk where we assess others' actions and speculate about their motivations in their absence.

Brady also reports his own mood when, in lines 12–15, he says: 'I <u>have</u> to say er I never thought I'd say this you know (.) er:: fifteen mo- more or less fifteen years competing against the BBC (.) the idea of <u>beating</u> them every day is what propels me out of <u>bed</u> in the morning'. Through this, Bradby imbues his talk with a sense of commitment that contributes to turning him from the category of media personnel to media personality – a transition assisted by television's keenness to highlight its authors and signatures (Caldwell 1995). Although Bradby's is a familiar face and voice for ITV News viewers in the UK, Derham still identifies him before the live two-way as 'our UK political editor . . .' (line 01).[7] Bradby, for his part, further signposts viewers about his standing in the field (lines 13–15), using his professional experience to inject humour into his report and hopefully construct an attractive personality within his professional role. His having been propelled out of bed for the past fifteen years to beat fellow BBC journalists makes an easy joke to share with Derham (note her audible outburst of laughter in line 16) and the viewers, as the competition between the BBC and ITV is well known in the UK. The combination of mood reporting and humour in Bradby's small talk thus creates a sense of playful complicity, a certain closeness, in a shared present time between the editor on site, the newsreader in the studio and the viewers at home.

In addition to its potential for affective engagement, Bradby's small talk is also useful in keeping his live news update 'alive'. As already mentioned, Bradby finds himself having to go live without any new development on which to report – a position not uncommon for journalists in a liveness-saturated news environment. To avoid an absence of talk/sound, he repeats old information (that he is waiting for things to happen), produces factually irrelevant talk (e.g. his getting out of bed) and 'noise' (e.g. frequent speech disfluencies). He replaces, in short, 'concrete' with 'metaphorical' silence (Jaworski 1993, 1997).

This practice is commonplace in live news reports on television. McGregor (1997), for example, conducted a detailed case study of coverage of a major breaking news story during the first Gulf War (1991), namely the British Cabinet and the home of the Prime Minister in Whitehall (London) coming under terrorist fire. He observed a noticeable use of metaphorical silence (not his term) in live two-ways covering the news story, as his description below illustrates:

> Shortly after 11:00 CNN feature a second dispatch from reporter Brian Cabell in Whitehall. [. . .] This is followed immediately by the CNN anchor in Atlanta reading out to him an Associated Press report stating that smoke had been seen coming from the back of Number 10 Downing Street [the Prime Minister's residence]. Cabell replies that he cannot see that far and therefore cannot confirm the report. He stresses that there is no access to the area and that no clear picture has yet emerged, suggesting sensibly that it may be as long as an hour before it will. (McGregor 1997: 94)

In this example, Cabell clearly had no further news to report but a report to give. He thus chose negative reporting – a form of metaphorical silence to fill airtime. Similarly, Hoskins (2004a: 61) describes one of the live reports during the second Gulf War (2003) as follows:

> NBC's correspondent Chip Reid with the US First Marine Division reported in a very quiet voice to avoid disturbing the rest of those he was embedded with: "forgive me for speaking very quietly but I am in the field of sleeping marines right now, it was a very long day, they got up well before dawn this morning and have spent the entire day moving north." (MSNBC, live, 23 March 2003)

Continuous news coverage of war means that live reports are often shot on the battlefield by embedded journalists – or 'embeds' – who may frequently have very little (if any) further news to tell. The embed in Hoskins's example resorted to metaphorical silence to avoid concrete silence: he provided audibly and visually evident information (that he was speaking quietly and that he was in the field with sleeping marines) and described an uneventful (by war standards) recent past (marines getting up early and moving north throughout the day). The whispering of his tone and the filming conditions constructed a sense of proximity between the marines and the embed, who did not wish to disturb them, and between the embed and the viewers, who watched the marines in their sleep.

Returning to Bradby's use of metaphorical silence in Extract 6.1, this also acts as a hook to create anticipation of the future. Faced with uneventful immediacy, conjectural imminence emerges as a very attractive reporting option in his live update. This is the case from the onset, with Derham opening the live two-way by explicitly asking Bradby to speculate about the future and to do so in emotional terms: 'Tom (.) what's your feeling? what's your gut instinct? will Greg Dyke resign?' (lines 03–05). Bradby obliges: 'well I I think he prob- he probably will I think (.) that's <u>certainly</u> the speculation (.) he doesn- I think he'll probably feel tha- (.) er it's <u>clear</u> tha- (.) er (.) he <u>doesn't</u> have much choice' (lines 06–09). Herein we can see an instance of different roles or identities occupying different 'slots' within the news discourse and having different 'fashions of speaking' associated with them. Specifically, presenters like Derham tend to 'assert' or 'avert', whereas correspondents and editors like Bradby tend to 'comment' or 'speculate' (Montgomery 2007).

Bradby's commenting on the imminent future displays 'liveliness' – note, for example, his disfluencies in lines 06–08. It is nevertheless performed so as to combine carefully assertiveness with tentativeness. His predictions are at times watchfully hedged, as though he were trying to avoid committing personally to an answer that might transpire to be incorrect. Thus, although expressed in a verbal tense (the future) that conveys certainty ('he . . . will [resign]' 'he will feel tha- . . .'), Bradby reduces his commitment to the truth value of part of his report through repeated use of the quality hedges 'probably' and 'I think'. At other times, however, he uses unequivocal terms, even if he implies that these are not his own predictions through third-person singular references, such as 'that's' in 'that's <u>certainly</u> the speculation' (lines 06–07) and 'it's' in 'it's <u>clear</u> tha- (.) er (.) he doesn't have much choice' (lines 08–09). Here the present tense is used and suprasegmental emphasis is placed on the adverb 'certainly' and the adjective 'clear', which strengthens their already assertive force.

The above blend of assertiveness and tentativeness reflects two mutually shaping needs in live two-ways: 'doing being interesting' and 'doing facticity'. In a highly competitive television environment, the news needs to engage and hold viewers. Talking about the imminent future – however tentatively – is one means of doing being interesting, just as gossiping about the actual and potential actions of others appears to be a common human pastime. But even in this competitive television environment, live news still seems to need to show some degree of connection to facts. Using strong assertions, or 'push structures', is a discursive means of doing facticity, however speculative the grounds for it may be, which may in turn explain the need to compensate for them with hedged statements, or 'pull structures' (Montgomery 2006).

Finally, although concrete silence is generally avoided in broadcasting, there are certain moments of maximum liveness on television where it is actually strategically used – admittedly often in conjunction with metaphorical silence. Paradigmatic instances of this include around-the-clock coverage of the immediate aftermath of unforeseen dramatic events, such as the assassination of Israeli athletes at the 1972 Munich Olympics, the terrorist attacks of 9/11 (US) and the Asian Tsunami and Hurricane Katrina, both in 2005. Coverage of these events is known as 'disaster marathons' (Liebes 1998) and it becomes a media event in itself – the main point of reference for all other news either directly or indirectly related to the initial dramatic event.

On the day of the 9/11 disaster, for example, images of a plane approaching and then hitting the World Trade Center South Tower whilst the North Tower was on fire were shown back to back and, on one occasion, even backwards by *BBC News 24*. According to Jaworski et al. (2005), such continuous reruns of the same video footage had a similar effect to that provided by still photographic images, with stillness acting as the visual equivalent of silence. The endless loops of moving images also contributed to their ensuing symbolism and iconicity (Zelizer 2002).

Another example of the strategic use of concrete silence in the *BBC News 24* coverage of the 9/11 disaster was the relative lack of sound in some of its video footage. The narrative commentary over the images of the North Tower on fire and the second plane approaching and crashing into the South Tower was accompanied by a slight whirring engine noise from the helicopter from which some of the images were filmed. Interestingly, the volume of the sound made by the helicopter engine remained constant when the footage was shown in slow motion (Jaworski et al. 2005). Restrained sound (or near-concrete silence) was presumably decided upon as the best way to capture the intensity of the live moment being shown. Further instances of concrete silence in the *BBC News 24* coverage of 9/11 included frequent and markedly long pauses in the reporters' live pieces, which conveyed their sense of trauma and awe at the event that they, too, were witnessing (rather than simply reporting).

## 6.4 Conclusion

The concept of liveness defies a single definition but emerges undoubtedly as highly popular and influential in today's television. Reality and news programmes, to mention but two examples, have become dominated by liveness, so much so that audiences have come to expect this to be the case (Hoskins 2004b). The popularity of liveness, moreover, currently seems uncompromised by potential questions about how real or preferred its effects are vis-à-vis those produced under unmediated, real-time conditions. This, some authors argue, is because liveness 'guarantees a potential connection to shared social realities as they are happening' (Couldry 2004: 355). It gives us 'a sense of connection to others through an experience we share' (Gitlin 2001: 128). Places, events, times, people: they are all made to enter a web of interconnectivity and, ultimately, closeness, through liveness.

As we have seen, live news uses a variety of means to connect us as 'live' viewers to each other, to the world out there and to others in that world (be it journalists or newsactors). It also connects us to our pasts, our presents and, increasingly, to our futures. Live images (whether in quick succession or simultaneously) confer the impression that we as viewers have access to the presentness of other places, people and, paradoxically, other times. The presents offered simultaneously on the screen may be temporally very different to our viewing presents – they may, for instance, include different time zones, all of them concomitantly offered as 'live'. Yet, they nevertheless continue to connect us to others in a broadcast moment that is produced as salient.

Similarly, live speech is constantly and self-reflexively performed in live news. The reporting of the present relies upon a particular performance of liveness in which sociable, small talk matters hugely. Such talk is often performed in ways that sound naturally occurring. It is also performed in ways which show that the speaker is personally committed to his/her words. Spontaneous-sounding talk and fresh talk are the two principal markers of broadcast authentic talk (see Chapter 4). When reporters' live pieces sound natural, rather than highly polished and rehearsed, their talk appears true to itself and, hence, authentic. And when mood reporting is used in live pieces, the result is the performance of talk that sounds true to experience and, in turn, also authentic. Furthermore, when reporters talk about their experiences, either as individuals or as propositional ventriloquists of wider groups, they imbue their live speech with a kind of authenticity that projects sociability rather than facticity at its base.

What is more, and as discussed in relation to disaster marathons, silence is often used strategically, in both its concrete and its metaphorical varieties, in live news. It serves to cover for an absence of new news, to instil emphasis or gravitas into given news items and events and, importantly for our discussion of closeness, to construct a shared emotional space in which collective feelings such as shock, grieving and wonder can be accommodated.

Whether or not viewers receive the currently fashionable, self-conscious (over)use of live images, live speech and live silence in news as genuine is open to debate – a point that is considered further in Chapter 14. What is certain, though, is that liveness has significantly contributed to taking news away from its traditionally claimed referential function. Regardless of how (un)critical one may ultimately be of the ways in which live news is nowadays performed and the consequences thereof, there is no escaping the fact that its ultimate imperative is a combination of immediacy and imminence. Television news is seemingly moving from disclosing and disseminating new factual information to providing affective and at times moral (Chouliaraki 2004) interpretations of present events and their likely developments in an imminent future. In so doing, live news is first and foremost becoming a case of 'close' news: a television context that keenly produces for viewers a sense of being in touch in the moment – often, actually, the next moment – with others within an imagined global community.

# 'Close' Talk and Moral Worthiness

7

We live, it is often stated in relation to the West, in a 'therapeutic culture' (Furedi 2004) – a culture in which talking to others about our mistakes and our attempts to overcome them is celebrated. We live, moreover, in a culture in which the media constantly manufacture feelings for personal gratification, contributing in this way to what Mestrovic (1997) calls a 'McDonaldization of emotions'. Following on from the discussion of closeness in live news, this chapter explores how television's 'therapy machine' (White 2002) creates an impression of proximity – even intimacy – between itself and viewers. It specifically explores the kind of self-disclosing/confessional talk in which ordinary people and celebrities alike often engage on television, as well as the systems of values and beliefs that seemingly underlie this talk. The analysis is primarily situated in celebrity chat shows and reality programmes. Despite their differences and hybrid nature, both share a keen interest in the revelation of emotions before the cameras. And since emotions are generally understood to be at the heart of one's 'core', both also claim to make directly accessible to viewers what truly happens to certain people and how these people really experience it.

## 7.1 Close chat

In their article 'Obsessed with the audience: Breakfast television revisited', Wieten and Pantii (2006) argue that this television format has gone to considerable lengths to get close to viewers. One of the main means of doing so has been to demystify itself. Camera crews, floor managers and other behind-the-scenes staff often come into view and at times participate in breakfast shows. Technical glitches are used as aesthetic choices to signify that, as in everyday life, things sometimes go wrong and that this is natural. Another means has been to construct a sense of relevance and belonging. The homely settings – the easy chairs, the seats in front of a fireplace, the kitchen tables – of breakfast television try to create the impression of familiarity, as do the presenters' professional identities, which generally rely on the performance of 'next-door-neighbour' roles and fit squarely into the general description of the presenters of ordinary television. They must disguise or disavow any signs of extraordinary intelligence, insight or high social status. In the case of male presenters, they must also lack exceptional good looks.[1] These presenters need, in short, to convey an appearance of unexceptionality.

When presenting teams on breakfast television interact with each other, too, they do so in reassuringly familiar ways. Frequently in the British breakfast show *GMTV* (*Good Morning Television*, ITV), for instance, presenters talk to each other about aspects of their lives that are assumed to be familiar to the viewers' daily experiences and, hence, ordinary: their pregnancies, their children's first day at school, and so forth. Presenters doing being ordinary often includes the disclosure of personal weaknesses and struggles. In keeping with the shows' reassuring familiarity and normality, these revelations are typically mundane and generally performed in a light-hearted, conversational style. A presenter, for instance, may nonchalantly 'confess' that he/she has failed to stay off chocolate following a previously made promise to camera to do so. Normality and familiarity, then, are pivotal to the impression that breakfast television shares viewers' experiences and feelings and that it is close to them – that 'it cares' (Wieten and Pantii 2006: 35).

Many other television contexts revolve around media professionals' self-disclosing talk in reassuringly familiar and/or ordinary fashion. We discussed in Chapter 4, for example, talk show hosts' selective personal revelations when interacting with participants. In this section of the chapter, we focus on a different variety of the talk show format: the celebrity chat show. This includes programmes such as *Parkinson* in the UK, in which presenters and a range of small- and big-screen personalities take self-disclosure 'seriously', which is not to say that the resulting talk lacks entertainment value. It also includes those other programmes, such as *The David Letterman Show* in the US and *Rove Live* in Australia and New Zealand, in which self-disclosing talk is generally used as a platform for banter and/or satire.[2]

Extract 7.1 (p. 82) reproduces part of a live video-conference interview by Australian presenter Rove McManus with Hollywood actress Drew Barrymore in *Rove Live*. It is preceded by a promotional trailer of Drew Barrymore's latest film, an informal greeting exchange between her and Rove, and a question by the latter about the film, which Barrymore has just answered.

Celebrities, in particular film stars, are said to achieve their 'charisma' through their screen appearances and the public's knowledge of their glamorous lifestyles (Dyer 1979). The latter is fuelled by an industry devoted to celebrity publicity (Ellis 1982) in the form of, for example, glossy magazine photos of their luxurious homes and promotional interviews like the one given by Barrymore to *Rove Live* in Extract 7.1. All this supplementary publicity generates a 'system of celebrity' (Marshall 1997) that exalts the glitzy world of film stars vis-à-vis both the familiar world of other media personalities (such as breakfast television presenters) and the mundane world of ordinary folk. An apparently inexorable attraction towards what the person behind the alluring celebrity mask may truly be like thereby ensues. This fascination seemingly transfigures viewers into 'detectives' in search of the 'real essence' of stars.

### Rove Live (New Zealand, TV3, 2004)

[Rove is standing on centre stage facing the studio audience. To his left, there is a wide screen showing a talking head (TH) of Barrymore against a superimposed background of an unspecified US city skyline at night. R: Rove; B: Barrymore; A: studio audience.]

| | | | |
|---|---|---|---|
| *LS – R's back, towards B* | 01 | R | in keeping with that (.) >'cos the theme of the |
| *on wide screen.* | 02 | | film is having to woo the same person every day< |
| *CU – B looks down coyly* | 03 | | (.) is that something that <u>you</u> try to do in your day |
| *and nods in agreement as* | 04 | | to day? just to try to <u>woo</u> the person you love |
| *she smiles shyly.* | 05 | | <<u>every</u>> <<u>single</u>> day of your life? |
| *CU – B looks up and* | 06 | B | <<u>ABSOLUTELY</u>> (.) er again although this |
| *smiles resolutely.* | 07 | | movie is a bright comedy in certain aspects (.) its |
| *LS – R's back, towards B* | 08 | | er er its underlying message is something |
| *on wide screen.* | 09 | | beautiful (.) how you do make love grow? [. . .] |
| | 10–19 | | *[B talks about love in general for about ten seconds.]* |
| *TH – B, to camera.* | 20 | | [. . .] it's so much fun to d- it's not only <u>not</u> |
| *CU – B looks down,* | 21 | | exhausting it's in<u>vigorating</u> (.) and er (.) er it- er |
| *as though shy.* | 22 | | er I'm such a <<u>hopeless</u>> ro<u>mantic</u> (.) |
| *LS – R's back, towards B* | 23 | | <<u>ABSOLUTELY</u>> (.) fall in love every day of |
| *on wide screen.* | 24 | | your life in <new> and <u>different</u> ways |
| | 25 | R | and what's the <u>most</u> romantic thing <u>you</u>'ve ever |
| | 26 | | done then? |
| *TH – B partially covers* | 27 | B | oh <u>GOODNESS</u> (.) er I er I I feel I (.) I er I <u>hope</u> I |
| *face with hands, looks* | 28 | | do [romantic things <u>all</u> the time |
| *up as if thinking and* | 29 | R | [*laughs* |
| *smiles demurely before* | 30 | B | er I like making things er I think something made |
| *continuing to talk.* | 31 | | is something that shows love and I <u>love</u> the |
| *MS – R nodding in* | 32 | | originality of that and the (.) creativity that goes |
| *agreement and smiling.* | 33 | | into it (2.0) and er and and (.) |
| *LS – R's back, towards B* | 34 | | just have fun with it and keep trying all the time |
| *on wide screen.* | 35 | | and and er and putting that effort in gives you <u>so::</u> |
| | 36 | | much in return even though <u>all</u> you're trying to do |
| | 37 | | is make someone else happy |
| | 38–47 | | *[R comments on B's wearing a T-shirt with the word Hawaii on it and asks her if she tried the Hawaiian way of life while filming on that island.]* |
| *CU – B, smiling broadly.* | 48 | B | I <u>DID</u> (.) I <u>DID</u> (.) a bunch of my girl friends |
| *TH – Gesturing with* | 49 | | came to stay with m- er it er it was the <u>one</u> |
| *hands.* | 50 | | location all my girl friends came to visit ['cos |
| *CU – R.* | 51 | R | [*laughs* |
| *TH – B's animated body* | 52 | B | of <u>beautiful</u> Hawaii and my girl friend ended up |
| *language and facial* | 53 | | staying for <<u>three</u> weeks> and er (.) w- er we |
| *expressions.* | 54 | | surfed <u>constantly</u> and er you know? it's |
| *MS – R smiling.* | 55 | | something I <u>never</u> thought I'd do (.) I'm like the |
| | 56 | | <u>biggest</u> dork (.) com<u>pletely</u> [<<u>uncoordinated</u>> er |
| *LS – A.* | 57 | A | [ *laughter* |
| *TH – B's animated body* | 58 | B | just er ri<u>diculous</u> and I <u>couldn't</u> believe I was |
| *language. LS – R's back,* | 59 | | ex<u>periencing</u> this (.) <<u>just</u> a dream come true> (.) |
| *towards B on wide* | 60 | | er it was <u>great</u> for the film 'cos that's why we |
| *screen.* | 61 | | were there er the backdr- this island [. . .] |

Some small-screen celebrities, as the analysis of Kilroy's personal-experience storytelling in Chapter 4 illustrated, ironise their media persona. For those others who follow the traditional performance of 'authentic stardom', the main issue at stake is to get things right in a celebrity climate in which 'yesterday's markers of sincerity and authenticity are today's signs of hype and artifice' (Dyer 1991: 137). How, then, is 'true celebrity' articulated nowadays? And what does it tell us about television discourse? Let us consider these questions through the example of Barrymore's interview in Extract 7.1.

In celebrity chat shows, true celebrity is often performed in celebrities' self-disclosing talk. This is because this form of talk generally includes aspects of their private lives, including their emotions. Together, emotion and privateness seem to project the image of celebrities' real essence being revealed through their talk. Barrymore, for instance, is asked whether *she* practises the romantic relationship style advocated in her film (lines 01–05, 25–26) and whether *she* tried the Hawaiian lifestyle whilst filming on that island (lines 38–47). Her answers are not only affirmative, and hence reveal aspects of Barrymore's private life, but effusively so: '<ABSOLUTELY>' (line 06), 'I'm such a <hopeless> romantic' (line 22), 'oh GOODNESS' (line 27) and 'I DID (.) I DID' (line 48). Note, in this respect, that the sentiment or emotion of her talk during these moments of the interview is maximally captured for the viewers through four camera close-ups of her looking down shyly (lines 03–05, 21–22) and of her smiling first resolutely (lines 06–07) and then broadly (line 48).

Barrymore's animated body language is, likewise, shown from a medium-close angle (talking head) as visual proof that she is speaking naturally, not from a script. She is shown in lines 27–28, for example, partially covering her face with her hands, which gives the impression that she has been somehow caught off-guard by Rove's personal questions and that she feels shy about disclosing her romantic self in front of the cameras. Barrymore's performance of 'fresh talk' (i.e. her occupying all three speaker roles of animator, principal and author) also contributes to the naturalness of her talk, as do the disfluencies in her delivery (e.g. lines 21–22 and 27). And Barrymore's conversational style projects a sense of informality – a certain interactional ease. This comes from her use of colloquialisms (e.g. 'just have fun with it', line 34; 'a bunch of', line 48; 'ended up', line 52), broken syntax (subject ellipsis in <just a dream come true>, line 59), conversational tags ('and er you know?', line 54) and youth talk markers (non-standard 'like' in 'I'm like the biggest dork . . .', lines 55–56). The distinctive gesturing, the liveliness and the conversational flavour of her self-disclosing talk, then, all add to the impression that direct access to Barrymore's real essence is being gained by watching and listening to her.

Paradoxically, though, the content of Barrymore's self-disclosing talk is quite guarded. She provides only a few glimpses of her private self, which she skilfully combines with talk about her latest film. Her combination of privateness and publicness is characteristic of the celebrity chat show interview context, where celebrities often trade moments of personal, and at times emotional, talk for airtime to promote their public selves. Viewers know this. 'Investigative' interest lies in their being able to identify those precise moments during the interviews in which celebrities may drop their promotional masks. Celebrities know it, too. Their job is to ensure that they achieve the right balance between private and public talk. In Goffman's (1981) terms, their job is to manage how much – and what type of – 'backstage material' they include in the otherwise very much 'frontstage' context of the celebrity chat show interview.

In his study of radio talk, Goffman (1981) explains how disc jockeys (DJs) sometimes take listeners figuratively behind the scenes during their shows. Matters that are normally concealed from listeners, such as production hitches, are commented upon. Talk that is, in theory, not meant to be broadcast becomes heard. On these occasions, Goffman explains, backstage talk is being fronted. Goffman's concepts of frontstage and backstage talk, moreover, extend beyond the context of radio DJ chatter. They are at the very heart of Goffman's 'theatrical' or 'dramaturgical' metaphor, which sees the presentation of self in everyday life as closely linked to enactment.[3] In their everyday interactions, Goffman argues, people present dramas to audiences, rather than provide information to recipients. When telling a personal anecdote, for example, 'what the individual presents is not himself but a story containing a protagonist who may happen also to be himself' (1974: 541). These performance rituals, he further observes, tend to conform to an individual's place in the social hierarchy. As social actors, we are all expected to – and generally do – base self-presentation upon the situational frame, footing and 'the normatively specified conduct' (1981: 3) of a given social event.

Situational or interactional frames are particular sets of principles of organisation that define the meaning and significance of social events (Goffman 1963). Footings are the particular alignments that we take up in interaction in relation to our own words and those of others. And normatively specified conduct makes certain kinds of talk, and certain forms of delivery, suitable (frontstage) or otherwise (backstage) for public reception within given frames and footings. Swearing, for example, is not regarded as frontstage material on British television before the so-called 'watershed' at nine o'clock in the evening. It is, in fact, considered backstage material across a number of (un)mediated social events in a number of cultures. Emotional self-disclosure is another example of material generally associated with the private – or backstage – regions of the self. Unlike swearing, however, the practice of baring one's soul in public is commonplace on television. Emotional self-disclosure, especially if confessional in nature, constitutes an expected-to-be-fronted type of backstage material across a number of television contexts and by a number of television performers.

In the interview from which Extract 7.1 comes, Barrymore alternates between backstage and frontstage talk. Interestingly, she does so even when responding to questions on private aspects of her life. Barrymore's answers to questions on her romantic self (lines 01–05, 25–26), for example, deftly interweave fleeting references to her experiences into comparatively more developed general and/or promotional remarks. Her initial and resolute '<ABSOLUTELY>' (line 06), for instance, provides a directly relevant response to Rove's first question. The micro-pause and hesitation ('(.) er') that follow, however, signal a change of footing. Barrymore now becomes the animator of a polished, and typically frontstage, sales-pitch about her film, which includes a definition of its genre ('this movie is a bright comedy in certain aspects', lines 06–07) and 'underlying message' (line 08). The latter she animates through a generic question ('how do you make love grow?', line 09) that she proceeds to answer, also in generic terms (lines 10–19). When asked by Rove to front more backstage material ('and what's the <u>most</u> romantic thing <u>you</u>'ve ever done then?', lines 25–26), Barrymore initially obliges (lines 27–28, 30–33). A subsequent two-second pause and several speech disfluencies (line 33), though, revert her talk to frontstage regions. Note, for instance, her use of the second person 'you' in a generic sense: 'just have fun with it and keep trying all the time and and er and putting that effort in gives you <u>so::</u> much in return even though <u>all</u> you're trying to do is make someone else happy' (lines 34–37).

When backstage material is actually fronted, moreover, Barrymore's style of delivery transforms it into talk-as-spectacle. A case in point is her self-deprecation in lines 54–58: 'it's something I <u>never</u> thought I'd do (.) I'm like the <u>biggest</u> dork (.) com<u>pletely</u> [<u><uncoordinated></u> er just er ri<u>diculous</u>'. Here, she reveals personal limitations but she uses a witty hyperbole to do so, which she animates with emphatic stress and a markedly slow delivery rate. This secures her a smile from the presenter (lines 55–56) and supportive laughter from the studio audience (line 57). It also turns her talk away from personal revelation to entertainment. By providing glimpses of her private self and delivering these as public talk, Barrymore can be seen both to fuel viewers' detective-like fascination with her privateness during the interview and to promote her publicness.

Emotion and private talk are, then, associated with the revelation of one's real essence in celebrity chat shows, even though both are often simply the carrot in the celebrities' public talk stick. But are all kinds of emotional self-disclosure seen as markers of true celebrity? The answer to this question depends largely on the given celebrity and/or chat show in which it is performed. Two kinds of performance, however, seem to be particularly favoured currently: 'doing being-ordinary' and 'doing being moralistic/motivational' (Tolson 2006).

In theory, doing being ordinary sits uncomfortably with the very concept of celebrity, which rests upon the possession of some extraordinary trait and means. This may explain why some media personalities ironise the whole idea of their being ordinary, as we saw in Chapter 4 in relation to talk show host Robert Kilroy-Silk. In practice, it can provide the appealing illusion that, despite all the surrounding glitz and success, the person beneath is really like the rest of us. Thus, for example, in Extract 7.1 Barrymore presents herself as a young female who, like most ordinary young females, enjoys spending time with 'a bunch of [. . .] girl friends' (line 48). These friends are, also like most ordinary girl friends would be, thrilled about a holiday on an exotic island. This surfaces in Barrymore's explanation that Hawaii 'was the <u>one</u> location all my girl friends came to visit' (lines 49–50) and that one of them 'ended up staying for <u>three</u> weeks>' (lines 52–53). Barrymore also presents herself as a person who moulds to her surroundings. Her anecdote about surfing with friends in Hawaii projects an ordinary, 'when in Rome' attitude, not a diva one. In this anecdote, she also presents herself as someone who, like ordinary people, is not perfect (e.g. 'the <u>biggest</u> dork com<u>pletely</u> <<u>uncoordinated</u>>', lines 55–56), even if her exaggerated self-mockery somewhat ironises her doing being ordinary at this point. Barrymore, too, presents herself as someone who, despite possessing extraordinary means, doubts her ability to fulfil her otherwise rather ordinary dream to practise surfing whilst on holiday in Hawaii – one of the most popular surfing places in the world: 'and er you know? it's something I <u>never</u> thought I'd do (.)' (lines 54–55), 'and I <u>couldn't</u> believe I was ex<u>periencing</u> this (.) <<u>just</u> a dream come true>'(lines 58–59). All in all, her backstage talk projects an ordinary self that reaches out to viewers for shared experiences and emotions.

As for doing being moralistic/motivational, this is not only a case of an increasing number of small- and big-screen celebrities publicising their status as ambassadors and/or sponsors of humanitarian organisations. Nor is it limited to their frequent appearances on a number of reality shows to raise funds for charity. It is also, and importantly considering the appeal of all things celebrity, a case of their fronted backstage talk increasingly carrying moralistic and/or motivational messages. Emblematic of this is Oprah Winfrey, who has been regarded as the personification of contemporary celebrity (Marshall 1997). Her frequent revelations to camera emphasise the self-transformation and rehabilitation power of emotional expressiveness. They tend to highlight ordinary aspects of her life – when it suits her to do so – and therefore seek to build a rapport between her and the viewers (Peck 1995). Her having conquered 'ordinary' weaknesses (e.g. weight problems) partly through talk, moreover, is used by Oprah Winfrey to claim a moral high ground from which she can counsel and instruct others in similar positions. As a number of celebrities nowadays do, Oprah Winfrey performs 'a motivational, even moral, discourse of personal achievement' (Tolson 2006: 155). Given the fascination that the role of celebrity *per se* seems to exert on some viewers (Bell and van Leeuwen 1994), these performances contribute to naturalising the speech and moral ideal of emotional expressiveness.

Unlike Oprah Winfrey, in Extract 7.1 Barrymore is neither confessing sins nor disclosing personal struggles that she has managed to overcome. But her backstage talk does turn personal experience into lessons about personal achievement. Following on from her enthusiastic approval of a particular romantic style (line 23), for example, she provides explicit instructions for others to follow suit: 'fall in love every day of your life in <new> and <u>different</u> ways' (lines 23–24) and 'just have fun with it and keep trying all the time' (line 34). Barrymore's romantic style, what is more, appears particularly worth emulating, not least because of the rewards that it supposedly brings: 'it's so much fun to d- it's not only <u>not</u> exhausting it's in<u>vigorating</u>' (lines 20–21) and 'putting that effort in gives you <u>so::</u> much in return even though <u>all</u> you're trying to do is make someone else happy' (lines 35–37). By transforming personal experience and emotion into rewarding lessons for others, celebrities like Barrymore market their public and their private selves whilst selling emotional expressiveness as desirable and morally worthy.

Doing being ordinary and being motivational/moralistic emerge as two recurrent markers of authentic talk in the context of celebrity chat shows. Both rely on the performance of emotional, self-disclosing talk and thus seemingly offer viewers direct access to the backstage regions of glamorous selves, where their real essence is assumed to lie. The association between privateness and authenticity is something of which celebrities are, of course, fully aware, as Barrymore's skilful combination of frontstage and backstage material in Extract 7.1 has shown. After all, celebrities' ultimate power is 'to sell the commodity that is themselves' (Turner et al. 2000: 128). In the remainder of this chapter, we continue to explore this privateness–authenticity relationship, but within a different form of talk (confessional monologues to camera) and in a different television context (reality shows).

## 7.2   Close talk, 'alone'

Reality television uses a variety of forms of talk to assert a direct link to reality, including multi-party conversations, dyadic interactions and single-person speech situations.[4] Of these forms of talk, the latter is generally regarded as its 'truth hallmark', despite the overtly scripted nature of monologue in other non-fictional television contexts, such as political speeches (see Chapter 12) and stand-up comedian performances. The emotional revelations of ordinary folk to closely positioned cameras in reality shows are generally treated as proof that direct access to these people's true selves is being gained. It is probable that this truth value of monologue in reality television has benefited from its use in established literary and film genres. In drama, prose and *film noir*, for example, monologue is typically used to reveal characters' true selves, especially when confessing to morally objectionable behaviour and/or engaging in soul-searching work.

Let us explore this monologue–true-selfhood relationship in reality television by examining Extract 7.2 (see p. 88), taken from the series *You are What You Eat* (Channel 4, UK). In the episode from which it comes, two ordinary people – Gregor and Helen – undergo a typical rehabilitation journey. This entails moving from being 'obsessed' with unhealthy food (and psychologically and physically affected by their obsession) to being 'in control' of their relationship with food (and emotionally and physically happier as a result). The catalyst for their emotional and physical rehabilitation is the presenter of the series and nutrition guru, Gillian McKeith. Her regime consists of an initial phase, in which participants like Gregor and Helen undergo a training session on healthy eating and fitness at her base, followed by a two-month (self-)monitoring phase. During the latter, participants receive 'unexpected' visits from the presenter to their homes and workplaces and are also given portable cameras to video-record the emotional ups and downs of their rehabilitation journeys.

Although reality television treats all forms of close talk 'alone' as truth signs, it favours a specific variety: confessional monologue. As its name indicates, this consists of single-speech situations in which a person revisits his/her moral

**EXTRACT 7.2**

**You Are What You Eat (Channel 4, 2007)**

[The extract takes place at the start of the second half of the episode, once Gregor and Helen have concluded their training session with Gillian McKeith (M: Gillian McKeith; G: Gregor; H: Helen.]

| | | | |
|---|---|---|---|
| *LS – G in kitchen peeling* | 01 | M | just <u>one</u> week after he's left the house and my |
| *a cucumber.* | 02 | (vo) | porky protégé Gregor has hit a hurdle (.) |
| *MS – To camera, as he* | 03 | G | what I'm <u>really</u> struggling |
| *blends cucumber and* | 04 | | with it's the er it's the juices th- (.) |
| *pours it into a glass.* | 05 | | to me (.) er mm (.) |
| *G drinks* | 06 | | I must admit it's it's <u>pretty</u> <u>vile</u> (2.0) |
| *and heaves. G in* | 07 | | I <u>CAN'T</u> stand cucumber |
| *kitchen, captions with* | 08 | M | <u>I</u> can't stand <<u>whingers</u>> (.) |
| *vitamin and mineral* | 09 | (vo) | cucumber is packed with the vitamins and |
| *names loop on screen.* | 10 | | minerals Gregor is missing [. . .] |

[The episode continues for a further fifteen minutes or so. The part of the episode reproduced below corresponds to one of the presenter's allegedly *impromptu* visits to Gregor three weeks into the (self-)monitoring phase of his rehabilitation.]

| | | | |
|---|---|---|---|
| *LS – G sitting in a café.* | 40 | M | Gregor is struggling to curb his cravings |
| *CU – plate with healthy* | 41 | (vo) | |
| *food being brought to G's* | 42 | G | last week was er <u>just</u> <u>horrific</u> er I <u>just</u> craved |
| *table.* | 43 | | chocolate (.) cakes and biscuits (.) that's what |
| *CU – G, to camera.* | 44 | | I was <u>really</u> craving (.) that's what I <u>really</u> |
| | 45 | | wanted er (.) I want to be good (2.0) |
| *CU – G's empty plate.* | 46 | | I'm er I'm sticking to it (.) |
| *LS – G, in flower shop* | 47 | M | <u>agh</u> (.) what a <<u>moaning</u> <u>minnie</u>> (.) he needs |
| *standing on stepper* | 48 | (vo) | to change that chocolate high for a serotonin |
| *behind the counter.* | 49 | | high and do some exercise so I've sent him a |
| *MS – G arranging.* | 50 | | stepper so that he can step at work (.) |
| *flowers. CU – G, to* | 51 | G | the stepper (.) I think it's a lot of shit (.) I'm |
| *camera, then looking* | 52 | | just standing all day on the stepper but I'm (.) |
| *down unimpressed in the* | 53 | | to me er it's <u>not</u> practical and I've got a shop |
| *direction of the stepper.* | 54 | | to run (.) I can't be <<u>faffing</u> around> with |
| | 55 | | doing (.) exercise on the stepper and stuff |
| *LS – M coming out of* | 56 | M | Gregor's negativity won't get him anywhere |
| *train station and meeting* | 57 | (vo) | so I'm enlisting Helen's help for some morale- |
| *Helen (H). The two hug* | 58 | | boosting |
| *and kiss on the cheek. MS* | 59 | M | Gregor is driving me <u>mad</u> that's why I wanted |
| *– H and M talking outside* | 60 | | you to come with me today (.) he's <<u>such a</u> |
| *train station. To H.* | 61 | | <u>whinger</u>> = |
| *CU – H, to M.* | 62 | H | = OH he <u>IS</u> [. . .] |

worthiness vis-à-vis his/her actions, thoughts, emotions and relationships with others. Unlike emotional self-disclosure in, for instance, talk shows, confessional monologue in reality television is, in theory, self-induced. It may ultimately have a therapeutic – even cathartic – value for its authors and/or the viewers, but it is not prompted by, for example, a talk show host's questions.

Instead, in a number of reality television programmes, participants are asked to keep video diaries so that they may 'spontaneously' confess their weaknesses, character flaws and other sins to portable cameras in the privacy of their own homes. Participants are, of course, aware that they are not really talking alone. Their addressing a camera means that they know that their seemingly self-induced, private processes of confession will evolve into other-appraised, public products. The occasional presence of the presenters and other members of the production teams likewise means that at least some of these confessional monologues to camera are actually prearranged.

Gregor's talk in Extract 7.2 includes three brief monologues to camera (lines 03–07, 42–46 and 51–55). All three are confessional in so far as they all contain self-examination talk. In the first one, Gregor talks emotionally about his struggles in following the presenter's instruction to drink healthy juices. In the other two, he acknowledges dwindling willpower when it comes to chocolate, cake and bicuits and an unwillingness to use a stepper in work, respectively. Only the first of these monologues, however, is performed as self-induced: it takes place in Gregor's kitchen and in conditions of no physical co-presence. The other two, offering footage of Gregor in a café and his shop, are filmed by another person at a specifically agreed moment in time. They are, therefore, other-induced, and possibly steered by specific interviewer prompts that have been edited out.

Gregor's confessional monologues in Extract 7.2 pander to reality television's promise of closeness and truth in that they reveal the emotional inner struggles of an ordinary person. Thus, throughout the extract, Gregor makes no secret of his difficulties in following the presenter's regime. He uses the emphatically delivered and prequalified superlative adjectives: 'pretty vile' (line 06) and 'just horrific' (line 42). He also emphatically delivers a number of verbal phrases through added stress and/or a raised voice, for example: 'I'm really struggling' (line 03), 'I CAN'T stand' (line 07) and 'I was really craving' (line 44). All of this leaves no doubt as to the intensity of the emotions being revealed to camera by Gregor.

The truth sign of Gregor's monologues lies, too, in his seemingly appearing untroubled by the close presence of the camera, of which his heaving after drinking cucumber juice in lines 06–07 is indicative.[5] Consider, too, his fronting of typical backstage talk in lines 51 and 54. Although relatively mild, the expressions 'a lot of shit' and '<faffing around' might be seen as socially improper. The use of these words despite the presence of a closely positioned camera contributes to the impression that Gregor's privateness is being 'blurted out'. This is important to some reality shows' claim to provide direct access to the real feelings of real people. Just as importantly, Gregor's confessional monologues provide the show with the building blocks from which to construct its own version of both truth and moral worthiness, as we discuss next.

In *The History of Sexuality*, French philosopher and historian Michel Foucault (1978) argued that today's Western man is a confessing animal. Confession in the West, he wrote, 'has spread far and wide':

It plays a part in justice, medicine, education, family relationships, and love relations, in the most ordinary affairs of everyday life, and in the most solemn rites; one confesses one's crimes, one's sins, one's thoughts and desires, one's illnesses and troubles; one goes about telling, with the greatest precision, whatever is most difficult to tell. One confesses in public and in private, to one's parents, one's educators, one's doctor, to those one loves; one admits to oneself, in pleasure and in pain, things it would be impossible to tell to anyone else, the things people write books about. (1978: 59).

Although nothing like today's reality television existed at the time when Foucault wrote *The History of Sexuality*, one cannot help but see in this form of programming's pervasive performance of close talk 'alone' a poignant reminder of Foucault's views on the West's confessional mania. Ever since the Middle Ages, Foucault further argued, Western societies have made confession one of the 'most highly valued techniques for producing truth' (1978: 58–59). This is because, through confession, individuals purportedly become authenticated by the discourses of truth that they voice about themselves. Such authenticating of the self, in turn, acts as a sign of their emotional determination to reach moral worthiness. In the Catholic Church rite of confession, for example, penitents acknowledge their wrongdoings and thereby communicate their intention to change (to improve) and to become good Catholics. This is why confession, Foucault (1978: 61) also observes, 'exonerates, redeems, and purifies him [the speaking subject]; it unburdens him of his wrongs, liberates him, and promises his salvation'.

In shows like *You Are What You Eat,* confessional practices seem to be driven, too, by participants' determination to become better selves – by the show's standards, that is. In Extract 7.2, for instance, Gregor's monologues to camera reveal not only his struggles to be good but also his determination to overcome his difficulties. In lines 06–07, he is seen drinking the cucumber juice that he so much despises. In lines 40–43, a plate with healthy food is served to him at a café and is soon afterwards shown empty (line 46) alongside Gregor's statement of determination and will power: 'I want to be good (2.0) I'm er I'm sticking to it' (lines 45–46). And, although he shows no intention of using the recommended stepper in work, he justifies this infringement of the presenter's regime on 'practical' (line 53) grounds: 'I've got a shop to run' (lines 53–54). A determination to improve, whether genuine or otherwise, thus underlies Gregor's confessional discourse before the camera.

In the so-called 'Diary Room' of the *Big Brother* house, too, participants regularly perform emotional self-disclosure (*Big-Brother*-induced) and/or confessional (self-induced) monologues.[6] The purpose of these monologues is essentially to come across as 'good housemates' – as moral selves within the parameters of the *Big Brother* house. Being a good *Big Brother* housemate is discursively realised through the performance of sociability, sympathetic circularity and selfhood (Tolson 2006). Sociability involves creating the impression that one cares about getting along with one's housemates, despite also wanting to beat them in the competition and wanting to entertain the viewers.

Sympathetic circularity seeks to generate benevolent understanding of one's behaviour from the viewers and the other housemates. It is implemented through 'sympathetic circularity markers' (Bernstein 1971; Montgomery 1986), such as 'you know?', 'you know what I mean?', and tag questions (e.g. 'I couldn't do anything else, could I?'). Through these, the housemates invite their interlocutors to sympathise with their talk (and behaviour). In the context of fierce competition for a significant cash prize and the possibility of becoming a celebrity, the *Big Brother* housemates' apparent negotiation of selfhood through such sympathetic circularity markers belies self-promotional talk. As for the performance of selfhood, this refers to the housemates' decisions about whether or not to show consistency between, on the one hand, the frontstage sociability that they are expected to display towards the other housemates and, on the other, their backstage confessions of manipulation, game tactics, and so forth in the Diary Room, which they also know need to be fronted since they are already known to the viewers.

Although different in some respects, shows like *You Are What You Eat* and *Big Brother* share a preoccupation with accessing ordinary people's real essence through the latters' talk 'alone' to camera. This talk is often confessional in nature: it reveals their authors' weaknesses, aspirations, struggles and inner demons. The moral worthiness of its authors is subsequently often also publicly judged within some of these shows. Once again, it is instructive here to consider Foucault's thesis on confession rituals.

Ever since the Middle Ages, Foucault (1978) explains, confession has acted as a form of regulation. Confession always takes place in the presence of another, whose role is first to listen and then 'to judge, punish, forgive, console and reconcile'. The power, or 'agency of domination', in confession therefore lies not within the speaking subject, through his/her authentication of selfhood, but within 'the one who listens [. . .] the one who questions and is not supposed to know' (1978: 61–62). In reality television, the invisible others are, in theory, the viewers. Gregor's confessional monologues in Extract 7.2, for example, are broadcast as moments of close talk, involving only him and the camera. Through the latter, viewers are positioned as those who listen but who are not supposed to know. In practice, however, viewers are only offered the position of vicarious agents of domination. It is normally the shows' presenters who appraise, impose penitence and, towards the end of the shows, generally absolve those ordinary people who have confessed to camera.

Whilst initially performed as private moments of self-evaluation, post-production editing techniques in many of these shows ensure that the ordinary people's talk 'alone' becomes public *and* accountable through the discourse of their presenters. In Extract 7.2, for instance, Gregor's confessional monologues are sandwiched between narrative voice-overs in which McKeith relays in no uncertain terms what she thinks about his claims to moral worthiness. These voice-overs are combined with her on-screen appearance in lines 59–61, in which she judges Gregor's performance in conversation with Helen. McKeith therefore exercises her agency of domination at will from within narrative positions of character in a play and voice of God. Within the latter, in particular, she provides a form of social regulation that relies on the teaching of cautionary lessons.

McKeith's appraisal of Gregor's confessional talk in Extract 7.2 is harsh and unsympathetic. It resembles the no-nonsense style of advice offered by the experts/presenters of a number of counselling shows like *Loveline* and *Good Sex! With Dr. Ruth Westheimer,* courtroom shows like *Judge Judy,* talent contests such as *Pop Idol* and *The X Factor* and 'reality-cum-cooking' shows like *(Ramsay's) Kitchen Nightmares.*[7] Common to them all is, as White (2002: 320) argues, their reliance on 'quick diagnostic and barbed exchanges about what is or is not "normal" behaviour'. The presenters of these shows engage frequently in derisive or dismissive commentary on ordinary folk's attempts at moral worthiness for entertainment purposes. This they do either in the presence of the ordinary people concerned (see Chapter 9) or, as in Extract 7.2, through voice-overs that are added at post-filming time. Either way, it normally entails the explicit, intentional transgression of socially accepted interactional norms such as discourse politeness.[8]

A central feature of discourse politeness in Anglo-Saxon cultures is the avoidance of behaviour that threatens one's co-interactants' need to be liked, appreciated and valued, that is, of behaviour that threatens their 'positive face needs'. McKeith's talk in Extract 7.2 contains several examples of this kind of facethreat. She, for instance, comments on Gregor's lack of will power ('just <u>one</u> week after . . . Gregor has hit a hurdle', lines 01–02) and on his 'negativity' (line 56). She refers to '<u><whingers></u>' (line 08) and calls Gregor 'a <u><moaning minnie></u>' (line 47). The latter makes him someone who is 'driving me <u>mad</u>' (line 59) and, once again, <u><such a whinger></u>' (lines 60–61). McKeith's face-threatening behaviour is, moreover, very explicit. Colourful, alliterative expressions such as 'moaning minnie' (line 47) and 'porky protégé' (line 02) are typical of what, drawing on Brown and Levinson's (1987) notion of politeness, Culpeper (1996, 2003, 2005) calls bald, on-record impoliteness. They are expressions that target one's co-interactant's face needs 'in a direct, clear, unambiguous and concise way'. Because these expressions are performed through verbal wit (e.g. alliteration, comical lexis), what is more, they concomitantly attend to McKeith's positive face needs, specifically her desire to come across if not as a good nutritionist, certainly as an entertaining presenter.

Is McKeith's talk really impolite, though? Authors such as Culpeper (2005) argue that the kind of bald, on-record impoliteness featured in 'exploitative' shows is so rare in naturally occurring interaction that, once performed, it is rather difficult for it not to override considerations of contextual appropriateness (see also Bousfield 2008). Impoliteness, however, is socially and contextually defined: it is behaviour that contravenes, and thus goes beyond, what is expected in a given social/interactional context (Watts 2003). If the public humiliation of ordinary folk is constitutive of the talk-as-spectacle that a number of reality shows routinely provide, then McKeith's talk may be seen as contextually appropriate, or 'politic' (Watts 2003), rather than impolite.

Lastly, presenters' talk in many of these shows also seeks to implement the shows' motivational and/or moral ethos, which is seemingly intended to save ordinary folk from their own 'helplessness'. Note, in this respect, that each of McKeith's jibes at Gregor in Extract 7.2 includes a lesson. Her echoic 'I can't stand <whingers> in line 08, for example, is followed by her narrative voice-over: 'cucumber is packed with the vitamins and minerals Gregor is missing' (lines 09–10). This spiel on nutrition is rendered over images of a pensive Gregor in the kitchen and captions with the names of vitamins and minerals looping on the screen. In line 47, she dramatically dismisses Gregor's statement of emotional determination thus: 'agh (.) what a <moaning minnie>'. This abrasive comment is followed by the instructive remark: 'he needs to . . . so I've sent him a stepper . . .' (lines 47–50). And after having patronisingly recast Gregor's view of the recommended stepper as 'negativity [which] won't get him anywhere' (line 56), she cheerfully reveals the next motivational trick up her sleeve: 'so I'm enlisting Helen's help for some morale-boosting' (lines 57–58).

The performance of confessional monologues to camera by ordinary people is, then, actively promoted in some varieties of reality television because it seemingly provides direct access to these people's real selves through their innermost emotions. At the same time, though, it is exploited for entertainment value, often harshly appraised and subjected to practices of social regulation which realise the shows' moralistic/motivational ethos.[9] A slightly different, yet equally telling, example to the one analysed in this part of the chapter arose during the 2006 edition of *UK Celebrity Big Brother*. One of its participants, Jade Goody, made racist remarks on camera about housemate and Bollywood actress Shilpa Shetty. Social outrage towards Goody soon erupted. Even the then British Chancellor of the Exchequer, Gordon Brown, was asked to comment on Goody's verbal behaviour and had to defend 'Britishness' during an official visit to India at that time. Viewer ratings also soared, as did criticism of Channel 4's decision to select, from their around-the-clock coverage of the *Big Brother* house, talk that potentially revealed fissures in Britain's proclaimed multicultural society. Goody's talk before the cameras had, in fact, been consistent with her progressively acquired media personality. Since her first appearance in 2002 as an ordinary *Big Brother* contestant, she had 'authenticated' the image of a brash yet 'dopey' female: someone with a big mouth but, basically, an innocent, good heart. Unintentional brashness was indeed the explanation that, once evicted from the house, Goody gave for her speech act of 'moral unworthiness' towards Shetty. Having become famous for her dim-witted, brassy self in ordinary *Big Brother*, she now became infamous for performing it instead of a morally worthy self in *Celebrity Big Brother*.

## 7.3    Conclusion

The analysis presented in this chapter has highlighted the role of emotional, private talk in celebrity chat shows and reality television. In the former, glimpses of true celebrity are seemingly offered in the course of presenter–celebrity interviews. These are, of course, carefully constructed and performed. In the latter, ordinary folk deliver confessional monologues to camera, in which they front their problems and their attempts to overcome them in the hope of being favourably appraised within the shows' standards of moral worthiness. In both contexts, the performance of emotional, private talk is offered to viewers as a truth sign – as a signifier of true selfhood.

Close chats between presenters and stars in celebrity chat shows are performed so as to quench viewers' alleged investigative thirst. Presenters intersperse questions about the celebrities' personal lives within these otherwise most public and promotional interactional contexts. Celebrities react to these questions 'naturally'. In Extract 7.1, for example, Barrymore appeared surprised to be asked questions about her romantic self but was nevertheless willing to reveal in her answers some of her real essence.

Similarly, ordinary people in reality shows are seen to be given an opportunity to authenticate their selves through confession rituals. Gregor's confessional monologues to camera in Extract 7.2, for example, were constructed so as to give the impression that they provided direct access to his true self. Viewers may have been more or less impressed about the moral consistency of his confessions. For example, he claimed to 'want[ing] to be good' (line 45) but also made it clear that he was unwilling to use the recommended stepper. Yet it is precisely in the emotional confession of internal contradictions that participants like Gregor may seen to reveal their true selves. It is in their morally inconsistent close talk 'alone' that the impression may have been convincingly created that viewers were able to assess a key characteristic of their authenticity: their 'integrity and credibility when it comes to feelings' (Aslama and Pantii 2006: 181).

Last but not least, this chapter has also shown that emotional, self-disclosing talk on television can be an interactional means to an ideological end. Celebrities use the fascination exerted by their celebrity status to endorse particular forms of moral worthiness and/or motivation. In the case of celebrities such as Oprah Winfrey, these emphasise ordinariness and personal achievement. In the reality shows considered in the second half of this chapter, the implementation of their moralistic and motivational ethos rests firmly with the presenter, for ordinary people are generally cast as incapable of solving their own problems. Both celebrities like Oprah and presenters like McKeith provide advice and counselling within the confines of their shows. Moreover, their doing so on the premise that a little assistance will liberate ordinary folk from their 'helplessness' enables them to square a circle inherent in these types of programme. An 'emphatic endorsement of individual agency and control' (Macdonald 2003: 85) allows moral worthiness still to be vested in self-help and self-management regimes (Squire 1997). Viewers, for their part, are both given the position of vicarious confessor/interlocutor and held at arm's length by the presenters' self-conscious performances, by television's also self-conscious strategies of mediation and simulation, and by the participants' own performativity (White 2002).

# Part III

## Conflict

# Conflict . . . or the Rise of Spectacular Incivility

> I'm paid to walk the line, I'm paid to go over the line. I'm paid to be provocative and to provoke discussion. And I've walked a pretty damned good line over the years. (Paul Holmes, 3 April 2004).

Paul Holmes is one of New Zealand's most popular and controversial broadcasters. His various shows on different television channels over the years have extensively drawn upon emotionalism and provocation. The latter is evident in Holmes's proud statement above, which comes from an interview with the Wellington-based newspaper *The Dominion Post* to mark the fifteenth anniversary of his show *Holmes* (1989–2004). In a programme that made considerable use of the interview format, 'to go over the line' and 'to provoke discussion' meant, respectively, to antagonise interviewees and to pursue argument. The first night of the *Holmes* show in 1989, for example, featured a hostile interview that resulted in the interviewee walking out of the studio. This was totally unexpected in New Zealand's hitherto deferential television interview climate. Holmes, in fact, made a national impact that night: 'When Dennis Conner [the interviewee] stormed out of a television studio on April 3, 1989', the *Dominion Post* reported, 'the word Holmes entered the national vocabulary.' (*Dominion Post* 2004: 6). The same newspaper article provided a more recent example of Holmes hitting the headlines in March 2004 'with a quip during a live discussion on ZB about the killing of Hamas spiritual leader Sheik Ahmed Yassin "They've got balls, those Israelis, haven't they, but not foreskins"' (2004: 6).[1]

*Holmes*, it seems, was less concerned with rational argumentation than with provocation and the free flow of 'negative' emotions, such as contempt and dislike for others. In this, neither *Holmes* nor its presenter is alone, of course. Veteran British broadcaster Jeremy Paxman's popularity, too, rose in the UK after a television interview in which he asked the same challenging question fourteen times of a cabinet minister. Paxman actually won one of the 1997 British Academy of Film and Television Arts (BAFTA) awards for his interviewing style. Since then, his explicit pursuance of conflict has remained impervious. If anything, it has been variously adapted by others to a number of news and political interviewing contexts on British television.

The adversarial style that characterises a number of televised political interviews may be ascribed to the inherently asymmetric turn-taking system under which they operate, specifically to the part played by the interviewer, who is able to shape the content and tenor of the interaction through the type of questions that he/she asks. However, this aspect of the political interview turn-taking system also applies to other types of interview on television, such as those in celebrity chat shows. And, as we saw in Chapter 7, whilst these too revolve around the performance of emotional talk, they display an affiliated rather than adversarial style. A more plausible explanation, then, for the adversarialness of political interviews lies in television's (and other media's) construction of its relationship with politics as fundamentally antagonistic. The main goals of the news interview, particularly in its political variety, are to seek controversy and encourage opposition, rather than to obtain information and to build consensus.[2] Generally conducted by experienced broadcasters, political interviews on television often place interviewers in the role of 'agent provocateurs' or 'hunters' and politicians as deliberately evasive but self-promotional 'prey' (Partington 2003). As the analysis of various forms of talk involving politicians and broadcasters on television in Chapters 10 and 12 shall show, however, both parties benefit from the performance of adversarialness.

Adversarialness also features regularly in talk and reality shows, where it is often performed in particularly explicit and visceral ways. In talk shows, conflict is maximised through a number of interactional devices. Many heated disagreements in shows featuring lay participants and experts, for example, occur at points where the latter relinquish their institutional (expert) footing and adopt 'lay' ways of arguing. These involve emotional disagreements, instead of the kind of rational consensus-building that is traditionally associated with discourses of expertise. Such emotional disagreements, crucially, are facilitated by the hosts' partisan control of the speaking floor. Rarely after a lay participant's complaint regarding a social service, for instance, did talk show host Robert Kilroy-Silk defend the right of the representative of that social service in the studio (the expert) to counter the lay participant's point uninterrupted. Far from a celebration of laity vis-à-vis expertise, however, such host-management of the turn-taking system seeks to meet the genre's demand for entertainment through confrontation (Lorenzo-Dus 2001a; Wood 2001). It seeks to deliver, in other words, televisual 'confrontainment'.

The entertainment value behind the performance of anger, contempt and other 'negative' emotions in talk shows is most evident in their 'tabloid' variety. The overall structure and the participation framework of these shows are specifically designed to be primarily received as spectacle. In the likes of *The Jerry Springer Show* (US) and *Trisha* (UK), a parade of guests ('victims') come on to the stage to complain about their being the target of some wrongdoing. Next, a procession of, this time, accused guests ('villains') are brought from backstage to give their drastically different but equally accusatory versions of events. Hostile arguments often erupt at this point, during which the hosts normally remain with the studio audience, opposite the guests, and intervene only to stop the guests' arguments once they are deemed to have generated sufficient confrontainment. This point of intervention varies from show to show and results in some of the shows bleeping certain forms of verbal aggression – for example, swearing at others – but making the most of its non-verbal counterpart, including on occasion physically attacking others.

'Tabloid' talk show hosts regularly draw attention to aspects of the guests' stories that are likely to trigger strong, hopefully 'negative' emotions. When they problematise their guests' experiences, the hosts often create further space for confrontainment, especially since their contributions involve considerable theatrics. Loud, emphatically delivered 'ouch-es', 'nos' and expressive hand and/or facial gesturing following a 'victim's' accusation, for instance, are designed not only to evaluate the latter but also to incite multi-party confrontations between victim, villain and studio audience. In addition, towards the end of some episodes, the shows' experts (self-help gurus, counsellors, and so on) are invited on to the stage to advise victim and villain about how to rid themselves of their anger towards each other. From start to finish, then, these shows frame their guests' contributions not only as positional stories (see Chapter 4) but as 'complainable matters' (Hutchby 2001). The studio sets become ideal sites for their performance of visceral conflict talk.

In a number of reality shows, adversarialness is also explicitly and emotionally performed. Leaving aside for a moment possible fifteen-minutes-of-fame reasons, ordinary people in theory participate in these shows because they wish either to master a skill or to achieve a personal goal: to pass an army instruction course (e.g. *Bad Lads' Army*), to become a (better) chef (*The F Word*), to settle a dispute (e.g. *The People's Court* and *Judge Mathis*), to lose weight (*You Are What You Eat*), to secure a highly paid job (*The Apprentice*), to become a pop star (*Pop Idol*), and so forth. In some, for instance the quiz show *The Weakest Link*, participation is also driven by the possibility of winning a cash prize. In practice, however, the prospect of reaching some kind of self-understanding, improvement and/or achievement becomes largely secondary: 'It is replaced instead by successful participation in a performative interplay of celebrity, authority and media technologies' (White 2002: 320) – an interplay that often contains a healthy dose of harsh appraisal and disdain towards the ordinary folk that the shows are claiming to help (see Chapter 7).

Conflict talk is thus commonplace in 'serious' (political interviews) and 'banal' forms of television, and this begs the question: why? Is it because television mirrors the 'argument culture' – a culture that thrives on automatic contentiousness to accomplish all kinds of personal and social goals – in which we are said to live nowadays? (Tannen 1999). Robin Lakoff talks of a significant coarsening of political and public discourse in the US from the last decade of the twentieth century onwards. She nevertheless argues that 'public incivility' is anything but new and expresses her longing 'at times for that hypothetical golden age when Americans all shared each other's interests, or if they didn't, were demure about it' (2003: 43).

The problem with the performance of both consensus and demurred dissent on television, of course, is that neither seems capable of generating half the entertainment that disagreements do, especially when viscerally performed.

Rather than a spectacular rise of incivility on television, what the medium seems to display is a rise of 'spectacular incivility' – of incivility-as-spectacle. This is not so much a case of frequent instances of shouting, provoking and confrontationally interrupting others featuring on television as it is a case of these types of behaviour being explicitly staged for their entertainment value – hence their assumed purchase on a medium that depends on viewer gratification for its survival.

Related to the above, Culpeper (2005) posits four generic factors for the entertainment value of conflict talk on television, specifically in shows where presenters ridicule ordinary participants. First, viewers seem to gain an intrinsic pleasure from the potential for violence that such talk already generates: 'we don't need actual fisticuffs: the mere suggestion of fisticuffs can cause the thrill' (2005: 45). Secondly, watching human weaknesses seems to give viewers voyeuristic pleasure. This, of course, assumes that shouting and other forms of emotional decontrol are a sign of human weakness – something which may be true in Anglo-Saxon societies but is certainly not universal, unlike the popularity of these shows. Thirdly, true to the German concept of *Schadenfreude,* viewers apparently enjoy watching others in a worse predicament than they are – for example, being shouted at or being made the subject of humiliating jokes. Fourthly, viewers derive pleasure from experiencing the risk of being potentially involved in confrontation at a safe distance. They may feel secure whilst watching a pub fight in a film, but watching a similar fight close to them in a pub may trigger feelings of insecurity and/or fear.

In addition to these four generic factors, conflict talk is useful to reality television because, as in fiction, it helps to further narrative plot and to build characters (Culpeper 1998). Developing an idiosyncratic style of adversarialness, for example, is particularly effective for the presenters of many reality shows. The UK host of *The Weakest Link*, Anne Robinson, regularly counters contestants' turns with witty, denigrating one-liners. And it is her scathing talk that is behind much of the show's success in the UK and other countries to which the show, and the presenter's caustic style, have subsequently been exported, including Australia, Denmark, New Zealand, Italy, Mexico and the US. Across languages and cultures, it seems, 'raw' conflict talk – especially if performed through verbal cleverness – provides an effective route to entertainment.[3]

There is here, though, something of a paradox. Conflict talk is pervasive across a number of television formats because of its entertainment value. Yet, in many societies where it makes popular viewing, especially Anglo-Saxon ones, the emotions that surface in this kind of conflict talk (contempt, rage, anger, etc.) are appraised negatively. This negative view of conflict has been echoed in, and further promoted by, a highly influential model for the study of interpersonal communication: discourse politeness.

Discourse politeness has indirect origins in Goffman's theory of social interaction and, specifically, in his notion of 'face'. For Goffman (1967: 5) face is 'the positive social value a person effectively claims for himself by the line others assume he has taken during a particular contact'. In order to protect their face, Goffman argues, individuals present self-images that are as consonant as possible with the relevant interactional frames of different social events. For example, the frame governing self-presentation in the course of an informal chat between two friends differs significantly from that in which the same two people might engage were they the interviewer and interviewee in a celebrity chat show. In the former, amongst other things, both can perform the interactional activities of 'doing asking' and 'doing answering'. Even within the informal interactional frame of the latter, turn-taking is inherently asymmetrical: only one of them (the interviewer) is expected to elicit information (through the activity of 'doing asking') and only the other one (the interviewee) is expected to deliver information (through the activity of 'doing answering'). Generally speaking, therefore, the interviewer may not present aspects of his/her own personal self, whilst the interviewee may use 'doing answering' to present and promote particular aspects of both his/her public and private self.

Partly drawing upon Goffman's social interaction theories, especially upon his concept of face, Penelope Brown and Stephen Levinson published in 1978 an article on politeness across cultures. An extended version of their work was published in book form nine years later (*Politeness: Some Universals in Language Usage*, 1987) and soon became the foundation for many studies on interpersonal communication. Brown and Levinson's model rests upon three principles:

1.  Every individual is equipped with a public self-image: face.
2.  Communication is a series of speech acts that damage the speaker's and hearer's face: face-threatening acts (FTAs).
3.  In order to alleviate the threatening act of communication, individuals engage in strategic talk that attends to their own and others' face: politeness strategies.

Brown and Levinson's notion of face consists of two 'wants' or 'needs' that individuals attribute to one another and that every member of society knows that every other member desires: positive face needs and negative face needs. Positive face needs, as introduced in Chapter 7, designate a person's desire to feel liked, respected or admired. Negative face needs concern a person's desire to remain free from imposition by others.

Like Goffman, Brown and Levinson saw face as a mutually beneficial enterprise: everyone's face depends on everyone else's face being maintained. Like Goffman, too, they stressed the strategic nature of human interaction. Individuals routinely deploy a series of politeness strategies through which they try to present to others a desirable self-image. Strategies aiming at attending to others' face needs to be liked and appreciated (their positive face needs) are known as positive politeness strategies, and those aimed at attending to others' face needs not to be imposed upon (their negative face needs) are known as negative politeness strategies.[4]

Given the importance attached in work influenced by Brown and Levinson's model to saving one's face through protecting the face of others, it is no wonder that the analysis of conflict talk has at times been approached in terms of a transgression of discourse politeness.[5] Opposing the views of others, as happens in disagreements, for instance, constitutes an attack on their positive face needs: it clashes with their desire to have their views appreciated, admired or respected. It also poses a threat to their needs to remain free from imposition – that is to their negative face needs – since often in the course of disagreements each party tries to ensure that his/her views prevail. Courtroom show judges, for instance, often interrupt litigants' testimonies with catch phrases such as 'I wouldn't believe you if your tongue came notarised! and 'What part of "stop" didn't you understand?' (Judge Milian, *The People's Court*, US). These confrontational interruptions threaten the litigants' negative face needs: their interactional right to testify. They also attack their positive face needs to be treated as honest and/or competent testimony-givers. Similarly, when interviewers in accountability news interviews of politicians preface their polar (yes–no) questions with damaging presuppositions about their interviewees, they threaten the negative and positive face needs of the latter. The yes–no format puts pressure on the politicians to follow a specific topical agenda and therefore curtails their rights to full self-expression. And the presuppositions associate the politicians with traits that are unlikely to make them be liked, admired or valued as politicians and/or people.

Conflict talk has thus often been seen as face-threatening *ergo* impolite behaviour. As we argued in Chapter 7, however, contextual and social appropriateness is vital when it comes to deciding on the (im)politeness or otherwise of given discourse behaviour. The view that certain speech acts are inherently (im)polite is untenable. Even speech acts that have a rather stable relationship with face-enhancement, such as compliments, have been found to threaten the face needs of their intended recipients if used in an inappropriate context: ironically, and so forth (Lorenzo-Dus 2001b). Likewise, speech acts that have a rather stable relationship with face-threat, such as expletives and insults, can help to build a rapport amongst members of certain groups in certain contexts. This is the case of expletives amongst young white males doing small talk (Cameron 1997) and insults amongst young speakers of black English vernacular doing ritual banter (Labov 1972b), to give but two well-known examples. In other contexts, the speech act of swearing can be used to enhance one's face, for example by acting as a truth sign of one's talk. Recall, for instance, Gregor's use of mild expletives in his monologues to camera (Chapter 7).

The belief that certain forms of talk are intrinsically impolite is, too, flawed. Arguments, for example, consist of action–opposition sequences that originate and develop when (1) speaker A makes a proposition; (2) speaker B (speaker A's co-interactant) regards this proposition as contestable, that is, as an 'action move'; (3) speaker B then opposes speaker A's action move, that is, he/she produces an 'opposition move'; (4) speaker B's opposition move is regarded as a new action move by speaker A, who opposes it with a new opposition move, and so forth (Maynard 1985). Each of these moves is face-threatening insofar as it challenges the views of one's interactional opponent.

But arguments are also constitutive of certain 'activity types' (Levinson 1992), such as political debates in the British House of Commons (Harris 2001; Pérez de Ayala 2001) and storytelling in some audience discussion shows

(Lorenzo-Dus 2007). In these, opposing others' views is contextually appropriate – it is unmarked, politic behaviour. Only if other factors co-occur, such as explicit violation of the British Parliament code of practice or direct attacks on the personal rather than interactional roles of other talk show participants, might arguments become an inappropriate, or impolite, form of talk.

The influence of activity types on the production and interpretation of behaviour as either politic or impolite is therefore paramount. Developing Austrian philosopher Ludwig Wittgenstein's view that to understand the meaning of an utterance one needs to know the activity in which this utterance plays a role, Stephen Levinson (1992: 69) defines an activity type thus:

> any culturally recognized activity, whether or not that activity is coextensive with a period of speech or indeed whether any talk takes places in it at all [. . .] In particular, I take the notion of an activity type to refer to a fuzzy category whose focal members are goal-defined, socially constituted, bounded events with *constraints* on participants, settings, and so on, but above all on the kinds of allowable contributions. Paradigm examples would be teaching, a job interview, a jural interrogation, a football game, a task in a workshop, a dinner party, and so on. (original emphasis)

Activity types help to ascertain how 'what one says will be "taken" – that is, what kinds of inferences will be made from what is said' (Levinson 1992: 97). Our knowledge of given activity types means that we are aware of the dos and don'ts of their performance, as well as the likely inferences that others will draw about us from our decisions.

Not all conflict talk is impolite, then, not even that which uses bald on-record, without redress FTAs. If it were, it would always break down, for it is discourse politeness that helps to lubricate the wheels of social interaction. Instead, within a particular activity type, a given sequence of talk is impolite if: '(1) the speaker communicates face-attack intentionally, or (2) the hearer perceives and/or constructs behaviour as intentionally face-attacking, or a combination of (1) and (2).' (Culpeper 2005: 38).

The above definition overcomes the traditional association of any type of face-threat (intentional or otherwise) with impoliteness. Yet, it presents some important challenges in relation to the television medium. We argued in Chapter 7, for example, that the talk-as-spectacle dimension of some reality shows rendered their presenters' intentional FTAs (Culpeper's factor (1) above) politic, rather than impolite. These presenters occupied the production role of animator, but the role of author remained partly at least with the shows and their performance of provocation and conflict. Remember in this respect, too, Holmes's quote: 'I'm paid to walk the line, I'm paid to go *over* the line . . .' (emphasis added). In other words, he is paid to be 'the sounding box' of deliberately face-threatening talk authored by the shows in order to entertain their viewers.[6]

As for the validity of hearer-interpretation considerations (factor (2) in Culpeper's definition above), this is also problematic because of the different layers of 'hearers' for whom television talk is intended. Consider, for instance, the typical case of two guests arguing heatedly with each other in a talk show. Each of them may indeed interpret as impolite the other's deliberate, and explicit attacks on their respective face. The studio guests, spurred on by the host's dramatisation of the guests' talk, may also interpret the latter's reciprocal FTAs as impolite. They may even provide their own deliberate counter-attacks, in the form of challenging questions and harsh evaluations (e.g. collective booing) of the guests' conduct. The host and the producers, though, may see such a flurry of bald, on-record FTAs as appropriate (politic), indeed accomplished, performances of conflict talk in their shows. Routine performance of this kind of conflict talk, what is more, may lead some viewers to treat guests' displays as the interactional norm – as politic behaviour. Yet other viewers may – as argued by Culpeper (2005) – be so taken aback by the 'markedness' of the guests' conflict talk that they forget its openly staged properties and thus interpret it and the guests as impolite. Even then, though, these viewers may disagree in their interpretation of which precise instances of deliberate face-threat are impolite and just how severe the guests' impoliteness actually is.

In light of the above, the next two chapters examine conflict talk on television from the dual premise of (1) its contextual sensitivity and (2) its knowing performance. They consequently pay particular attention to the different activity types in which this talk is staged. Chapter 9 explores conflict talk in 'tabloid' talk shows and courtroom shows. In both, and despite their non-fiction programming status, conflict is not only emotionally performed but also used as a platform from which certain social values are promoted and others are represented as worthless or deviant. Chapter 10, for its part, analyses the performance of conflict talk amongst politicians (political debates) and between politicians and broadcasters (political interviews) on television. This chapter assesses the role of political adversarialness in a mediaised political climate. It argues that, faced with an increasingly cynical and/or apathetic electorate in many countries, television showing politicians arguing passionately with one another can 'spice up' politics and its media coverage. Similarly, moving political interviews away from traditional 'formal neutralism' may be an effective means to promote interest in politics and hold viewers' attention.

# Emotional Conflict Talk and Reality Television

**9**

In 'tabloid' talk shows, guests are often seen shouting at each other, angrily accusing one another of all kinds of wrongdoings and even physically attacking one another. Proven cases of fraudulent posturing by hoax guests, of guest coaching to ensure the regular performance of heated arguments, and of wooden delivery styles have all led to increasing levels of viewer scepticism regarding the 'authenticity' of guests' conflict talk. Yet in today's 'tabloid' talk shows, guests continue to shout at, accuse and attack one another on a regular basis. In light of this, the first part of this chapter examines some of the recurrent features of the performance of conflict talk by these guests. The analysis highlights the importance of camera work in maximising the entertainment value of ordinary people's emotional displays and exposes the myth that such intense emotionalism is constitutive of the discursive category collectively known as laity.

The second part of the chapter moves on to a related aspect: the performance of emotional conflict talk in reality television by the shows' presenters. In Chapter 7, we used the case of the 'lifestyle coaching' show *You Are What You Eat* to illustrate how ordinary people's confessional monologues to camera are subsequently used by the programmes' presenters (experts) to criticise and/or humiliate these people and to assert the shows' moralistic/motivational ethos. Focusing now on courtroom shows, the analysis here reveals some of the means by which the performance of conflict talk between litigants and judges in these shows contributes to upholding the traditional subordination of laity to expertise and to transforming private, 'negative' emotions into public, much-celebrated spectacle.

## 9.1    Ordinary folk out of control?

Together with personal-experience stories (see Chapter 4), arguments are the main contribution to talk shows' talk that is expected from lay participants. The argumentative style of some of these shows, moreover, is overtly visceral: it is designed and produced to be watched and heard as 'over the top' conflict. To do

---

### *Trisha* (ITV, Granada, 2004)

[Annette has come to the studio to try to convince her pregnant teenage daughter Donna to 'dump' the latter's partner, Craig, whom Annette has accused of being a 'useless father'. After listening to Annette, Trisha asks Craig to join Annette and Donna on stage. As he does so, there is a round of applause and some booing from the studio audience. C: Craig; T: Trisha; A: Annette; D: Donna.]

| *LS – C approaches A and D* | 01 | C | ca- can I just er can I say one thing before we |
|---|---|---|---|
| *and, still standing, addresses T.* | 02 | | start?= |
| *LS – D, A and C on stage.* | 03 | T | = yeah = |
| *To A. LS (from behind A) – A* | 04 | C | = you know (.) Donna and I split [up bec- the |
| *stands up and walks towards C* | 05 | A |                                  [NO there's |
| *with letter in hand. MS – A and* | 06 | | (.) <u>NO</u> here's the <u>letter</u> (.) here's the |
| *C, face to face, angrily pointing* | 07 | | <u>PROOF</u> (.) <u>you</u> <u>ruined</u> our family (.) <u>you</u> ru- |
| *at each other. LS – A and C,* | 08 | | [THERE (.) <u>you</u> say it ther- (xxxx) |
| *very annoyed. A throws letter* | 09 | C | [<u>you</u> don't know (.) <u>SHUT UP</u> YOU = |
| *at C's feet, then walks away. LS* | 10 | A | = you've [destroy- NO (.) <u>YOU</u> shut- (xxxx) |
| *– A, C and D. D picks up letter* | 11 | D |             [mum (.) MUM (.) <u>no</u> (.) MUM |
| *from floor. CU – A and C,* | 12 | C |            [now (.) (xxxx) LISTEN (.) you |
| *defiant looks from both.* | 13 | | (xxxx) LISTEN [you (xxxx) |
| *MS – A turns away from C.* | 14 | A |                  [NO (.) don't want to know = |
| *CU – C, pointing at A and very* | 15 | C | = the REASON we [split up |
| *annoyed. LS – A turns towards* | 16 | A |                [NO don't want to <u>know</u> |
| *C and points towards his face.* | 17 | | (.) <u>NO</u> (.) [you're a <u>LAZY</u> <u>rotten</u> fath- you |
| *LS – A and C facing each other.* | 18 | C |           [you just (xxxx) you don't [. . .] |

---

so, the shows rely principally on ordinary people displaying in the most unmitigated of ways their anger and disdain towards each other. Extract 9.1 above, from *Trisha*, is characteristic of the shows' portrayal of ordinary folk seemingly out of emotional control.

The sequence of conflict talk between Annette and Craig in Extract 9.1 transgresses British norms of discourse politeness, even by conflict-talk standards. It makes no attempt to mitigate, let alone avoid, face-threat. The explicit hostility and the emotional opposition performed by these two guests, nevertheless, are characteristic of a significant number of instances of conflict talk on our television screens. For example, in Scott's (2002) study of the CNN news talk show *Crossfire*, 'foregrounded disagreements' significantly outnumbered 'backgrounded disagreements'. These were respectively distinguished on the grounds of their explicit or implicit nature, as measured by a set of linguistic strategies, grammatical categories and lexical items typically found in verbal arguments, namely: absolutes (e.g. 'all', 'every'), negation, discourse markers ('but', 'now' and 'well'), emphatics (e.g. 'a lot'), floor bids (i.e. phrases that indicate an attempt to stop others from talking), flow (i.e. confrontational latching and interrupting), indexical second-person pronouns (e.g. accusational use of these pronouns), modals (necessity, prediction and semi-modals), repetition,

**Table 9.1  Types of foregrounded disagreements in *Crossfire***

| | *Type* | | |
| --- | --- | --- | --- |
| *Feature strength* | *Collegial disagreements* | *Personal challenge disagreements* | *Personal attack disagreements* |
| Strong | Flow, questions | Questions, negation | Negation, flow, repetition |
| Moderate | Repetition | Flow, repetition, emphatics | Second-person pronouns |
| Tendency | Negation, discourse particles, modals | Second-person pronouns, modals | Discourse particles |

*Source*:  Adapted from Scott (2002: 314)

questions (challenging), turn length (i.e. short turns as potential indices of disagreement) and uptake avoidances (e.g. non-answers to challenging questions).[1] Foregrounded disagreements in *Crossfire* contained different degrees of hostility. As shown in Table 9.1, these were ranked, from weakest to strongest, as collegial disagreements, personal challenge disagreements and personal attack disagreements.

All three types of foregrounded disagreements were accompanied in Scott's data by a considerable degree of conversational turbulence, characterised by the presence of short speaker turns, raised voices and multiple speakers trying to speak at the same time. The main difference between personal-challenge and personal-attack disagreement styles was the relative lack of questions in the latter. In these, the possibility of indirect criticism through questions tended to be replaced by bold statements and negative labels. In addition, personal-attack disagreements were often accompanied by 'looks of shock, narrowed eyes, and/or dramatic gestures' (Scott 2002: 322).

The sequence of conflict talk between Annette and Craig in Extract 9.1 contains most of the defining features of foregrounded disagreements, especially of those in the personal-attack type. Both participants display their contempt for each other in a highly explicit and intense fashion. Apart from Craig's initial question, which is actually directed at the host, there are no attempts to indirectly criticise the other's position through the speech act of asking questions. Instead, in the less-than-half-a-minute stretch of talk that Extract 9.1 reproduces, there are raised voices (lines 05–17), overt denials of accusations (lines 05–06, 10), commands (lines 09, 12–13), emphatics (lines 05–06, 09, 16–17), accusational second-person pronouns (lines 07, 09, 12–13, 17–18), repetitions (lines 05–06, 12–13, 14–16) and insults (line 17). Interaction is fast-paced throughout, the first opposition move (line 05–08) appearing within the first turn exchange and already showing anger being freely released. There is no single turn exchange that it is not either confrontationally interrupted or sharply latched over. As for dramatic gestures, these are evident in Figures 9.1–9.4, which include a selection of the camera angles used in lines 05–10:

'NO there's (.) NO ...'

*Figure 9.1*

'... here's the letter (.) here's the PROOF (.)'

*Figure 9.2*

'you ruined our family (.) you'

*Figure 9.3*

C: 'you don't know (.) SHUT UP YOU =
A: = you've [destroy- NO (.) YOU shut-'

*Figure 9.4*

**Camera angles and the performance of raw conflict talk by ordinary people in 'tabloid' talk shows**

In lines 05–10, Annette produces the alledged material evidence for her anger towards Craig in the form of a letter (Figure 9.1), which she proceeds to wave angrily at him (Figure 9.2). Note, next, the bitterness and challenge of her facial expression in Figure 9.3, as well as her invasion of Craig's physical space. Having furiously thrown the letter at Craig's feet, Annette then dramatically turns away from him – only to pivot around, again most dramatically, as soon as Craig shouts at her: 'SHUT UP YOU (line 09). What follows, and as Figure 9.4 partly shows, is a most intense display of anger, including intimidating commands and threatening pointing and finger-waving.

The two guests' anger, in particular Annette's, is obvious to anyone physically co-present during this sequence of conflict talk. But it is the camera work that ensures that their reciprocal incivility becomes plainly visible to the viewers – that it becomes, in other words, 'spectacular incivility' (see Chapter 8). During the sequence of conflict talk reproduced in Extract 9.1, several camera close-ups show in full detail the intensity of sentiment on Annette's face, whereas various long-range shots successfully capture the overall sense of fast emotional release. For example, as shown in Figure 9.1, a long-range angle from behind Annette shows viewers her visceral reactions, specifically her springing out of her seat to argue with Craig as soon as he asks for the speaking floor to justify his case. The camera is positioned below stage level and close to Annette at this point, which makes her appear more powerful in her contempt. Figure 9.4, also reproducing a camera long-range shot, captures the compelling moment of Annette and Craig shouting and angrily gesturing at each other whilst a heavily pregnant Donna bends over with much difficulty to pick up the letter, and a static audience and host watch from a safe distance. The from-above shot used here positions the guests as powerless in relation to the camera, which is situated within the studio audience. Camera work in Figure 9.4 also emphasises the theatricality of the argument by offering a view of the talk show studio that resembles very closely the spatial arrangements of a theatre house.

The kind of emotional release in Extract 9.1 and Figures 9.1–9.4 has been likened to 'the orgasmic cum shot of pornographic films' (Grindstaff 1997, 2002). In talk shows and pornographic films, it is argued, the performance of intense feelings seeks to create the impression that those on the screen are making visible their moments of 'letting go, of losing control, of surrendering to the body and its "animal" emotions' (Grindstaff 2002: 19–20). In pornographic films, professional actors are responsible for such performances. In talk shows, it is the participatory category of laity which has generally been seen to provide the 'money shot' through their 'willingness to sob, scream, bicker and fight on television' (Grindstaff 1997: 169). Pornography performs 'a kind of low-brow ethnography of the body [. . .] Like pornography, daytime talk exposes people's private parts in public. It demands external visible proof of a guest's inner emotional state' (1997: 169).

As well as being a profitable source of entertainment, ordinary people's 'exhibitionism of emotions' (Biressi and Nunn 2005: 30) in talk shows has been regarded as indicative of a revalorisation of lay knowledge in modern societies and in their media (Livingstone and Lunt 1994).[2] This revalorisation has seemingly taken place alongside a devaluation of the type of knowledge provided by experts, as Table 9.2 (see p. 110) shows.

Each of the terms in the second column of Table 9.2 is not only undoubtedly positive but also directly applicable to the performance of conflict talk in Extract 9.1. This conflict talk originates and develops because two ordinary people (Annette and Craig) hotly disagree about a private matter: Donna's 'reckless sex'. A social subject, sexual promiscuity, is thus discussed through the personal-experience stories of an individual. The particular facts of these stories, for example Craig's letter to Annette's family, are treated as real, meaningful and relevant to the general discussion.

That the kind of emotional, personal talk performed by Annette and Craig

**Table 9.2  The evolution of lay and expert knowledge from pre-modern to modern societies**

| Lay Knowledge | | Expert Knowledge | |
|---|---|---|---|
| Pre-modern societies | Modern societies | Pre-modern societies | Modern societies |
| Subjective | Authentic | Objective | Alienated |
| Ungrounded | Narrative | Grounded in data | Fragmented |
| Emotional | Hot | Rational | Cold |
| Particular | Relevant | Replicable and general | Irrelevant |
| Concrete | Grounded in experience | Abstract | Ungrounded |
| Motivated | Meaningful | Neutral | Empty of meaning |
| Supposition | Practical | Factual | Useless |
| Obvious | Real | Counter-intuitive | Artificial |

*Source*:   Adapted from Livingstone and Lunt (1994: 102)

in Extract 9.1 is valued is evident from its recurrence in talk shows like *Trisha*. It is also evident in the fact that participants almost invariably are granted the speaking floor even though the shouting and interruptions often render a significant proportion of their talk indecipherable (e.g. lines 08, 10, 12 and 13). It is manifest, moreover, in the resistance faced by those participants who fail to perform in the expected lay fashion in these shows. When ordinary people in talk shows try to have their say in general terms, for example, they are often instructed to become personal and emotional. A pattern ensues, in fact, whereby those lay participants who try to have their say in non-specific terms are quickly steered by the host towards the telling of personal experiences of grievance, as Extract 9.2 (see p. 111) illustrates.

In lines 01–04 of Extract 9.2, Kilroy asks a general question. He uses the generic second-person pronoun 'you'/'your' (line 02) and the inclusive first-person plural pronoun 'we' (line 04). The lay participant's response, however, soon reveals the actual perlocutionary effect (i.e. the intended effect on the participant) of Kilroy's question to be the elicitation of a personal-grievance story. The participant's references in lines 05–07 to 'some people', 'certain positions for example management' and 'a matter of playing the rules of the game' seem to signal his initially being unaware of expectations to deliver personal-grievance talk. But his 'I mean if you're talking about my personal situation because I guess otherwise I wouldn't be here [would I?' (lines 07–09) makes it plainly obvious that he knows what is required of him as a lay participant in the show. He seems to be keen, moreover, to expose the show's attempts to influence the content and delivery style of lay participants' talk.

Unsurprisingly, therefore, the host takes the participant's remarks in lines 07–09 as contestable – as the basis for an argument. This may be further encouraged by these remarks co-occurring with a knowingly ironic smile from the participant (lines 08–09) and being immediately followed by an outburst of

**EXTRACT 9.2**

## Kilroy (BBC, 1999)

[The extract comes from an episode on the importance or otherwise of a dress code in the workplace. Talk show host Robert Kilroy-Silk is sitting next to a woman who has been criticising, through a personal-experience story, those companies that insist on their employees wearing a uniform. The lay participant in this extract is the first trombone of a classical music orchestra. K: Robert Kilroy-Silk; T: first trombone; A: studio audience.]

| | | | |
|---|---|---|---|
| LS – K gets up and | 01 | K | but there's rules that say there's something im<u>por</u>tant |
| walks down a set of | 02 | | about the way you dress for your profession (.) isn't |
| centrally positioned | 03 | | there? (.) is there <u>something</u> im<u>por</u>tant about the way |
| stairs in the studio. | 04 | | we dress? |
| MS – K sits next to T. | 05 | T | well (.) er for <u>some</u> people in <u>certain</u> positions for |
| | 06 | | example management it's it's a matter of playing the |
| | 07 | | rules of the game (.) I mean if you're talking about <u>my</u> |
| CU – T smiles | 08 | | personal situation because I guess otherwise I wouldn't |
| ironically. | 09 | | be here [would I? |
| LS – A. | 10 | A | [laughter |
| MS – K and T. | 11 | K | [THAT'S RIGHT (.) otherwise <u>I</u> wouldn't be |
| CU – K, rolls eyes | 12 | | talking to <u>you</u> (.) <now> (.) <u>don't</u> make |
| and smiles at A. | 13 | | [things difficult for me |
| CU – K looks | 14 | T | [otherwise you wouldn't [be interest- |
| annoyed, gesticulates | 15 | K | [oh <u>COME ON</u> (.) <u>SPEAK</u> |
| with hands, | 16 | T | er I (.) er it's been a <u>major</u> source of stress for me and |
| encouraging T to | 17 | | my family (.) I've recently concluded a legal battle |
| speak. MS – K and T. | 18 | | against a certain orchestra [. . .] |

supportive laughter from the studio audience (line 10). In lines 11–13, Kilroy interrupts the participant in a loud, clearly irritated voice. Note his emphatic 'you' (line 12), the markedly slow delivery rate of '<now>' and the subsequent, also emphatic, '<u>don't</u> make [things difficult for me' (lines 12–13). In this turn, the host opposes the participant and tries to realign the studio audience with him. He, for example, rolls his eyes theatrically as he smiles in an attempt to gain their sympathy for his having to deal with such an awkward participant.

Possibly emboldened by the audience's laughter and despite the host's prior instruction not to obstruct his talk-monitoring, this participant decides to continue to challenge the show's preference for a particular type of talk. In line 14, he interrupts the host: '[otherwise you [the host] wouldn't [be interest-'. Kilroy takes the bait, as it were, and in a rare performance in this show, loses his composure. Loudly and visibly irritated, he produces a further opposition move: 'oh <u>COME ON</u> (.) <u>SPEAK</u>' (line 15). At this point, the participant gives way and performs as required. He engages in painful self-disclosure ('it's been a <u>major</u> source of stress for me and my family', lines 16–17) and uses the expected personal-experience story format ('I've recently concluded a legal battle against a certain orchestra [. . .]', lines 17–18).

By getting ordinary people to have their own say on a range of issues in personal and/or visceral ways, talk shows claim to contribute to the current revalorisation of lay knowledge. The analysis of Extracts 9.1 and 9.2 has illustrated that lay participants in talk shows are indeed allowed to express their views in these programmes. But it has also, and instructively, revealed that this is only the case when these participants adhere to expectations about what they – as members of the discursive category of laity – should say, and how. Authors like Fairclough (1995) argue that television talk shows represent a form of political and social manipulation of lay participants, studio audiences and viewers alike. The alleged revalorisation of lay knowledge in these programmes only responds to a superficial shift in power relations in favour of the lay person. Underneath, power rests firmly with the various institutional figures of the shows: the hosts, the production teams, and so forth. Claims that talk shows give ordinary people a public voice are, therefore, only literally true.

Can ordinary people be said to be *really* out of emotional control in talk shows, then? It does not seem so. Their arguments on camera certainly appear to show them letting go of their anger rather than conforming to, say, societal norms of discourse politeness and rational discussion. Yet these arguments are strongly encouraged – and carefully staged – by the shows. Through hosts' talk-monitoring, selective use of camera angles, strategic placement of participants with opposing views next to one another, and so on, these programmes facilitate – even manufacture – the entertaining decontrolling of lay participants' behaviour within the highly controlled setting of their studios. The view that visceral conflict talk is constitutive of the discourse of laity cannot therefore be supported beyond the latter's role of animators of that talk.

In the next part of the chapter, a related aspect is explored, namely the appropriation of emotional conflict talk by some expert figures on television. This may be seen as an inevitable corollary of the alleged revalorisation of lay knowledge in modern Western societies and media. The collapse of expertise as 'awesome, distant or threatening authority' (Chaney 2002: 109) in these societies has prompted an increasing number of 'small scale authorities' (Biressi and Nunn 2005) or 'everyday experts of subjectivity' (Hawkins 2001: 418) on our television screens to foreground their lay, ordinary selves. This 'layisation', or 'ordinaryisation', of expertise has also resulted in some of these experts releasing 'negative' emotions before the cameras. At first sight, this seems to confirm the triumph of the discourse of laity, which appears to be emulated even when it entails the performance of interpersonally undesirable behaviour. On closer inspection, though, things are rather different, as the case study of conflict talk in television courtroom shows next reveals.

## 9.2   Experts out of control?

Together with talk shows, US courtroom shows offer one of the clearest examples of the visceral performance of conflict talk on television. This is partly because the unmediated communication context that these shows emulate, US small claims courtrooms, is inherently oppositional. They revolve around a defendant and a plaintiff presenting contradictory versions of reality and a judge deciding whose version is true and pronouncing his/her verdict. In the plethora of courtroom shows on US syndicated television, however, this interactional frame is only loosely adopted.

Courtroom shows generally begin with a presenter's dramatically phrased voice-over introduction of a court case synced with images of defendants and plaintiffs entering the courtroom. Next, judicial arbitration takes place before approximately thirty members of the general public, who sit behind the litigants and their witnesses, facing the judges. Once the litigants have presented their cases and the judges have concluded their cross-examinations, the latter pronounce their verdicts. On leaving the courtroom, the litigants are asked to comment on the ruling to camera. In some shows (e.g. *The People's Court),* people standing outside the courtroom studio building are also asked for their views on the on-going cases and/or verdicts.

Most of the interaction in courtroom shows revolves around sequences of conflict talk. For example, analysis of over sixty court cases from *Texas Justice, Judge Mathis, Judge Joe* and *The People's Court* reveals that foregrounded disagreements comprised between 78 per cent (for *Texas Justice*) and 63 per cent (for *The People's Court*) of the total amount of talk examined (Lorenzo-Dus 2008). These foregrounded disagreements constituted primarily the personal-challenge and personal-attack types (Scott 2002). Tellingly, over half of them involved the litigants *and* the judges.

Judge–litigant conflict talk is generally performed through a combination of (1) personal challenges and attacks from the judges, and (2) attempts to negate the judges' moves by the litigants. Judicial cross-examination, for instance, includes a considerable number of challenging – rather than merely informa-tion-seeking – questions, such as 'are you <u>really</u> telling me that you knew <u>nothing</u> at all about this money? (.) that you <simply <u>forgot</u> to pay it back>? (.) <that you <u>really</u> had <u>no idea</u>>?' (Judge Milian, *The People's Court,* 2006). In this exam-ple, the lexical upgraders 'really' and 'simply', a slow speech rate that intensifies face-threat, and marked stress on key items (e.g. '<u>nothing</u>', '<u>forgot</u>', '<u>really</u>' and '<u>no idea</u>') leave no doubt as to the judge's scepticism of the litigant's testimony. Also, on those occasions when the litigants oppose the judges' challenges with emphatic negations, the latter usually trigger further challenges and/or discred-iting remarks by the judges: e.g. 'oh COME on (.) >ok ok ok< (.) try again (.) this time tell me <the story and nothing but the story> (.) with <u>some</u> truth along with it' (Judge Dohorty, *Texas Justice,* 2006).

Extract 9.3 (see pp. 114–15) shows a typical sequence of conflict talk between a judge and a litigant in US television courtroom shows. Here, Judge Greg Mathis conducts the final part of his cross-examination (lines 01–33) and prepares the ground for – and pronounces – his verdict (lines 34–64). A personal challenge style of disagreement predominates in the cross-examina-tion part of the extract. Various questions are asked by the judge, which strongly imply the defendant's guilt (lines 01–04, 06–07, 09–10, 12–14, 17 and 19). A respective number of emphatic denials are produced by the defen-dant (lines 05, 08, 11, 15 and 18), but only one of these actually includes

**_Judge Mathis_ (AND Syndicated Productions (Warner Bros), 2006)**

[The court case from which this extract comes involves a defendant in his twenties being accused of defaming his mother – the plaintiff – on a website that she had contracted him to build for her business. The defendant's criminal history as a burglar and wife beater has been mentioned earlier in the case, as well as his intention to buy an expensive motorbike at the time of the defamation incident. The defendant has just explained that his mother demanded rent from him despite their prior agreement that his work on the website would offset this. J: Judge Mathis; D: defendant, P: plaintiff; A: courtroom studio audience.]

| | | | |
|---|---|---|---|
| MS – J, to D. | 01 | J | is that <u>your</u> excuse for de<u>fam</u>ing your <u>mother</u> |
| | 02 | | with the <u>worst</u> names? (.) for saying <the <u>worst</u> |
| | 03 | | things>? (.) the <<u>worst</u>> <<u>human</u>> <<u>words</u>> |
| | 04 | | created to her? = |
| LS – D and P. | 05 | D | = ye- er er <u>no</u> (.) <u>no</u> 'cos [ I'v:::e liv- no (xxxx) |
| MS – J, to D. | 06 | J | ['cos you wanted the |
| LS – courtroom. MS – J, to | 07 | | money to [buy a motorcycle? |
| A. MS – D, to J. | 08 | D | [<u>NO</u> (.) <u>NO</u> <u>NO</u> (.) <u>NO</u> 'cos I [want- |
| LS – J's back, D, P and | 09 | J | [there's |
| amused A behind litigants. | 10 | | <u>another</u> excuse [then? |
| CU – D, looks agitated. | 11 | D | [<u>NO</u> (.) that's <u>not</u> true [<u>no</u> (.) <u>no</u> |
| MS – J, sits up, raises his | 12 | J | [in your |
| arms in despair, and leans | 13 | | excuses (.) <I'm just curious> (.) how <u>far</u> |
| on desk as he addresses D. | 14 | | would you <u>go</u> for [ that motorcycle? |
| MS from above – D, who | 15 | D | [<u>NO</u> (.) <u>NO</u> that's not tr- it |
| appears 'cornered'. | 16 | | [wasn't the (xxxx) |
| | 17 | J | [would you have <u>beaten</u> [her? (.) would you've |
| CU – D, looking angry. | 18 | D | [no no no it wasn- (xxxx) |
| CU – J, visibly annoyed. | 19 | J | <u>killed</u> [her? |
| CU – D, to J, angrily. | 20 | D | [no no it wasn't ab- NO you're <u>wrong</u> = |
| MS – J, looks at A, | 21 | J | = O::::H (4.0) |
| exaggerated surprise. CU – | 22 | | it <<u>wasn't</u> about the motorcycle> (.) |
| J, mimics D's voice. LS – | 23 | | <what was it about <u>then</u>?> <u>what</u> [was it tha-? |
| amused A. MS – J, lifts files | 24 | D | [the <u>respect</u> (.) |
| and waves them as if in | 25 | | 'cos it's my <u>mom</u> (.) my <u>mom</u> (.) how |
| angry despair. LS – amused | 26 | | [am I gonn-? |
| A. MS – J, sceptically. | 27 | J | [you're showing <u>respect</u> for <u>her</u>? = |

→

a direct rejection: 'NO you're <u>wrong</u>' (line 20). This opposition move is immediately countered by the judge, who in line 21 produces an evaluation token that dramatically signals his reaction to the defendant's accusation: '<u>O::::H</u>'. The ensuing four-second pause is used by the judge to capitalise on the talk-as-spectacle value of his evaluation token. During this pause, he looks with exaggerated surprise towards the studio audience, who look visibly amused by the judge's performance (lines 21–23). This reaction probably spurs the judge to continue to entertain the studio audience. In lines 22–23, he ventriloquises the defendant's speech, using mocking paralanguage to mimic his attempted denial ('it <wasn't about the motorcycle>'), before proceeding to challenge him ('<what

| | | | |
|---|---|---|---|
| *Screen splits into two equal size fragments. Fragments show CUs of P and D.* | 28 | D | = no (.) her respect for <u>me</u> 'cos we wer- we |
| | 29 | | never had a deal that I owed her any money (.) |
| | 30 | | WE NEVER HAD [A DEAL I owed her any |
| *MS – J, looking annoyed.* | 31 | J | [oh (.) you n- |
| *CU – D, to J, defiantly.* | 32 | D | money from the bank <u>OK</u>? (.) so we never had |
| | 33 | | [any deal th- |
| *MS – points at D with index finger, angrily* | 34 | J | [OK (.) <u>right</u> (.) <u>quiet</u> (.) QUIET (.) I DON'T |
| | 35 | | NEED TO HEAR ANY MORE OF <u>YOUR</u> |
| | 36 | | NONSENSE (.) I'm asking <u>you</u> WHY YOU |
| *CU – D, looks down as though embarrassed.* | 37 | | DID IT (.) you tell me 'cos she <u>disrespected</u> |
| | 38 | | YOU [ so my question is HOW FAR WOU- |
| | 39 | D | [ no (.) that- that's n- |
| *MS – J, angrily.* | 40 | J | WOULD YOU GO? <WOULD YOU <u>BEAT</u> |
| | 41 | | YOUR MOTHER FOR [DISRESPECTING |
| *Screen split into two equal-size fragments, showing CUs of D (looking annoyed) and P(smiling).* | 42 | D | [no that's [ n- |
| | 43 | J | [YOU? (.) |
| | 44 | | WOULD YOU [KILL |
| | 45 | D | [NO she's [n- |
| | 46 | J | [YOUR |
| | 47 | | MO[THER? |
| | 48 | D | [no (.) she's [N- |
| *MS – waves case paperwork angrily in the air while looking at A.* | 49 | J | [YOU REFERRED TO HER |
| | 50 | | DEATH SO THAT <u>MILLIONS</u> OF <u>PEOPLE</u> |
| | 51 | | COULD SEE WHAT YOU THINK OF <u>YOUR</u> |
| *CU – J, to D.* | 52 | | MOTHER (.) that's <u>how far</u> you'd go? OK (.) |
| *LS – A, amused by J's performance.* | 53 | | there's <u>nothing</u> a mother could <u>do</u> to <u>you</u> to make |
| *MS – J, to D.* | 54 | | you <u>call</u> her <<u>all these names</u>> is there? (.) <u>NO:::</u> |
| *CU – D, staring at J.* | 55 | | OTHER MAN <<u>IN THEIR RIGHT MIND</u>> |
| *CU – J, to D.* | 56 | | would <u>ever</u> do <u>that</u> to their mother (2.0) but you |
| *MS –D, to J, defensively.* | 57 | | <u>AIN'T</u> [IN YOUR <u>RIGHT MIND</u> |
| | 58 | D | [N- I <u>am</u> a moral man (.) I <u>AM</u> A |
| | 59 | | [MORAL M- |
| *MS – J, looks at A, then points accusingly at D.* | 60 | J | [NO YOU <u>AIN'T</u> (.) YOU <u>AIN'T</u> and you need |
| | 61 | | to be <u>locked up</u> again |
| *LS – J, to an amused A.* | 62 | | (.) <u>five thousand dollars</u> for the <u>defamation</u> (.) |
| *J stands up and begins to leave room.* | 63 | | [you ought to be <u>ashamed</u> (xxxx) |
| | 64 | A | [*cheering and applauding* (4.0) [. . .] |

was it about <u>then</u>?> <u>what</u> [was it tha- ?'). Throughout the remainder of the extract, the defendant mainly continues to try to deny the raft of hostile personal attacks and challenges that the judge throws at him. Most of the shouting (lines 34–38, 40–41, 43–44, 46–47, 49–52, 55–57, 60), emphatic delivery of offensive remarks (lines 35–36, 55–57) and angry non-verbal behaviour (e.g. lines 24–26, 34–35, 49–50) in the extract come from the judge.

Judge Mathis's performance in Extract 9.3 is indicative of the belittling faced by ordinary people in courtroom shows. This differs radically from the 'reality' that these shows claim to emulate, namely US small claims arbitration courts. In these, judges actively discourage emotional outbreaks of anger and intense confrontation, let alone being dragged into it themselves (García 1991). Judge Mathis's performance differs, too, from the ways in which their closest broadcast 'cousins' – talk show hosts – generally relate to ordinary folk. In talk shows, hosts interact with lay participants in rational – and only occasionally emotional (Extract 9.2) – ways. These hosts also tend to, at least superficially, affiliate with lay participants in their studio, for example, by defending their interests when they clash with those of the experts (see Chapter 8).

The situation is different in courtroom shows, where judges regularly and openly humiliate ordinary folk and, in so doing, are themselves at times responsible for some of the shows' most spectacular money shots. Male judges, for instance, often use patronising forms of address ('sweetie', 'honey', 'hon') towards litigants of the opposite sex. They frequently use verbal cleverness in their personal attacks, leaving the litigants lost for words and the studio audiences visibly amused. In a 2006 episode of *Texas Justice*, for example, an enraged Judge Dohorty makes the studio audience laugh by dismantling the rationale behind the plaintiff's $2000 claim for mental anguish thus: 'for starters (.) you've got to have <u>some mental capacity</u> to suffer from anguish (.) my ruling is for the defendant'. Courtroom show judges also draw upon a number of catch-phrases, much in the style of game-show presenters but considerably less nice, to chastise litigants. Judge Milian's (*The People's Court*) infamous sayings and quotes, for example, include: 'not <u>here</u> (.) not <u>today</u> (.) and <u>not</u> in <u>my</u> courtroom' and 'you redefine <u>chutzpah</u>'. Some of the judges' most celebrated catch-phrases are in fact recorded and played on the programmes' official websites.[3] This indicates how much effort these shows invest in creating memorable, often flamboyant, 'star judges'.

The entertainment value of the judges' performance of conflict talk is evident when one considers how closely both the contributions of the judges and the subsequent reactions of the studio audience are followed by the cameras. In Extract 9.3, for example, several medium-range shots highlight the judge's (non)-verbal dramatisation of his anger (lines 21–22, 24–26, 49–51, 60–61). A corresponding number of long-range shots follow, which show the audience's positive reaction to the judge's theatricality (lines 23–24, 26–27, 53–54, 62). This kind of camera work confirms the confrontainment value behind the judges' performances.

There is no doubt, then, that courtroom show judges' conflict talk is explicitly designed and strategically produced as emotional, over-the-top performance for televisual entertainment. Their reactions of, for example, surprise, scepticism or displeasure about the litigants' testimony are often plainly exaggerated; their questions are often worded in overly dramatic style; and their interaction with the audience in the courtroom studio (frequent direct gaze and address) is frequent and clearly intended to make the latter laugh. This being the case, and similarly to the situation with lay participants' emotionalism in talk shows examined in Section 9.1, courtroom judges cannot be said to be *really* out of emotional control in their shows. Instead, their visceral displays serve as vehicles for viewer entertainment.

The above is not to say, however, that conflict talk should be seen merely as a form of spectacle in courtroom shows. For starters, and as we noted earlier, the judges of these shows cultivate their own idiosyncratic styles of confrontainment, which their respective programmes make a point of promoting through their official websites. Importantly, too, conflict talk in courtroom shows mediates public expression, deliberation and reflection. It does so, what is more, in ways that differ markedly from rational expression and consensus-building, that is, from the interactional means traditionally associated with the Habermasian concept of the 'public sphere'.[4] In their place, these shows choose to show intense anger, contempt, frustration, rage and other 'negative' emotions when discussing a range of social and personal matters in public. In Extract 9.3, for instance, the judge's performance of contempt makes public the realm of family life, specifically aspects of family members' behaviour that might cause disgrace to their families and the need to show respect towards one's elders (parents). A further example is provided in Extract 9.4.

In Extract 9.4, Judge Milian uses a combination of verbal wit and expressive paralanguage and body language to question the practice of body-piercing. Note, for instance, her exaggerated intonation of surprise (lines 02–03), her ironic smile (line 04) and her raising her arms (lines 07–08). Camera work capitalises on the spectacle potential of such a dramatic performance. A quick alternation between medium-range and close-up shots results in footage in lines 01–09 that effectively captures the reactions of all parties, including those of the studio audience. The plaintiff's initial attempt to explain her case (line 03) is silenced by the judge's interruption in line 04 ('<u>well</u> <u>well</u> [<u>well</u>') and by the almost instant outburst of laughter that it triggers in the studio (line 05). The judge's punchline, as it were, is also quick to materialise in the form of a

---

**EXTRACT 9.4**

### *The People's Court* (Ralph Edwards/Stu Billet productions, 2006)

[The plaintiff in this episode is a woman in her mid-forties who claims that the defendant – the owner of a body-piercing business – was negligent in her work, causing the plaintiff's lip to become infected. The extract corresponds to the first intervention by Judge Milian in the episode and follows her asking the plaintiff to confirm her name. J: Judge Milian; P: Plaintiff; A: courtroom studio audience. D: defendant.]

| | | | |
|---|---|---|---|
| *CU – To P.* | 01 | J | <u>right</u> (.) er so you you're suing the defendant |
| *MS – To A, exaggerated* | 02 | | because she's pierced your lip negligently? = |
| *intonation of surprise.* | 03 | P | = yes but yo[ur hon- |
| *CU – J (ironic smile* | 04 | J | [<u>well</u> <u>well</u> [ <u>well</u> |
| *at A). LS – P (serious),* | 05 | A | [ *laughter* |
| *D (smiling), and amused A.* | 06 | J | I <u>knew::</u> no good could <<u>ever</u>> come from |
| *MS – J, raising arms* | 07 | | making a hole in a place God did not give you |
| *theatrically.* | 08 | | [one |
| *MS – P looking* | 09 | A | [*laughter* (3.0) |
| *embarrassed. LS – P, D* | 10 | P | [(xxxx) when er when I I went to have my lip |
| *and A.* | 11 | | pierced [. . .] |

sarcastic remark in lines 06–08 whereby she implies that it ought to be self-evident that body-piercing carries some risks. Milian uses a colloquial expression ('making a hole in a place God did not give you one', lines 07–08), to imply that humans should not interfere with God's creation. Through verbal cleverness and theatrics, then, the judge in this extract places the litigant in the passive role of recipient of a humiliating lesson.

It is worth noting in respect of the above that courtroom show judges' lessons are taught with equal zeal in relation to serious and frivolous issues. The moral worthiness of the most trivial aspects of the litigants' behaviour is often closely scrutinised, even when the relevance of such aspects to the court cases being judged is seemingly non-existent. A judge may, for example, ask a plaintiff suing his neighbour for the damage caused by her dog, 'Do you spend quality time every day with your family?'. The answer – the judge most likely knows – is negative and serves to expose flaws in the litigant's moral character. This enables the judge to qualify, to classify and to punish these 'guilty' individuals in the shows. It allows him/her to establish over them 'a visibility through which one differentiates them and judges them' (Foucault 1977: 184). The intensely individualised form of surveillance exerted by courtroom show judges constructs 'a logic of personal responsibility' within which the most trivial and irrelevant habits are treated as leading to 'unwise choices, irresponsibility, and lack of self-control or discipline' (Shugart 2006: 87). In doing this, courtroom shows provide, as one might expect, a form of social regulation. However, they do so from within an 'emotional public sphere' (Lunt and Stenner 2005) that promotes the expression and evaluation of personal-identity questions and various social issues in visceral, unrestrained ways.

## 9.3   Conclusion

In courtroom and talk shows, disputes that may not break out at all without the presence of the cameras become emotionally performed sequences of conflict talk precisely because of the presence of the cameras. Performing conflict talk in these shows often means making moments of letting go obvious: knowingly releasing one's anger, airing one's grievances blamelessly, displaying one's contempt for others unreservedly, and so on. None of this is the interactional norm in naturally occurring, unmediated sequences of conflict talk in Anglo-Saxon societies, which favour the avoidance of direct face threat to one's co-interactants. As Lunt and Stenner (2005: 65) observe in relation to *The Jerry Springer Show*: 'In an ironic reversal, rational critical discussion would disrupt the potential for conflict, the revelation of secrets and the escalation of emotions, and so has to be constrained and managed.'

The performance of conflict talk in the television contexts examined in this chapter is not intended to come across as 'real' vis-à-vis real life. Instead, it is designed and produced to be received as the performance of uncontrolled 'negative' behaviour in highly controlled settings and thus as only 'real' vis-à-vis these television contexts. These shows make no secret of their staging of 'negative' emotionalism. Camera close-ups that explicitly and overtly publicise expressions of anger and contempt are frequently used when filming guests' quarrels. In courtroom shows, for example, the television screen is at times split into two, equal-size windows, each of which offers a close-up of one of the litigants looking angrily in the direction of the other, shouting at each other, and so forth. Such windowed style artificially minimises the physical distance that exists between the participants in the studio (see Chapter 6) and thus maximises the emotionalism of their arguments. At other times, visual collages comprised of video stills of enraged/shocked participants are offered over dramatic verbal renditions of disputes to come. There is an explicit emphasis in both talk shows and courtroom shows, then, on the choreographing and packaging of 'negative' emotions as a style of talk most conducive to viewer gratification. Conflict talk produces 'real' (entertainment) effects in these shows precisely because it is openly constructed and dramatic.

Alongside its spectacle dimension, the performance of conflict in talk shows and courtroom shows projects an emotional public sphere. Lay participants are strongly encouraged – even instructed at times – to adhere to the speech and moral ideal of emotional expressiveness. This values the public's sharing of private emotions, including – as we have seen in this chapter – those denounced in the very societies in which their broadcasting is celebrated (anger, disdain, intolerance of others' views, and so forth). Hosts and presenters, too, are encouraged – possibly instructed – to jump on the 'negative' emotional expressiveness bandwagon. In courtroom shows, for example, judges regularly provide virtuoso displays of anger, which they use both to promote their media personae and to expose litigants.

What drives this emphasis on 'raw' conflict talk? Well, viewers may enjoy watching members of a discursive category traditionally seen as the vanguard of rational critical argumentation (experts) being dragged down to shouting, interrupting, insulting, and so forth. Alternatively, they may be attracted by the voyeuristic, possibly morbid, pleasure of watching members of their own discursive category (laity) being publicly humiliated by members of a different discursive category (experts). After all, portraying ordinary folk in an ungainly light is by no means a new form of broadcast entertainment. First-wave talk shows, for example, used experts to assist those ordinary people who could not solve their problems and struggles by themselves to become better, emotionally expressive selves. Make-over shows, as we will discuss in Chapter 13, have continued this trend and often portray ordinary people in an unseemly light through the negative evaluation of their taste in interior decoration, their gardening skills, and so forth. Often, though, such portrayals are performed from discourse positions of rational argumentation, rarely, face to face. The next step, we have seen in this chapter, has been the explicit display of 'negative' emotionalism by experts at the expense of the lay person and directly to his/her face.

However, regardless of where the attraction of the public humiliation of ordinary folk may lie, the performance of conflict talk before the cameras tells us much about the alleged revalorisation of lay knowledge in modern societies and media. Across varieties of reality television nowadays, lay ways of communicating are in theory being revalorised such that the performance of 'negative' emotional release by experts and presenters is both a frequent and a legitimate aspect of conflict talk. Yet these same experts use such ways of communicating openly to demonstrate contempt for, and frustration with, the figure of the lay person. Moreover, their theatrical impersonations of ordinary folk and witty mockery of their arguments, for example, demonstrate how they exploit their status as expert and media *savoir-faire* to belittle the ordinary (wo)man. In short, 'lay' ways of communicating are being skilfully and selectively adapted by media-savvy experts to keep lay people in their traditionally subordinate place. That this is frequently sanctioned as part of television's confrontainment agenda only highlights further the importance of this particular feature of television discourse.

# Conflict Talk and Politics

10

Having examined in Chapter 9 the performance of conflict talk in 'banal' television contexts, this chapter proceeds to analyse this talk in two 'serious' television contexts: political debates and political interviews. Conflict talk develops in political debates through action–opposition sequences that are arbitrated by an institutional agent: the moderator of the debate. These debates are often figuratively presented as boxing rings in which members of different political parties, or different factions within the same party, try to 'knock out' their opponents dialectically. As the analysis in the first part of this chapter reveals, however, behind reciprocal opposition and the discrediting of one's opponent lurks a more pressing goal: self-display. In political interviews, conflict talk follows a question–answer format, which is said to be bounded by a demand for impartial yet critical inquiry. To meet this demand, journalists and politicians tend to rely on the performance of 'formal neutralism'. Yet a considerable number of accountability interviews of politicians on British television are nowadays explicitly adversarial and adopt a 'populist stance in which interviewers – like tribunes of the people – ventriloquise on behalf of a presumed sceptical public' (Montgomery 2007: 179). In light of this, the second part of this chapter explores what I argue may be regarded as a 'formal coarsening' of the political interview.

## 10.1 Conflict talk in political debates: 'Politic' arguments and self-display

Whether occurring in Congress/Parliament or in television studios, disputes amongst politicians are one aspect of politics that television is particularly keen to capture. In the UK, two television contexts that regularly feature such disputes are parliamentary debates, specifically *Prime Minister's Questions (PMQs)*, and panel debates in political affairs programmes. The former take place in the British House of Commons and involve Members of Parliament (MPs) questioning the Prime Minister on his Government's policies. *PMQs* is covered by radio and television, and a written record of these and other parliamentary debates is compiled in *Hansard*, which is accessible on the web. MPs' contributions are thus intended to be seen and heard not only by the members of the House of Commons but also, and importantly, by the general public. MPs know, for example, that particularly adversarial sequences within these debates, especially those wittily delivered, are regularly used as sound-bites in news reports. It is in their interest, therefore, to perform these sequences in ways that help them to project attractive personalities. As for panel debates, these feature in a number of political affairs shows, including the *Newsnight* programme. First aired in 1980, and currently shown on BBC2 Monday to Friday immediately after the 10:00 p.m. news, *Newsnight* broadcasts extended news reports, political interviews and political debates and is generally regarded as 'the intelligent person's guide to the day's key stories, often covered from a provocative angle' (Born 2004: 414).

Whilst different in some respects, *PMQs* and *Newsnight* provide two typical examples of adversarial political communication on television. Officially, the aim of MPs' questions during *PMQs* is to obtain information about Government policies. Their underlying objective, however, is to attack the Government (Harris 2001).[1] Likewise, *Newsnight* has gained over time a reputation for challenging – rather than merely informing viewers about or debating – policy-making. In *PMQs* and *Newsnight* debates, therefore, conflict talk is commonplace.

In both broadcast contexts, too, conflict talk generally begins, develops and ends in accordance with specific practices with which the politicians involved are fully familiar. MPs, for example, are expected to – and generally do – follow the British parliamentary code of practice, known as the *Erskine May Treatise* (or, simply, *May*). This regulates the structure of discussions in the House of Commons. For instance, *PMQs* always opens with a pre-tabled question to the Prime Minister, to which the latter always responds in part. This initial turn exchange is followed by one supplementary question, which has not been tabled beforehand and therefore allows an element of spontaneity. *May* also regulates various aspects of the participation framework governing Parliament, such as the fact that MPs are expected to address each other via a moderator known as the 'Speaker', which in practice means their using third-person (pro)nominal forms of address.[2]

Panellists in *Newsnight* are, likewise, expected to interact with one another according to specific practices. These are neither as explicit nor as rigid as *May*'s but they nevertheless regulate how and when politicians can disagree with each other in the course of debates. They stipulate, for example, that politicians may counter-argue each others' points directly and that the programme's moderators may introduce points for discussion and reset the agenda of debates as deemed necessary. The latter entails, especially since the late 1990s, finding opportunities to hold politicians to account and to 'uncover and animate significant disensus rather than to confirm consensus' amongst political factions (Born 2004: 428).

In *PMQs* and *Newsnight*, then, debating politics is generally an adversarial 'activity type' (Levinson 1992). This makes conflict talk a constitutive feature of these debates and threats to a politician's face needs politic behaviour – so long, that is, as conflict talk and face-threat are conducted in observance of the constraints of their respective activity type. Doing so, as Extracts 10.1 below and 10.2 (see p. 124) illustrate, is essential if politicians wish to 'make a good showing' (Goffman 1967: 237). Extract 10.1 comes from a *PMQs* session held six weeks before the 5 May 2005 UK General Election, and Extract 10.2 reproduces part of a *Newsnight* debate amongst six members of the Conservative Party, which lost the 2001 UK General Election.

In both extracts, politicians perform a number of FTAs. In Extract 10.2, for instance, Clarke implies that Smith engaged in convenience campaigning at the 2001 General Election (lines 25–27) – an FTA that Clarke's non-verbal

---

**EXTRACT 10.1**

### PMQs (BBC, 2005)

[In the extract below, the then Deputy Prime Minister John Prescott answers questions on behalf of former Prime Minister Tony Blair, who was attending a European Union Council meeting on that day. A: Conservative Party MP Michael Ancram; P: John Prescott; M: Members of the House of Commons (HC).]

| | | | |
|---|---|---|---|
| MS – A. | 01 | A | [. . .] let me ask the Deputy Prime Minister another question (.) |
| LS – HC. | 02 | | after <eight years> of Labour Government (.) |
| MS – A. | 03 | | how many school children play truant? |
| MS – P | 04 | P | it's hard to jump from crime to truancy (.) but presumably that is |
| smiling. | 05 | | the kind of jump that a Tory Administration would want to make |
| LS – HC. | 06 | | (.) the right honourable and learned gentleman still has to face |
| | 07 | | the fact that under this Government crime's been reduced [. . .] |
| MS – A. | 08 | A | again (.) the right honourable gentleman did not answer the |
| | 09 | | question [. . .] let me ask the Deputy Prime Minister another |
| LS – HC. | 10 | | question (.) after <eight years> of Labour Government (.) |
| MS – A. | 11 | | how many asylum seekers whose claims and appeals were |
| LS – HC. | 12 | | rejected have managed to stay in the country? |
| MS – P. | 13 | P | again (.) the number of applications from asylum seekers has |
| LS – HC. | 14 | | fallen [. . .] to be fair to the right honourable and learned |
| MS – P. | 15 | | gentleman (.) he gave us this quote (.) quite honestly (.) I go to |
| | 16 | | Germany now and they say to me (.) I wish we had your |
| | 17 | | unemployment (2.0) employment has increased by <one |
| P smiles | 18 | | hundred and eighty thousand> since he made that statement (.) |
| ironically | 19 | | are you thinking what we're thinking? = |
| at A. LS – | 20 | M | = heckling, laughing and cheering |
| HC. MS – | 21 | A | oh well (.) we always know that the right honourable gentleman |
| A, smiling. | 22 | | is blustering when he answers a different question from the one |
| | 23 | | that was asked (.) the reality is that a <quarter of a million> |
| | 24 | | failed asylum seekers have managed to stay in this country |
| | 25 | | under this Government [. . .] does he not understand that when it |
| | 26 | | comes to crime (.) when it comes to truancy (.) when it comes to |
| | 27 | | asylum (.) people feel totally let down by this Government and |
| | 28 | | can hardly wait for the fifth of May to send them packing? |

### Newsnight (BBC, 2001)

[The extract centres on the Conservative Party's decision at the time not to campaign extensively on public service issues but on distancing the UK from Europe instead – a decision subsequently found to have contributed to the Party's defeat and to have prompted the search for a new leader. The two politicians in the extract, Kenneth Clarke and Iain Duncan Smith, were running for the position of UK Conservative Party leader at the time of the debate. C: Kenneth Clarke; S: Iain Duncan Smith.]

| | | |
|---|---|---|
| *MS – round* | 01 C | I don't think there's anybody more Eurosceptic in the |
| *table, six* | 02 | Conservative Party than Iain (.) the position that we spent the first |
| *politicians.* | 03 | three months with a polic- expressing a policy for the foreseeable |
| | 04 | future (.) >we <u>did</u> actually have a party conference where I was as |
| *MS – table.* | 05 | much in accord with the policy as <u>you</u> were< °I thought° (.) then |
| *MCU – C,* | 06 | <u>you</u> and <u>David</u> [(xxxx) said we m- [(xxxx) <u>well::</u> |
| *pointing at S,* | 07 S | [Ken (.)                    [Ken (2.0) |
| *mockingly.* | 08 C | [it's <u>not</u> for the Parliament |
| *CU – S.* | 09 S | [with respect (.) that's not the case (.) the truth was that what |
| *CU – C shakes* | 10 | William had stood on (.) >the position on Europe< |
| *head in denial.* | 11 | (.) go back and check this (.) |
| *MS – table.* | 12 | I promise you (.) |
| *CU – S.* | 13 | there's no point in getting in dispute about this (.) this is <u>all</u> |
| *MS – table* | 14 | in the past (.) [. . .] <that was all> (.) I <u>didn't</u> have a huge |
| *CU – C,* | 15 | drive to do it more than anyone else (.) it was the fact that |
| *sceptical look* | 16 | until this was clarified it would lead to difficulties (.) that's |
| *on his face. CU* | 17 | the past though Ken = |
| *– S. CU – C.* | 18 C | = I don't want to dispute tha- I don't think it's relevant now (.) <I |
| | 19 | mean> going back to what's just been revealed by Liam Fox that |
| | 20 | before the election the decision was taken <u>NOT</u> to campaign on |
| *CU – C,* | 21 | <u>HEALTH</u> and <u>EDUCATION</u> and these issues (.) it was decided to |
| *mockingly,* | 22 | campaign on Europe (.) TWELVE DAYS TO SAVE THE |
| *dismissing S* | 23 | POUND and all that kind of thing (.) <u>now</u> (.) I had been advising |
| *with hand* | 24 | William (.) I'd been advising colleagues (.) we should fight on the |
| *gesture. MS –* | 25 | <u>big domestic issues</u> (.) health and so on (.) but <u>you</u> were amongst |
| *table. CU – C,* | 26 | those who made the decision <<u>not to campaign on health and</u> |
| *points* | 27 | <u>[education></u> |
| *at S. MS – table* | 28 S | [with respect Ken (.) there were <u>three days</u> allocated and launched |
| *CU – S,* | 29 | for education during the campaign (.) <u>three times</u> that Theresa |
| *emphatically* | 30 | May and others actually stated our education policies (.) there |
| *raising right* | 31 | were other moments when we did pension- a <u>whole</u> variety of |
| *arm. CU – C,* | 32 | issues (.) the problem was >as I think you can understand< that |
| *shaking head in* | 33 | there was less interest in getting on to what <u>I</u> consider to be the |
| *denial.* | 34 | major subjects and <I agree with you here> (.) I think we <u>do</u> agree |
| *CU – S.* | 35 | about thi- that (.) <u>actually</u> (.) <u>what we need to do as a party</u> is to |
| *MS – table.* | 36 | get on to those public service issues [. . .] |

behaviour (finger-pointing in lines 26–28) further underscores. And in Extract 10.1, the design of Ancram's questions turns them from attempts to elicit information to challenges against Prescott and his Government. In lines 02 and 10, he uses the same contextualising proposition, namely 'after <eight years> of Labour Government', as a platform on which to build responsibility for the embedded presuppositions in his subsequent questions. These questions ('how many school children play truant?', line 03; and 'how many asylum seekers whose claims and appeals were rejected have managed to stay in the country?', lines 11–12) treat as 'given information' that the Government's policies on school truancy and asylum are problematic, for it is the extent of and control over school truancy and illegal immigration, not their existence, that Ancram enquires about. Both Ancram's contextualising propositions and embedded presuppositions thus serve to challenge, rather than merely pose questions, placing Prescott in the position of having to respond to, rather than simply answer, them. In lines 25–28, Ancram also frames one of his questions using negative interrogative syntax ('does he not understand . . .'). This facilitates a preferred answer in the minds of those listening, namely that Prescott indeed does not understand the country's social 'reality'. The expressions to 'feel totally let down' (line 27) and 'can hardly wait for the fifth of May to send them packing?' (line 28), including Ancram's use of marked stress on the two intensifying adverbs 'totally' and 'hardly', leave no doubt as to the weightiness of the FTA being performed through this question.

In Extracts 10.1 and 10.2, therefore, politicians' FTAs on their opponents result in the latter being cast in a negative light: as devious, incapable of understanding the electorate, failing to reduce school truancy, and so forth. Interestingly, though, both extracts also contain a number of attempts at minimising face-threat through a range of politeness strategies. In other words, in both extracts, politicians engage in the performance of face-work. In Extract 10.1, for example, Prescott and Ancram use the noun-phrase 'the right honourable (and learned) gentleman' (lines 08, 14–15, 21) to refer to each other, which conveys respect. And in Extract 10.2, Smith uses on three occasions (lines 07, 17 and 28) the familiar, shortened version of Clarke's first name ('Ken' for 'Kenneth'), which conveys an impression of camaraderie.

Further instances of face-work include several attempts at emphasising common ground. In Extract 10.2, for example, Smith uses various rapprochement-seeking expressions: '>as I think you can understand<' (line 32), '<I agree with you here> (.) I think we do agree about thi- that actually (.) what we need to do as a party' (lines 34–35). He also gives Clarke a reassurance token: 'I promise you' (line 12). And he and Clarke use variations of the formula 'there's no point in getting in dispute about this (.) this is all in the past' (Extract 10.2, lines 13–14, 17 and 18), in order to minimise their differences.

Extracts 10.1 and 10.2, then, reveal a combination of face-threat and face-work. Such a combination, which may seem odd vis-à-vis the view of political debates as boxing rings, makes perfect sense vis-à-vis the view of political debates as arenas for, primarily, public self-display. Other-directed face-threat and face-work are far from incompatible with one another because both are subsidiary to politicians' work on enhancing their own face through their media appearances. This is evident in two, related, aspects.

First, in political debates face-threat is generally conducted within the parameters of contextual appropriateness, and therefore serves to display politicians' debating know-how. The seemingly flattering terms of address used by MPs in Extract 10.1, for example, are formulaic. *May* (1989: 380) identifies expressions such as 'the right honourable (and learned) gentleman' (lines 06, 14–15, 21) as appropriate forms of parliamentary address. They are therefore politic rather than polite terms of address. Also, the reciprocal FTAs by Prescott and Ancram in Extract 10.1 are filtered through the Speaker, to whom they orientate their body language and address their turns. Note that they use third-person singular nouns to refer to each other. Note, too, that all the FTAs in Extracts 10.1 and 10.2 target politicians' public face, in either its positive or its negative dimension. A politician's public positive face designates an image of self as 'a rational, trustworthy person whose political ideas and actions are better fitted to the wants and demands of the general public than those of his opponents' (Gruber 1993: 3). His/her public negative face, in turn, refers to the right to remain free of imposition in political domains (Pérez de Ayala 2001). Attacks on either aspect of politicians' public face are not only allowable contributions but also constitutive of the activity type of debating politics in public. They are important, moreover, for the latter's confrontainment value in the context of television.

Secondly, politicians' face-work in televised debates is often placed within stretches of talk that either cancel its otherwise mitigating function or emphasise positive traits of their own face.[3] Prescott's addressing of Ancram in Extract 10.1 as 'the right honourable and learned gentleman' (line 06; lines 14–15), for example, precedes respectively the challenging statement that he [Ancram] 'still has to face the fact that under this Government crime's been reduced' (lines 06–07) and a mockery of his opponent (see below). These otherwise flattering terms of address are in this way cancelled out not only by their formulaic nature, as aforementioned, but also by the explicit FTAs that often follow.

Politicians' references to closeness and commonality of views, likewise, often occur within utterance contexts that deny their literal meaning. Clarke's minimisation token in line 18 of Extract 10.2 ('I don't want to dispute tha- I don't think it's relevant now'), for instance, develops into a FTA that brings to the fore the very past that he had just dismissed as not 'relevant now' and uses it to discredit Smith (lines 19–27). And Smith's reassurance token in line 12 ('I promise you') is framed between an imperative that explicitly threatens Clarke's negative face needs not to be interactionally imposed upon ('go back and check this', line 11) and an emphatic self-justification that asserts his own position: '<that was all> (.) I didn't have a huge drive to do it more than anyone else' (lines 14–15).

Consider, furthermore, Prescott's and Clarke's ventriloquising of their opponents in, respectively, lines 19 (Extract 10.1) and 22–23 (Extract 10.2). As explained in Chapter 3, Goffman's (1974) concept of ventriloquising designates a speaker's playful representation of the discourse of either 'lovable' objects or prelinguistic children. Evidently, the latter aspect of Goffman's definition does not apply to the mock representations of Prescott and Clarke, for Ancram and Smith are very capable of producing their own discourse and are physically present in the debates to do so. Instead, on both occasions, ventriloquising is made to serve a purpose different from that identified by Goffman. Let us take a closer look.

In Extract 10.1, lines 15–17, Prescott prepares the ground for his subsequent act of ventriloquism by recalling a quote apparently from Ancram: 'quite honestly (.) I go to Germany now and they say to me (.) I wish we had your unemployment'. He next presents a statistic on rising employment that turns Ancram's quote against him and in favour of Prescott's party: 'employment has increased by <one hundred and eighty thousand> since he [Ancram] made that statement' (lines 17–18). Prescott follows this up by recalling the Conservative Party slogan during the 2005 General Election campaign: 'are you thinking what we're thinking?'. This slogan was used in broadcast and print advertisements, where it followed a long list of alleged failures by the Labour Party and therefore strongly presupposed an answer along the lines of: 'yes, I'm also thinking that it's time to vote Conservative'. Prescott's invocation here, though, of the slogan after stating his party's allegedly successful record of employment turns it cleverly against its original author, namely Ancram and the Conservative Party.

In Extract 10.2, Clarke reproduces a campaign slogan which was authored by the faction of the Conservative Party led by Smith in 2001 and proved to be a failure in terms of its ability to lure the electorate: 'TWELVE DAYS TO SAVE THE POUND' (lines 22–23). Clarke's paralanguage is face-threatening (raised voice) and so is his body language, which is captured in close-up and shows him patronising Smith with a dismissive hand gesture (lines 21–25). Clarke's act of ventriloquising thus serves to challenge the position held by his opponent in the context of a political debate.

The representations by Prescott and Clarke of their opponent's discourse are delivered in a playful style, though, which makes them particularly useful resources for debating politics on television. Prescott's mock delivery is not very close to Ancram's voice but it teasingly emulates the imagined collective voice of the latter's party, which is portrayed as full of self-importance. Clarke's rendition, for its part, is audibly close to Smith's grave tone of voice and is also delivered in a mocking manner. Prescott and Clarke convey, by the style of their delivery, the impression that their otherwise face-threatening acts of ventriloquising are simply instances of innocent banter between them and other members of the same discursive category: high-ranking politicians. Consider in this respect, for instance, the medium-range shot of Ancram in lines 21–22 of Extract 10.1, which shows him smiling as he amiably returns Prescott's jibe through a reference to the latter's 'blustering' when answering the wrong question.

Yet the same playful style of delivery that characterises the strategy of ventriloquising sets an effective interactional trap for those whose discourse is being represented. In the cases considered here, Ancram and Smith cannot take offence against this seemingly light-hearted mockery without appearing politically thin-skinned. The mock dimension of the strategy of ventriloquising, then, enables Clarke and Prescott to challenge their opponents without having to appear to be really doing so. Crucially, too, it affords them an excellent opportunity for impression management because such displays of verbal cleverness allow them to score 'wit points' off their opponents.

So, the analysis of Extracts 10.1 and 10.2 reveals that, if appropriately performed, conflict talk can facilitate political self-display. Through action–opposition moves in which the public face needs of one's political opponents are seemingly, and simultaneously, threatened and protected, politicians work first and foremost on constructing appealing political images of themselves. By complying with particular debating rules, they display more their skills as debaters than genuine concern not to impose upon their opponents' face needs. Under the guise of banter, they display their witty selves rather than attend to the face needs of their opponents. Rather than as adversarial boxing rings, then, televised political debates may be seen as self-promotional platforms from which politicians can sell their images to audiences. It is persuasion rather than adversarialness that drives the activity type of debating politics before the cameras. Put differently, other-directed face-threat and face-work are discursive means to a more important end: the construction of attractive personalities in a mediated political arena (see Chapters 11 and 12).

## 10.2   Conflict talk in political interviews: An argumentative feast for all

Political interviews on British television often reflect the hunter–prey relationship that purportedly exists between the media and politicians. When interviewing politicians, journalists try to hold the latter to account, often in a non-deferential, no-nonsense style. They frequently also try to get politicians to say something that they may subsequently regret and/or that may reveal their political 'trickery'. At the same time, though, journalists are expected to elicit information from the politicians whom they interview: neither to affiliate with them – as is, for example, the case for many celebrity chat show presenters (see Chapter 7) – nor to disaffiliate from them through hostility or partisanship. They are, in short, expected to appear impartial.

In political interviews on television, then, journalists face the seemingly impossible task of being 'impartial agent provocateurs'. On closer inspection, though, this is quite easily achieved by their drawing upon a particular notion of impartiality known as the neutralistic stance (Heritage and Greatbatch 1991). This neutralistic stance describes 'a manner or style of interviewing; it refers to patterns of IR [interviewer] conduct which can escape formal charges of bias – whether in the interview context itself or beyond' (Greatbatch 1998: 167).

One strategy that interviewers often use to achieve such positions of formal neutralism is to distance themselves personally from their opinions and/or challenging questions by attributing them to a third party. In third-party attributions, interviewers cite or evoke an individual, a group or an anonymous collective as the author or originator of their words and retain only the production role of animator. During an interview with a politician supportive of Bosnian refugee camps, for example, an interviewer might ask the following question: 'people have used the phrase concentration camps; and the Bosnians themselves have used that phrase. Do you believe there's any justification for that at all?'[4] Within this question, the interviewer shifts footing, abandoning temporarily the role of author of the questions posed and keeping only that of animator. Authoring is ascribed to an anonymous, generic group: 'people'. The negative remark that Bosnian refugee camps are similar to concentration camps is, as a result, invested with neutrality at a formal level: the interviewer cannot be said personally to have compared Bosnian refugee camps to concentration camps, let alone to have accused the interviewee of supporting the latter. A subjective, damaging, comparison between the camps that the interviewee supports and concentration camps has nonetheless been made.

Crucially, the pursuit of neutralistic stances by interviewers cannot be successful without the collaboration of politicians. The latter tend to accept both the basic premise of a shift of footing by interviewers, namely that journalists are speaking on behalf of others, and the expectation that they should respond to journalists' questions but not to their provocations. Politicians use a number of overt and covert interactional devices that downplay or even deny the possibility that the challenging questions and remarks that they are presented with may be those of the interviewer(s). For example, politicians often cite the same third party as the interviewer as being responsible for a particular viewpoint, refer to the disputed viewpoint without attributing it to anyone in particular, or ignore the previous viewpoint and simply present a contrasting argument.

Preserving positions of formal neutralism in the course of a political interview through third-party attributions and other interactional devices has been seen to benefit journalists. Clayman and Heritage (2002: 177) observe that '[w]hen interviewers are seen as having an axe to grind, they risk damaging their journalistic reputations, alienating a segment of the audience, and incoming negative sanctions from various interested parties'. For their part, politicians risk damaging their political image if they interpret questions as personal attacks rather than in the context of journalists' alleged spirit of advocacy. To respond to journalists' provocations might, after all, signal that politicians have hidden agendas that the journalists have successfully exposed.

Given the above, it is unsurprising that neutralistic stances are often found in televised political interviews. That said, there have always been exceptions. Clayman and Heritage (2002), for instance, demonstrated through a comprehensive study of the political interview broadcast genre in the UK and the US that interviewers' contributions are not always characterised by defensible (i.e., neutralistic) questioning and an absence of personalised editorial commentary. They also showed that politicians do not always play along with journalists when they present challenge as genuine information-seeking and negative remarks as other-authored. However, it seems reasonable to suggest also that over the past ten years or so it has become increasingly common to see occurrences of explicitly hostile questioning and antagonistic answering, at least on

## Question Time (BBC, 2005)

[Tony Blair is being questioned in the extract below about his decision to support the US invasion of Iraq in 2003 despite the then British Attorney General expressing reservations in a written report about the legality of the action. The report's leaking to the press caused Blair to face strong criticism in Parliament. A1, A2 and A3: individual members of the live studio audience. A: studio audience; TB: Tony Blair.]

| | | | |
|---|---|---|---|
| LS – A. MS – | 01 | A1 | it's very interesting that you decide to disguise as po<u>lit</u>ical |
| A1, to TB. | 02 | | your decision to::: support (.) your <u>best</u> mate (.) George Bush |
| CU – TB looks | 03 | | but [ bu- (xxxx) you always s- but you <u>always</u> say |
| down, resigned | 04 | A |     [ *cheering and laughing* (5.0) |
| smile. MS – A1, | 05 | A1 | <u>oh</u> it's ok because Saddam Hussein is a <u>really</u> nasty guy (.) |
| to TB, mocking | 06 | | clearly that's <u>self-evidently</u> <u>true</u> (.) |
| intonation. CU | 07 | | it's also <an academic point> (.) the reality is that George |
| – TB, stern | 08 | | Bush would have removed Saddam Hussein |
| look. MS – A1. | 09 | | <u>with</u> or <u>without</u> your support = |
| LS – A. MS – | 10 | A | = [ *general applause* |
| TB staring at | 11 | TB |    [(2.0) (xxxx) (3.0) |
| A1 as he waits | 12 | | |
| for applause to | 13 | | it <u>wasn't</u> (.) it wasn't an academic point |
| fade out. CU – | 14 | | for the hundreds of thousands of Iraqis |
| TB, to A1, | 15 | | who lost their lives under Saddam Hussein (.) |
| speaking with | 16 | | it was very imp<u>ort</u>ant to them (.) |
| soft intonation. | 17 | | |
| MS – A1, looks | 18 | | <u>now</u> (.) |
| sceptical. CU – | 19 | | you may say I took the action simply for America (.) I <u>didn't</u> |
| TB, assertively. | 20 | | (.) I took it because <u>I</u> believed it was in the <u>interest</u> of this |
| CU – TB, | 21 | | country (.) |
| humbly, then | 22 | | I <u>took</u> the decision in good faith and (.) <u>sometimes</u> (.) when |
| with stern and | 23 | | you're sitting in <u>my</u> seat as Prime Minister (.) you <u>have</u> to take |

→

British television (see also Montgomery 2007). Indeed, there appears to be an evolving symbiotic relationship whereby lay people and experts are appropriating similar interviewer and interviewee styles on television, which both reflects and reinforces a coarsening of the political interview genre.

Let us consider in this light Extracts 10.3 (see above and p. 131) and 10.4 (see pp. 132–3). Extract 10.3 reproduces part of an interview with the former British Prime Minister Tony Blair as the interviewee, and a group of members of the general public as the interviewers. The interview was part of a special edition of the BBC political affairs programme *Question Time* under the title 'Ask the Leader'. Extract 10.4 comes from an interview broadcast on Channel 4 (UK) of the then Labour Government Director of Communications and renowned spin-doctor Alistair Campbell by veteran news anchor Jon Snow.

A common thread runs strongly through the two political interviews from which these two extracts come: neutralistic stances are sacrificed at the altar of

| | | | |
|---|---|---|---|
| *resolute voice.* | 24 | | the decision (.) and <u>that's</u> the decision <u>I</u> took |
| *CU – A1,* | 25 | A1 | Prime Minister (.) it <u>is</u> your <u>job</u> to make the <u>right</u> <u>decision</u> and |
| *points angrily* | 26 | | <u>you</u> made the <u>wrong</u> <u>one</u> = |
| *at TB. LS – A.* | 27 | A | = [ *general applause* |
| *CU – TB,* | 28 | TB | = [ (xxxx) er (xxxx) well er (xxxx) |
| *stares towards* | 29 | | (3.0) well that's that's that- (.) that's your view (.) |
| *A.* | 30 | | but it's interesting isn't it? that today we actually have a |
| | 31 | | democratic government in Iraq |
| | [...] | | [*TB's response continues for approximately half a minute*] |
| *CU – A2 leans* | 57 | A2 | when you presented your evidence to the House of Commons |
| *forward, looks* | 58 | | you said it was <<u>authoritative</u>> and <<u>full</u>> <u>evidence</u> er uh |
| *very agitated.* | 59 | | >can't remember the exact words< (.) yet the intelligence said |
| *A2 points at TB* | 60 | | it was <<u>sporadic</u>> and <<u>patchy</u>> (.) THAT'S A <u>LIE</u> (.) <YOU |
| *accusingly with* | 61 | | <u>LIED</u> TO THIS COUNTRY> and THAT'S WHY WE <u>CAN'T</u> |
| *index finger.* | 62 | | SUPPORT YOU AT THE COMING [ ELECTION |
| *LS – A. MS –* | 63 | A | [ *general applause* |
| *TB looks down,* | 64 | TB | [ (xxxx) wel- |
| *resigned smile,* | 65 | | er (xxxx) |
| *waiting for end* | 66 | | well (6.0) er well you're going to have to make your decision |
| *of applause.* | 67 | | about that (.) <u>before</u> you make your decision <u>though</u> (.) |
| *CU – TB.* | 68 | | the inter<u>esting</u> point about the int<u>elligence</u> [. . .] |
| | 69–87 | | [*TB's response continues for approximately one minute. He refers to his having authorised an inquiry into the Labour Government's use of intelligence on Iraq's alleged WMD capabilities.*] |
| *LS – A. MS –* | 88 | A3 | why don't you have a <<u>full</u> <u>independent</u>> inquiry answering all |
| *TB raises hand* | 89 | | the [questions rather than the specific questions [<u>you</u> dec- |
| *to speak. CU –* | 90 | TB | [you know? d-? [<u>NO</u>::: (.) |
| *TB, angrily.* | 91 | | [AGH |
| *LS – A. MS –* | 92 | A | [*general applause and some cheering* |
| *TB, frustrated,* | 93 | TB | (5.0) you know how many inquiries [ we've had? (.) <u>FOUR</u> |
| *to A3. MS – A3,* | 94 | A3 | [ it's just th- you <u>decide</u> |
| *leans forward* | 95 | | the wording <<u>EVERY</u>> < <u>TIME</u>> = |
| *towards TB.* | 96 | A | = *general applause* [. . .] |

explicit adversarialness. Regardless of the fact that the interviewers in Extracts 10.3 and 10.4 are of different types, lay and professional respectively, there is, for example, only one instance of interviewer use of third-party attributions, namely Snow's in Extract 10.4, lines 46–47: 'you've heard the Foreign Secretary himself tell that committee that <u>that</u> dossier was a <u>horlicks</u>'. There is also only one instance of interviewer use of the mitigating strategy of depersonalisation, once again by Snow, who states in Extract 10.4, lines 09–10: 'the <u>reason</u> we don't know is that there's <<u>obfuscation</u>> and <<u>diversion</u>>'. Through this strategy, Snow distances his accusation of governmental obfuscation and diversion from Campbell (a senior representative of that government) and presents it instead as simply something that exists.

With the above exceptions, interviewing in Extracts 10.3 and 10.4 is overtly hostile. Even Snow's depersonalisation strategy in lines 09–10 is cancelled out by his subsequent accusation against Campbell, which is most emphatic: 'part

---

**EXTRACT 10.4**

### Channel 4 News (Channel 4, 2003)

[This extract comes from an interview conducted following the publication of a dossier with the findings of a Labour-Government-commissioned independent threat assessment of Iraq's alleged WMD capabilities prior to the 2003 Iraq war. For background to the story, see Chapter 6. The extract reproduces the first few minutes of the interview. S: Snow, C: Campbell.]

| | | |
|---|---|---|
| *MS – C and S* | 01 S | [. . .] the question you put to the BBC? (.) |
| *sitting at a table,* | 02 | do they <u>stand</u> by it? |
| *facing each* | 03 | the answer is <u>yes</u> (.) |
| *other. MCU – C,* | 04 | a robust [<u>yes</u> |
| *leans forward* | 05 C |       [ex<u>cuse</u> me (.) that letter is about as robust as Blackburn |
| *towards S. MS –* | 06 | Rovers were when they played Trelleborgs (.) I'll tell you (.) the |
| *C and S now* | 07 | answer to the question (.) <yes or no>? the answer to that question |
| *leaning closer* | 08 | is <u>NO</u> = |
| *towards one* | 09 S | = the answer to that question is <we <u>don't</u> know> (.) and the |
| *another.* | 10 | <u>reason</u> we don't know is that there's <obfuscation> and |
| | 11 | <diversion> (.) part of which we are seeing played out <u>right</u> <u>here</u> |
| | 12 | before us |
| | [. . .] | [*The interview continues for approximately one minute.*] |
| *MS – C and S.* | 46 S | you've heard the Foreign Secretary himself tell that committee |
| | 47 | that <u>that</u> dossier was a <u>horlicks</u> [ and someth- |
| *MCU – C, raises* | 48 C |       [ <u>SORRY</u> (.) <u>AGAIN</u> <deliberate> |
| *hand to speak* | 49 | conflation of two things = |
| *and gesticulates* | 50 S | = something he sa[id |
| *expressively. MS* | 51 C |       [<u>correct</u> <u>yourself</u> (.) <u>correct</u> <u>yourself</u> (.) it is <u>not</u> |

→

---

of which [the obfuscation and diversion] we are seeing played out <u>right</u> <u>here</u> before us' (lines 11–12). Snow also makes challenging requests for clarification (e.g. line 53) and explicit counter-attacks to Campbell's oppositional moves (lines 09–12, 60–62 and 65–67) and provides editorial commentary that both aligns him with positions contrary to Campbell's (lines 54–55) and presents damaging evidence against him (lines 60–62). Snow, too, largely ignores what is arguably the central feature of interviewing: to ask questions. His opportunity may have been somewhat limited by Campbell's aggressive conduct but Snow nevertheless actually asks only one substantive question during Extract 10.4: 'the question you put to the BBC? (.) do they <u>stand</u> by it?' (lines 01–02). This question transpires to be far from neutral as Snow himself immediately and emphatically answers it: 'the answer is <u>yes</u> (.) a robust [<u>yes</u>' (lines 03–04).

In Extract 10.3, members of the general public acting as interviewers also dispense with questions and engage instead in the performance of bald, on-record FTAs. Thus, for example, A1 threatens Blair's face when she states that he acted upon personal rather than professional considerations, specifically his supporting his '<u>best</u> mate (.) George Bush' (line 02). In doing so, A1 connects Blair's public (political leader) and private (friend) face. She explicitly accuses Blair, in fact, of falsely justifying his personal-friendship-based policy-making:

| | | |
|---|---|---|
| – C, points at S | 52 | the <u>same</u> document (.) do you accept that? = |
| with index finger. | 53 S | = which is not the same document? = |
| MCU – C, | 54 C | = you just said (.) the Foreign Secretary described the dossier as a |
| gesticulating with | 55 | [horlicks |
| clenched fist. | 56 S | [the dodgy do- dos[sier |
| | 57 C | [ex<u>cu</u>se me (.) we were talking about the |
| | 58 | weapons of mass destruction dossier [. . .] and <u>you</u> are <u>deliberately</u> |
| MCU – S, | 59 | con<u>flat</u>ing [the two issues |
| gesticulates with | 60 S | [the issue in play here today is <u>firstly</u> the charges that in |
| hand. MCU – C, | 61 | the first document in September (.) there were serious errors of |
| drinking water. | 62 | fact? [we now know |
| MS – S and C. C | 63 C | [so- <u>sorry</u> (.) the first (.) document in Septem- (.) |
| breaks off from | 64 | there were <u>serious</u> errors of fac- fact? and <u>what</u> were they Jon? |
| drinking water. | 65 S | the allegation in which er er the minister who was supposed to |
| MS – S and C. S | 66 | have signed the (.) nuclear purchasing order (.) had himself |
| illustrates signing | 67 | resigned <u>many</u> years be[fore |
| with hand. | 68 C | [y'kn- <u>you</u> know (.) do <u>you</u> Jon? that the |
| MCU – C, points | 69 | (.) that <u>that was</u> the basis on which British intelligence put that in |
| towards S with | 70 | the dossier (.) <u>you</u> know that <u>DO YOU</u>? (.) because if <u>you</u> <u>think</u> |
| pen in fist. | 71 | that (.) <u>you</u> <u>are</u> <u>WRONG</u> (.) there were <u>no</u> (.) <u>errors</u> (.) of <u>fact</u> (.) |
| | 72 | in the (.) wm- in the WMD dossier of [ September two thousan- |
| MS – C and S. | 73 S | [(xxxx) the the (xxxx) |
| | 74 | source was [nothing to |
| MCU – C, still | 75 C | [ex<u>cu</u>se me (.) it was a<u>no</u>ther country's intelligence |
| pointing at S with | 76 | and the <u>Brit</u>ish intel<u>lig</u>ence (.) put what they put in that dossier on |
| pen in fist. | 77 | the basis of <u>Brit</u>ish intel<u>lig</u>ence (.) <u>GET YOUR FACTS RIGHT</u> |
| | 78 | before <u>you</u> make serious allegations [. . .] |

'you decide to disguise as po<u>lit</u>ical your decision . . .' (lines 01–02). Possibly emboldened by the general support that her accusations receive (general cheering and laughter in the studio, line 04), A1 then further threatens Blair's face by accusing him of using academic points to justify his errors (lines 06–09). This FTA is prefaced by an instance of ventriloquism in which A1 uses mocking intonation, expressive paralanguage ('<u>oh</u>') and simplistic lexical representation ('it's ok because Saddam Hussein is a <u>really</u> nasty guy') to scorn Blair's discourse on Hussein. Given the considerable social distance and power imbalance that hold between A1 (a member of the general public) and Blair (the UK Prime Minister at the time), her act of ventriloquism is particularly face-threatening.

Far from accepting Blair's response in lines 11–24, moreover, A1 continues to oppose Blair in highly antagonistic fashion. In line 25, she reminds Blair that his job is 'to make the <u>right</u> decision', something in which she immediately portrays him to have failed: 'and <u>you</u> made the <u>wrong one</u> =' (line 26). Note that A1 does not mitigate the face-threat level of her statement through, for example, a discourse quality hedge such as 'in my opinion' or 'I think'. On the contrary, she uses emphatic stress on key lexical items ('<u>is</u> your <u>job</u>' '<u>right</u> deci-sion', '<u>wrong one</u>') and the distance-marking, official vocative 'Prime Minister' to signal a clear 'us' (the general public) versus 'you' (high-ranking politician) divide.

A2's contribution (lines 57–62), too, relies on the performance of bald on-record, without-redress FTAs and continues to ignore expectations that inter-viewers ask questions, especially in a programme entitled 'Ask the Leader'. A2 produces a rhetorically efficient, and most hostile, list of three: (1) Blair's previous answer is 'A LIE (.)', (2) Blair is a politician who has '<LIED TO THIS COUNTRY>'; and (3) THAT'S WHY WE CAN'T SUPPORT YOU AT THE COMING [ELECTION' (lines 60–62). Like A1 before and A3 afterwards, A2 both emphasises an 'us' versus 'you' divide and receives general support from the studio audience for his contribution. A2's body language, furthermore, is very aggressive. As soon as he accesses the speaking floor, and is captured in close-up, he menacingly leans forward towards Blair (lines 57–59) and accusingly points at Blair (lines 60–62). A2's paralanguage is equally hostile. Although he is the only person speaking with a microphone at this point, he raises his voice consid-erably, uses marked stress on the words that carry most face-threat, delivers some of his accusations at a noticeably slow rate and makes strategic use of micro-pauses in his tripartite charge.

A3 *does* ask a question: 'why don't you have a <full independent> inquiry [. . .]' (lines 88–89). This question, however, brings together in one single utterance the strategies of negative (e.g. 'Isn't it true, Mr. X that . . .') and accountability questioning (e.g. 'Why do you . . .?', 'why is it that you . . .?'). Negative and accountability questions fail to pose questions at all. Instead, they strongly proj-ect expected answers that contest and damage the interviewees' positions (Clayman and Heritage 2002). A3's question projects, indeed, a serious accusa-tion as a preferred answer (as confirmed by A3 in lines 89 and 94–95), namely that Blair decided on the content of allegedly independent inquiries into his government. It is therefore hardly an instance of defensible questioning. Moreover, following as it does the preceding array of individual accusations and supportive laughter, it is the one FTA that finally makes Blair 'snap'.

In lines 90–91, Blair confrontationally interrupts A3's turn and expressively shows his frustration: '[you know? d-? [NO::: (.) [AGH'. After yet another long round of applause and cheering from the studio audience in line 92, Blair next produces an adversarial opposition move in the form of a challenging question to A3: 'you know how many enquiries [we've had?' (line 93). Visibly irritated, he rushes to answer his own question in a loud, emphatic voice: 'FOUR' (line 93).

If there is an interviewee who really 'loses it', however, that interviewee is Campbell (Extract 10.4). Not only does he consistently fail to resist the inter-viewer's challenges but also actually uses these as platforms from which to counter-attack in the most explicit and personal of ways. In lines 05–06, for example, he dismantles Snow's initial question thus: 'excuse me (.) that letter is about as robust as Blackburn Rovers were when they played Trelleborgs'. Campbell is referring here to the annual Champions League European football competition. He is specifically comparing the robustness of the BBC's argu-ments to the poor performance of English premier league club Blackburn

Rovers when playing the theoretically weaker Swedish football team Trelleborgs during the 2003 round of this competition.

Most of Campbell's forceful rejections of Snow's points, moreover, are uttered even before the latter has had a chance to develop them fully. Campbell's confrontational interruptions (lines 05–08, 48–49, 51–52, 57–59, 63–64, 68–72 and 75–78) thus repeatedly threaten Snow's negative face-needs to have his interviewer turns respected. Campbell's rejections, too, are unmistakably articulated as bald on-record, without-redress FTAs. For instance, he uses the second-person pronoun 'you', sometimes in conjunction with marked emphasis and/or expressive hand gestures, to launch personal accusations against Snow: 'you are deliberately conflating [the two issues' (lines 58–59); 'y'kn- you know (.) do you Jon? that the (.) that that was the basis [. . .] you know that DO YOU? because if you think that . . .' (lines 62–72), 'GET YOUR FACTS RIGHT before you make serious allegations' (lines 77–78).

Further testament to Campbell's explicit antagonism are, ironically given his interactional role as interviewee, his questions to Snow. In lines 51–52, and following an emphatic order for Snow to 'correct yourself (.) correct yourself', he corners the latter through a polar (yes–no) question: 'it is not the same document (.) do you accept that?'. And in lines 63–64 and 68–70, in a kind of *crescendo* of adversarialness, he sets a questioning trap for Snow: 'so-sorry (.) the first (.) document in Septem- (.) there were serious errors of fac- fact? and what were they Jon?', 'y'kn- you know (.) do you Jon? [. . .] you know that DO YOU?'. Campbell's *coup de grâce* is quick to materialise: 'because if you think that (.) you are WRONG' (lines 70–71).

Campbell's paralanguage and body language are also hostile. On the one occasion in which Campbell depersonalises his accusations, his paralanguage communicates maximum face-threat: 'SORRY (.) AGAIN <deliberate> conflation of two things =' (lines 48–49). Note the loudness of, and marked stress on, 'sorry' and 'again', which convey irritation and complement his equally face-threatening body language (raising his hand to speak and gesticulating expressively).

A considerable number of camera medium close-ups (seven, to be precise, in the extract) skilfully capture the intensity of Campbell's face-threatening body language. During these, the camera zooms in on non-verbal behaviour that seemingly reveals visceral reactions from this otherwise infamously accomplished spin-doctor: intimidating finger-pointing (lines 50–53, 69–71, 75–78), fist-clenching (lines 54–59) and the reduction of physical space between him and Snow (lines 04–06). Note also the subsequent medium-range shot that shows interviewer and interviewee now closely facing each other (lines 06–12).

Did Campbell genuinely lose his cool during this interview? He had previously refused to give an interview to Channel 4 News but subsequently arrived at the news studios unannounced and ready to be interviewed. This suggests that he was not at his most rational. He was certainly not at his most politically sensible for through his performance in this interview he broke the first rule of spin-doctoring: never become the story. At the same time, however, it is of course possible that Campbell may have staged his out-of-emotional-control performance to take immediate pressure and media frenzy temporarily away from the government.

Regardless of the actual genuineness of Campbell's performance in Extract 10.4, this interview showed a politician openly and viscerally defying/attacking an experienced journalist. This is, within the traditional adversarial style of political interviewing in the UK at least, a rare display and one that challenges journalists' watchdog skills. It is also particularly powerful because the politician concerned is one of the most accomplished representatives of a political breed that epitomises self-control in public: spin-doctors.

Similarly, Extract 10.3 showed members of the general public 'bypassing' the established practice of neutralistic interviewing. This may be appealing in that it seemingly shows ordinary people subverting the system from within and bringing the kind of 'negative' emotionalism commonly found in 'banal' forms of television, such as those examined in Chapter 9, to the serious form of broadcasting that political interviews are seen to be. That the target of this adversarialness was a much more powerful person than they were – the highest-ranking politician in the country at the time, in fact – may arguably have provided an additional attraction.

## 10.3   Conclusion

Politics is conflict – or so television and politicians seem to want us to believe. In this chapter we have examined how conflict talk originates and develops in two activity types that are constitutively adversarial: televised political debates and televised political interviews. Face-threat is intentional in these debates but it is also generally conducted within the parameters of what is contextually appropriate and, hence, politic rather than impolite. British Parliamentary debates, for example, do not generally feature direct verbal attacks on politicians' face. Instead, challenges and criticisms are filtered through the figure of the Speaker. In panel debates, politicians tend to attack each other's public face. In both contexts, politeness strategies are often embedded within adversarial turns and this weakens the tempering function that these strategies would otherwise have in non-adversarial genres.

The alternating nature of face-threat and face-work in political debates, for its part, constitutes one of their most idiosyncratic features. Rather than clashing, contextually appropriate face-threat and face-work complement each other perfectly well in televised political debates. Face-threat seeks to construct conflict talk in these debates as genuine in the eyes of increasingly cynical viewers. Face-work, in turn, seeks to convey the impression that the business at hand, namely, debating political issues, can be safeguarded because opposing others' views is not so important as to override the imperatives of the activity type of debating politics on television.

Both face-threat and face-work, then, are meant to aid politicians' self-presentation in these debates. As discussed in Chapter 8, self-presentation describes the communicative process whereby individuals try to manage how others perceive them. It always involves, therefore, an element of performance. In televised political debates, such as *PMQs* and *Newsnight,* this is at its most explicit: the presence of the cameras in the House of Commons and the BBC studios is already a poignant reminder that politicians are on stage. In addition, in a mediatised political environment, politicians know that these public performances are closely scrutinised by the media and that they are thus of significance for their political image.

In Extract 10.2, for instance, spatial and sitting arrangements in the studio maximised the framing of the debate as 'gladiatorial'. Clarke and Smith were made to sit around a table facing each other directly and flanked by two political supporters each. In centre position was the moderator. A quick succession of (medium) close-ups of Clarke and Smith was juxtaposed with occasional medium-range shots of all participants across the table. These (medium) close-ups co-occurred with the politicians' FTAs. They therefore strengthened the impression of debating politics as a confrontational practice. For example, the medium-range angle of the politicians sitting at a round table that had been accompanying Clarke's turn in lines 01–04 quickly shifted to a medium close-up (lines 05–07) when he emphatically personalised his accusation against Smith through added stress on '<u>you</u>' and '<u>David</u>'. Clarke's emphatic head shakes denying Smith's words (lines 10–11 and 32–34) and his loud (lines 23–24, 25–26) and mocking (line 25–26) delivery were also shot in close-up. The visual and verbal cueing of conflict therefore reinforced each other and, in turn, the framing of televised political debates as knowing performance of adversarialness.

A similar need to self-advertise underlies conflict talk in accountability interviews of politicians on television. Here, however, the kind of formal neutralism that was once thought of as politic behaviour is seemingly being superseded by explicit adversarialness. Throughout the second part of this chapter we have illustrated some of the means by which lay people and journalists perform their role of interviewer in an openly hostile fashion. We have also shown a number of devices by which politicians respond in kind.

The increasing frequency of the above practices may turn them from marked (and at times impolite – Snow's reactions to Campbell's behaviour as interviewee certainly suggest so, as do Blair's to A3's as interviewer) to unmarked (politic). It may indeed gradually pave the way for, and eventually instate, a new interactional frame for the activity type of the televised political interview – one of formal coarsening. In this, interviewers would routinely project aspects of their own (or their institution's) identity through overtly subjective questions and editorial commentary, and interviewees would display explicit adversarialness through, amongst other strategies, strong rebuttals, insistent counter-questions and personal attacks.

Such a frame would tie in with television's projection of an emotional public sphere, in which both ordinary people and experts (here, politicians and journalists) opt for visceral ways of self-expression as avenues for social discussion and reflection. It would also fit television's promotion of confrontainment and, in the case of political talk on television, of 'politainment'. If explicit antagonism is allegedly what viewers want in an era of mediatised politics, then this may

be what those on the screen (ordinary folk, journalists and politicians) will ultimately strive to provide.[5]

Finally, the analyses presented in this chapter challenge the view that the
media–politics relationship is a hunter and prey interactional affair. Those in the
world of television (and other media) and those in the world of politics draw
upon discourses that have over the years undergone a considerable process of
convergence. They are therefore locked as much into a relationship marked by
struggle and adversarialness as by complicity and, above all, mutual need
(Fairclough 1998). The television–politics relationship is, therefore, a synergetic
one in which both parties benefit from the knowing performance of a number
of forms of talk, including various types of conflict talk.

# Part IV

## Persuasion

# Persuasion . . . or the Art of *Occultatio*

> I shall say nothing, either, about the financial ruin into which
> you will be plunged upon the thirteenth of this month.
> Instead, I shall turn to matters which relate
> not to the squalor of your personal depravities,
> not to the sordid tangle of your personal affairs,
> but to the supreme interests of our commonwealth.

The above passage comes from a political speech by Cicero in which the famous orator is scolding Catilina before the Roman Senate.[1] It is the passage selected by Robert Cockcroft and Susan Cockcroft (2005) in their book *Persuading People* to illustrate the rhetorical strategy known as 'passing over' or *occultatio*. The ploy around which this strategy works is to pretend that one does not mention what one is mentioning. At a local level, *occultatio* is just one more of the vast repertoire of strategies used to persuade others in and through discourse. At a more general level, it captures what this part of the book is largely about: television's covert selling of a raft of goods and services to its viewers.

Television's *occultatio* stems, in part at least, from an inherent feature of persuasion: its blurred boundaries with argumentation. All texts have 'argumentativeness', that is, they all try to convince their target audiences at some level (Lavandera 1992). But *the* communicative goal of persuasive texts is to convince. The line between argumentation and persuasion is relatively easy to draw vis-à-vis certain television contexts. Even when 'soft' (covert) advertising techniques are used, for example, viewer expectations of the activity type of advertising entail some awareness of its persuasive nature. Can we always tell, though, whether a news report on a politician's public speech portrays that politician in a particular light rather than persuades us to see him/her as so? And can we distinguish between the arguments offered by the presenters of travel shows in favour of, say, package deals for holidays abroad and their persuading us to partake of specific styles of doing tourism? The answer, as Chapters 12 and 13 reveal, is not always, and certainly not easily.

One possible way to distinguish persuasion from argumentation is to consider the difference between them as one of degree, rather than nature

**141**

(Pardo 2001). In the field of political oratory, for instance, politicians are known to deploy a substantial number and variety of strategies to convince their audiences, rather than simply to argue, that their views are better than those of their opponents. These strategies generally fall under one of the three Aristotelian 'means of persuasion', namely *logos, pathos* and *ethos* (Aristotle, 1926, 3–6).

Aristotle defines *logos* as persuasion by the speech itself. The term describes 'the process of identifying the issues at the heart of the debate; the range of diverse arguments in the discourse; the structure of thought these arguments compose; and the sequencing, coherence and logical value of these arguments' (Cockcroft and Cockcroft 2005: 18).

For Aristotle, *pathos* is persuasion by placing the hearer into a specific frame of mind. It designates the persuader's decision to orientate 'emotional appeals precisely towards audience and topic, and to found them on sources of feeling accessible to speaker and audience, writer and reader' (Cockcroft and Cockcroft 2005: 17). In their televised political appearances, for example, politicians may use several (non-)verbal communication signs, such as emotive gesturing or explicit references to their feelings, in order to appeal to viewers at an emotional (rather than a rational) level.

*Ethos,* for its part, is seen by Aristotle as persuasion by moral character. Echoing Aristotle, Cockcroft and Cockcroft (2005: 16–17) emphasise that persuasion through *ethos* 'must be due to the speech itself, not to any preconceived idea of the speaker's character'. For persuasion through *ethos* to work, moreover, the persuader's character has to be accompanied by a congruous *stance,* or attitude, towards the issues being talked about. Stance, in turn, is determined by *kairos,* or timeliness, which refers to one's ability to be constantly aware of the needs of one's audience and to be able to adapt to these needs by making the required changes in one's rhetoric.

Politicians need to ensure that their stance complements their moral character and to avoid appearing instrumental. Otherwise, politicians can easily be seen as lacking a sound and distinctive political programme and/or *ethos*. At the same time, pragmatism-driven adaptability is crucial to the success of political persuasion. Those politicians who engage in 'positive rhetoric' (Hunter 1984) shift or broaden their stance in response to their audience, rather than adhere to a single viewpoint (i.e. 'negative rhetoric'). As a case in point, recall the former British Prime Minister Blair's responses during a televised interview with members of the general public in the previous chapter (Extract 10.3), in which he defended his decision to support the US in its war with Iraq in 2003. However, as his interviewers kept criticising his stance, he made remarks such as: 'well that's that's that- (.) that's your view' (line 29) and 'well (6.0) er well you're going to have to make your decision about that' (lines 66–67). Through these remarks, he acknowledged the validity of other stances on that issue, even if he personally did not share them.

Drawing upon *ethos,* or its modern version 'image', has become a *sine qua non* in mediated political communication and has resulted in an 'explicit styling of politics' that, Corner and Pels (2003) argue, resembles that of popular culture. These authors compare political and popular music election campaigns, noting for instance that the 2002 final of the British talent show *Pop Idol* generated the biggest phone-in ever in the UK (8.7 million votes were cast – more than the Liberal Democratic Party had polled in the 2001 UK General Election). Manufactured pop has appropriated some of the conventions and paraphernalia of political campaigning. At the same time, '"official" politics has been catching up, blurring the boundaries and levelling the hierarchy between "high" political representation and "low" popular entertainment' Corner and Pels (2003: 4). Politics is nowadays a culture industry, resembling a talent show or popularity contest. This is despised by some critics as 'disabling' politics but in the eyes of others 'enables' a form of active citizen participation in politics.[2] Regardless of whether the mediatisation of politics is seen favourably or otherwise, the undeniable fact is that style is itself a gateway to politics and that it operates in ways not too dissimilar from those in other forms of popular culture. As such, it is strongly driven by personality and hence political image.

Currently favoured political images include that of the self-made man or woman turned into a successful politician. This image, which has been found to have global purchase, portrays politicians as individuals who have overcome personal hardships, are family-orientated and have deeply held, personal values, which they use to inform their political decisions (Stanyer and Wring 2004). Let us revisit Blair's performance in the televised interview examined in Extract 10.3 in Chapter 10 once again, specifically his response regarding his decision to go to war:

| MS – A1, | 18 | TB | now (.) |
|---|---|---|---|
| looks | 19 | | you may say I took the action simply for America (.) I didn't |
| sceptical. CU – | 20 | | (.) I took it because I believed it was in the interest of this |
| TB, assertively. | 21 | | country (.) |
| CU – TB, | 22 | | I took the decision in good faith and (.) sometimes (.) when |
| humbly [. . .] | 23 | | you're sitting in my seat as Prime Minister (.) you have to take |
| | 24 | | the decision (.) and that's the decision I took |

Blair referred to personal beliefs being the driving force of his decision-making. He used emphatic stress on both first-person singular pronouns ('I', 'my') and the verb 'believed' in order to persuade his (inter)viewers of the importance of him trying to do what he felt was 'in the interest of this country' (lines 20–21) and his acting 'in good faith' (line 22). He sought to appear, in short, personally committed to politics – driven by his values – thereby conflating the man and the leader within his political image.

Two other, related, images currently valued in politics are the 'cool' politician and the politician as an emotionally expressive individual. At a general level, 'cool' refers to a type of personality that revolves around three characteristics: narcissism, ironic detachment and hedonism (Pountain and Robins 2000). These three core aspects of coolness are at loggerheads with what being a politician is expected to be about, which is why for Pountain and Robins (2000: 171) 'cool is never political, and politics, almost by definition, can never be cool'. The political image of coolness thus relies on the performance of the kind of stylishly cool attitude that popular culture stars display and that may allow politicians to claim that they are in touch with popular culture.

As for the image of the emotionally expressive politician, this refers to the politician as someone who is able and willing to share his/her emotions with the general public. Viewers are known to judge politicians often on the appropriateness or otherwise of their emotional displays. Decisions about the authenticity of such displays are said to play a key part in viewers' assessment of the trustworthiness of the politicians and their political programmes (Bucy 2000). The consequent 'emotionalisation' of politics (Lilleker 2006) is one of the reasons why high-profile politicians are nowadays often regarded as one more type of celebrity.

Seeing politicians as celebrities owes to more than just their associations with the glitzy world of film and rock stars, of which former Hollywood star Arnold Schwarzenegger becoming Governor of California and former British Prime Minister Blair meeting U2 lead singer Bono to discuss world poverty are but two examples. It also owes to politicians joining the increasingly lengthy list of showbiz performers whose personal lives are publicly displayed across, and then closely scrutinised by, the media. Like film stars and chat show hosts, political leaders have made the speech and moral ideal of emotional expressiveness a regular feature of their public appearances – of indeed their ability to sell the cultural goods that they embody.

The increased media attention that the emotionally expressive, cool politician brings can be a double-edged sword. In his detailed account of the rise of mediated political scandal, Thompson (2000) notes the capacity of television to provide a most fertile breeding ground for what he terms today's 'society of self-disclosure'. He describes the latter as a society in which it is 'possible and, indeed, increasingly common for political leaders and other individuals to appear before distant audiences and lay bare some aspect of their self or their personal life' (2000: 40). Television's ability to broadcast high-quality sounds and close-up images, for example, has resulted in politicians and their PR teams planning in great detail aspects of their screen appearances that were hitherto reserved for those with whom they shared a relationship of close physical co-presence, such as their facial expressions, their mannerisms, their hand gestures and the different inflections in their voices.

The increased visibility that television has afforded political leaders, Thompson (2000: 108–9) further argues, is one of the main reasons for the rise of mediated political scandal in recent times:

> In this age of mediated visibility, political leaders (and aspiring leaders) know that they must use the media as a way of achieving visibility in the political field – without it, they will go nowhere. But mediated visibility can be a trap. The more visible you are, the more vulnerable you may be, because more visibility will generate more interest from the media and, however much you may wish to manage your self-presentation through the media, you cannot completely control it. [. . .] Political leaders may seek to manage the ways in which they appear through the media, but it becomes increasingly difficult for them to prevent the disclosure of potentially damaging information or images. Mediated visibility can easily slip out of their control and may, on occasion, work against them.

Sex scandals in the political field are good examples of this. And the Clinton–Lewinsky affair – arguably the most significant sex scandal in American political history – exemplifies how easily the image and career of even the most accomplished of political orators can potentially be derailed in a political climate of increased visibility. This scandal initially revolved around a 'first-order transgression' (Thompson 2000), namely the media's exposing of the illicit relationship between then US President Bill Clinton and White House intern Monika Lewinsky. It soon became, however, a scandal marked by 'second-order transgressions' (Thompson 2000), where media attention switched from the original sexual indiscretion to a series of subsequent actions, the aim of which was to hide the first-order transgression. Clinton's attempts to conceal his affair with Lewinsky thus gave rise to 'an intensifying cycle of claim and counter-claim that dwarf[ed] the initial offence and fuel[led] a scandal which escalate[d] with every twist' (Thompson 2000: 17). These second-order transgressions became more important – and more destructive of his political image – than the scandal regarding his affair.

The media, for their part, covered Clinton's each and every attempt to deny the affair, so much so that this scandal dominated the news for over a year. Such media coverage involved, amongst other things, Clinton's verbal statements of denial, such as the one on 26 January 1998, in which he appeared on television next to his wife and vehemently announced: 'I did not have sexual relations with that woman, Miss Lewinsky. I never told anybody to lie, not a single time – never. These allegations are false. And I need to go back to work for the American people.'[3] Clinton's choice of words (specifically, his first sentence in the above quotation) soon became one of the iconic sound-bites of the scandal – one to be endlessly relayed by different media across the globe, especially once it was found to be false.

Clinton's body language, too, was closely scrutinised by the media. His Grand Jury testimony video on 17 August 1998, released to the public on 21 September 1998, provided the media with a rich source of material not just on Clinton's actual testimony (his verbal behaviour) but, as Jaworski and Galasiński (2002) argue, but also on the way that he 'looked' and 'behaved' during it (his non-verbal behaviour). The latter were seen as particularly salient, possibly because of the primacy generally assigned to non-verbal over verbal signs of communication in terms of believability (Argyle et al. 1970; Lyons 1977; Richmond and McCroskey 2000), especially when the messages being simultaneously sent out by verbal and non-verbal signs are contradictory (Hetch et al. 1999).

Although non-verbal signs of communication are generally seen as more believable than co-occurring verbal ones, they are also notoriously more indeterminate and ambiguous. Verbal signs draw on a set of fixed and rather complex devices to indicate a number of connections, such as causality, similarity, difference, and so forth, whereas non-verbal signs are considerably less explicit about such relationships. Even those non-verbal signs normally associated with lying (e.g. fidgeting and averting one's gaze) cannot be unequivocally related to deception. The strong point of non-verbal signs such as images, for example, is precisely their implicitness. This is why soft-sell advertising techniques, which work through implicitness (verbal and visual), are generally believed to be more persuasive than their hard-sell counterparts (Cook 2001). Moreover, visual implicitness in advertising is often the only way forward when persuasion uses aspects of behaviour or identity traits that are either contentious or taboo, for instance smoking and sexual promiscuity (Messaris 1997).

The Clinton–Lewinsky scandal, then, illustrates not only the potential price to pay for increased visibility but also the potentially persuasive nature of television's language on the language of politicians. At a general level, the capacity of language to refer to, and comment on, itself is known as its 'metalinguistic' function. Mikhail Bakhtin's (1981, 1984, 1986) characterisation of language as heteroglossic is instructive in this regard. For Bakhtin, language always embeds multiple competing 'voices': from the present and the past, and from different socio-ideological groups and traditions. This makes language dialogic, rather than a set of single, isolated utterances.[4] It makes language usage, in turn, always a matter of choice. The choices one makes signal one's decisions to represent – to emulate, copy, or differ from – particular voices from the whole language pool. They are, in short, metachoices that are necessary to communicate.

But along with the linguistic capacity to refer to language use comes also a capacity for conscious linguistic manipulation, which Bakhtin calls 'heteroglossia with awareness' and which can be made to serve a number of purposes. Consider, for example, a group of people discussing how to translate the Bible into the Klingon language. Since Klingon is an imaginary alien language, there is strictly speaking no need to have such a Bible in the first place, let alone to have discussions over best translation practice (Cameron 1995, 2004).

Within educational settings, Jaworski and Sachdev (2004) provide the example of teachers' written references of pupils applying for university places in Britain. Some of these references included comments on the amount of talk that the pupils generated in class and evaluated loquacity positively and silence negatively. Given the influence of academic and character references in the process of accepting university applicants, the effects of these teachers' meta acts were most significant for the pupils. Their references were also unfair for some of these pupils, for there is no evidence of a positive correlation between loquacity and academic ability and/or achievement.

Instances of the strategic metarepresentation of the language of others are also often found on television. Nowadays, for example, most of us form our opinions of political (aspiring) leaders from the television coverage that they receive rather than, say, from thorough reading of their party manifestos (Corner 2003). During campaign periods, television pundits extensively discuss candidates' daily public engagements, often focusing on their impression-management techniques: their choice of words, the tone of their voices, their hand-shaking, their outfits, and so forth. What most of us may be less aware of, though, is that such metarepresentations contribute to portraying politicians in a given light. Journalists' metalanguage on politicians' (non-)verbal behaviour may indeed contribute to naturalising their (journalists') own ways of seeing and constructing both politicians' images and the field of politics.

In personal make-over shows, too, presenters often comment on and evaluate ordinary people's discourse of physical appearance. Given the expert status of these presenters, their metalinguistic acts are potentially persuasive resources for doing power. Through them, the shows persuasively project their aesthetic preferences with regard to clothes, hairstyles, and so forth as universal. In other words, they help naturalise certain aesthetic choices across a range of everyday life activities and spheres of personal and social action. Although these forms of television are ostensibly about disseminating skills and knowledge, on closer inspection they are about educating viewers in 'good taste'. What is more, make-over shows tend to make strong connections between tangible (e.g. a particular outfit) and symbolic (e.g. high self-esteem) products. They regularly present viewers with images and contexts designed to persuade them to see the material products on the screen as the gateways to appealing identities. In doing so, these shows not only reflect but also contribute to the transition from ways of life to lifestyles.

The latter requires some words of introduction, not least because lifestyles have been identified as one of the defining features of modern, mass-mediated societies. Lifestyles comprise a range of routinised practices embedded in habits of food and dress, ways of acting socially and in work, preferred places for meeting people, and so forth. A person's lifestyle thus encompasses a set of 'lifestyle sectors' or 'time–space slices of a person's overall activities, within which a reasonably consistent and ordered set of practices is adopted and enacted' (Giddens 1991: 83). Perhaps unsurprisingly, therefore, lifestyles have become chief markers of identity. People often draw on specific images and symbols associated with particular lifestyles as a means both to express their identities and to differentiate themselves from the identities and lifestyles of others. They embrace the practices that define a given lifestyle not only because they 'fulfil utilitarian needs, but because they give material form to a particular narrative of self-identity' (Giddens 1991: 81).

Lifestyles may also be presented as coping mechanisms that are available for us to choose from as we seek to negotiate our way through the multiplicity of contexts and options that modern societies have delivered to our doorsteps. They provide a form of ordered control (Chaney 1996, 2001). Some people may find this reassuring but, paradoxically, the apparent plethora of volitional lifestyles arguably denies us the choice not to select one or more of them. As Giddens' (1991: 81) puts it:

> The notion of lifestyle sounds somewhat trivial because it is so often thought of solely in terms of a superficial consumerism: lifestyles are suggested by glossy magazines and advertising images. But there is something much more fundamental going on than such a conception suggests: in conditions of high modernity, we all not only follow lifestyles, but in an important sense are forced to do so – we have no choice but to choose.

Finally, and returning to Cicero's opening quotation, this part of the book examines a range of semiotic resources used in two very different contexts of television in order to convince viewers that the various goods and services displayed – whether symbolic or material – are worth partaking of. Chapter 12 focuses on political persuasion on television. There is nowadays a saturation of media attention on politicians' public appearances. Confronted with this, viewers may normalise the meta acts of representation that such attention carries. And the persuasive force of television's metalanguage on politics and politicians may be easily obscured by the commentary that it provides on their on-screen appearances. Chapter 13 examines persuasion across varieties of lifestyle television. Many of these shows deploy a significant number of visual, aural and verbal strategies to showcase the desirability of certain ways of conducting aspects of one's life. Yet, they are also careful not to be seen to impose these lifestyles on viewers. Instead, they draw upon easily identifiable and purchasable material goods and services, which they present as the symbols of a range of appealing lifestyles and identities. The result is a lifestyle television environment where 'there is less and less of a clear distinction to be made between consumption of all kinds and the "consumption" of symbolic goods' (McQuail 2002: 427).

# Persuasion, Politics and Television

In the previous chapter, we noted the increased visibility of today's politicians – a phenomenon that may have had its origins in the advent of print but that was radically changed by 'the development of electronic media – radio and above all television' (Thompson 2000: 39). One of the corollaries of this phenomenon is a significant shift in politics away from traditional (e.g. Parliament and Congress) to new, media-accessible, sites. In the UK, for example, politicians have come to see their appearances within the House of Commons as secondary in importance to those just outside it – either on College Green (otherwise known as 'sound-bite heaven') or in the main television channels' studios at Millbank (Riddell 1998; Seaton 1998).

The increased visibility of politicians, moreover, has had to be professionally managed – a task that has been keenly embraced by different breeds of PR experts. Whilst pervasive nowadays, the 'PRisation' of politics is not entirely new. As early as the 1920s, for example, Walter Lippmann acknowledged the crucial intermediary role between politicians and the media of, then, a new type of professional communicator: the press agent (McNair 1999). In the 1930s and 1940s, US president F. D. Roosevelt was famous for his 'fireside chats' on radio with the American people – chats for which he was professionally coached.[1] And, in the 1950s, Eisenhower revealed himself as the first US political leader to understand the sheer importance of PR in politics. He was the first US President to have his television image 'made-over' by a team of media consultants, who turned him into a war hero (Jamieson 1984). In the UK, political PR made its first real entrance during Margaret Thatcher's government in the late 1970s and the 1980s (Louw 2005). Since then, and not unlike in the US and other modern democracies, the PRisation of British politics has become indispensable to journalists and politicians alike.

It is against the above background that this chapter examines political persuasion on television. The first part examines some of the key (non-)verbal resources used by politicians in order to sell particular political images to viewers. In the second part of the chapter, the flip side of the coin, as it were, is explored, namely television's use of a range of (non-)verbal communication resources also to project particular images of politics and politicians to viewers.

**149**

By examining both politicians' use of the television medium and television's use of the field of politics to attain their respective persuasion goals, this chapter further highlights the synergetic relationship that exists between politics and the media. Of course, whether the identified persuasion strategies used by either politicians or journalists actually succeed is a different matter, especially given the current debate about apathy and cynicism amongst the electorate in a number of Western democracies.

## 12.1   Of politicians and their television performances

If there is one television context in which managing one's political image matters greatly, it is that of election debates. These debates are incredibly popular in the US, where they are known to have an impact upon subsequent voting intentions and behaviour (Yawn and Beatty 2000). Because of this, every aspect regarding their conduct is agreed well in advance of their broadcast. From whether or not the candidates will be standing or sitting, will be allowed to walk up to the studio audience or will be able to address each other directly, to the number of commercial breaks and the duration of their opening and closing statements, televised presidential election debates in the US are nothing but carefully crafted persuasion exercises in which the candidates' verbal behaviour contains numerous classical oratory strategies, ranging from syntactic parallelisms (*isocolon*) and rhetorical questions to irony and personification (*prosopopoeia*).[2]

The candidates' non-verbal behaviour is, likewise, painstakingly planned. Before the candidates appear on these debates, professional PR teams are known to coach them explicitly on their posture, facial expression and so forth. The importance given to non-verbal communication here owes mainly to two factors. One is the primacy of non-verbal signs of communication over co-occurring verbal ones in terms of believability (see Chapter 11). It is very important for politicians that their body language, for example, does not 'betray' them during their statements of commitment to the party, the nation, and so on. The other factor is the high visibility (and audibility) that television affords politicians in these debates (see Chapter 11). Facial expressions, hand gestures and the specific intonation with which they deliver particular words all need to be performed just right because they can all be captured in minute detail by the cameras and microphones in the studios where the debates are held.

In light of the above, let us consider Extract 12.1 (see pp. 152–3), which reproduces the closing statements of the US Democrat presidential candidate Senator John Kerry and Republican President George W. Bush during the third and final presidential debate in the run-up to the 2004 US General Presidential election. Bob Schieffer, of the CBS television network, moderated the debate. It was broadcast amidst great media expectations, for it had been marketed as Bush's last chance to beat Kerry, whom media polls had proclaimed winner of the two previous debates. Schieffer opened the broadcast by announcing the debate's general topic (domestic affairs) and briefly explaining its rules. At the end, he gave the two candidates two minutes each for their closing statements.

Unlike in other extracts in this book, the left-hand column of Extract 12.1 only records hand gestures. This is because the type and number of camera angles was exactly the same in the two closing statements: approximately one third of them were close-up shots and the remaining two thirds were medium-range angles. Long-range shots were not used, although they had featured previously in the debate. The decision to use close-up and medium-range angles during the candidates' closing statements to camera was, then, most probably strategic. Through their simulation of close-range, prolonged eye-contact with the viewers, these angles added intensity to the candidates' performances and possibly sought to create a sense of parasocial interaction between them and the viewers (see Chapter 5).

The exclusive use of close-up and medium-range camera angles in the candidates' closing statements made facial expressions, gaze and hand gestures their three key non-verbal (visual) signs of communication. However, both politicians used facial expressions and gaze similarly. Other than brief smiles and glances at the moderator at the start of their statements to acknowledge his yielding the speaking floor to them (lines 03–05, 36–38), Kerry and Bush kept grave facial expressions and looked directly at the camera throughout. In terms of non-verbal behaviour, then, it was their hand gestures that were particularly noteworthy.

Politicians' hand-gesturing has been found to have a persuasive impact on viewers, regardless of whether it is spontaneous or coached (Kendon 1994). In a study of the 2000 US presidential debates, Cienki (2004) found that the hand gestures used by the candidates (Al Gore and George W. Bush) performed three, not mutually exclusive, functions: performative, discursive and referential. Performative gestures comprised a speech act, for example rejecting something with a hand dismissal. Discursive gestures presented or emphasised a point by, for instance, raising one's hand with the index finger pointing upwards to convey determination. As for referential gestures, these designated the form or behaviour of an entity. This entity could be concrete, for example a politician would point to his/her opponent. It could, alternatively, be metaphorical, whereby hand-gesturing was used to depict the source domain through which an abstract topic was being characterised. An example in Cienki's study was Bush's use of flat-handed gestures, in which the palms of both hands faced the body and the fingertips pointed at each other, as if using both hands to form a barrier. These gestures projected an image of strength, especially since they co-occurred with relevant verbal expressions such as 'and a {strong} military' and 'if we're a humble nation, but {strong}, they'll welcome us' (Cienki 2004: 427).

Table 12.1 (see p. 154) lists the hand gestures and co-occurring verbal expressions performed by Kerry and Bush in their closing statements. Half of Kerry's referential gestures pointed to a concrete entity (1, 2, 3). Specifically, they located the entity that was being spoken about (a person, a country, a political idea) in a given physical space ('out there', 'right', 'left', etc.). Whilst these gestures made Kerry's verbal rendition more vivid than had none been used, they actually carried relatively low emotive force. His metaphorical referential gestures (4, 8 and 9), for their part, were not particularly effective in terms of their potential to infuse his words with emotional force. In 4, he

## Closing Statements by Kerry and Bush (CBS, 2004)

[Curly brackets in the right-hand column below indicate the words with which the main 'stroke' phase of the hand gesture co-occurs. A brief description of the gestures is provided between curly brackets in the left-hand column. The notations '2H' and 'RH' designate two-handed and right-hand gestures, respectively. Neither politician used a single left-hand gesture in the closing statements below. S: Bob Schieffer; K: John Kerry; B: George W. Bush.]

| | | |
|---|---|---|
| S talking to K and B | 01 S | well (.) gentlemen (.) that brings us to the closing |
| on stage, opposite | 02 | statements (.) Senator Kerry I believe you're first |
| him. K looks up to | 03 K | (1.6) |
| camera, then to S, | 04 | my fellow Americans (.) as you heard from |
| smiling {RH out to S} | 05 | {Bob (.) Schieffer} a moment ago (.) America is being |
| | 06 | tested by division (.) more than <u>ever</u> (.) we need to be |
| {2H palms up and | 07 | united as a country (.) a::nd (.) like {Franklin Roosevelt} |
| out} | 08 | (.) I don't care whether an idea is a {<u>Republican</u> idea or a |
| {2H sway to R and L} | 09 | Democrat idea} (.) I <u>just</u> care whether it works for |
| | 10 | America and whether it's going to make us <u>stronger</u> (.) |
| | 11 | these are dangerous times (2.0) I believe I offer <u>tested</u> (.) |
| | 12 | strong leadership (.) that can calm the waters of the |
| {2H palms towards | 13 | troubled world (.) and {I believe} that we can (.) together |
| chest} | 14 | (.) do things that are within the grasp of Americans >we |
| | 15 | <u>can</u> lift our schools up (.) we <u>can</u> create jobs that pay more |
| | 16 | than the jobs we're losing overseas< (.) we <u>can</u> have |
| | 17 | health care for <u>all</u> Americans (.) <we <u>can</u> further the cause |
| {Index finger of RH | 18 | of <u>equality</u> in <u>our nation</u>> (2.0) {let me just make it clear} |
| up} | 19 | (.) <u>I</u> will never allow any country to have a veto over our |
| | 20 | security (.) just as <u>I</u> fought for our country as a young man |
| {2H palms up and | 21 | {(.) with the same <u>passion</u> (.)} |
| out} {RH held high} | 22 | I will {<u>fight</u>} to defend this nation that I love (.) and with |
| | 23 | faith in <u>God</u> (.) and with <u>conviction</u> in the mission of |
| {2H palms up and | 24 | {America (.)} I believe that we can reach higher (.) I |
| out} | 25 | believe we can do better (.) I think the greatest |
| | 26 | possibilities of our country (.) <our <u>dreams</u> and our |
| | 27 | <u>hopes</u>> are out there just waiting for us {to grab onto |
| {2H palms up and | 28 | them} (.) and I ask you to embark on that journey with me |
| out} | 29 | (.) I ask you for your <u>trust</u> (.) I ask you for your <u>help</u> (.) I |
| | 30 | ask you to allow me the <u>privilege</u> of <u>leading</u> this <u>great</u> |
| | 31 | nation of ours (.) of helping us to be stronger here at home |
| | 32 | and to be <u>respected</u> again in the world (.) and most of all |

➡

extended the palms of both hands towards his chest as he uttered the words '{I believe}'. However, his hands were directed to the chest, not to its left side – i.e. to his heart. And in 8 and 9, Kerry's gestures were slightly out of sync with the actual referents that they alluded to. Kerry's palms were up and out as he said the words 'America' and 'grab onto them', rather than when he uttered the more emotive, abstract terms '<u>conviction</u>' and '<u>dreams</u> and . . . <u>hopes</u>', respectively.

Kerry's non-referential gestures (5, 6 and 7) were, in principle, better placed

| | | | |
|---|---|---|---|
| | 33 | | (.) to be safer (.) forever (.) thank you (.) good night (.) |
| | 34 | | and God bless the United States of America |
| *S, to B.* | 35 | S | (2.0) Mr President? |
| *B, nods at S and* | 36 | B | (2.0) |
| *smiles. Looks down,* | 37 | | in the Oval Office there's a painting (.) by a friend of- |
| *then up to camera.* | 38 | | Laura and mine name- (.) by Tom Lee (.) and it's a west |
| | 39 | | Texas painting (.) a painting of a mountain scene and (.) |
| | 40 | | he said this about it >he said Sarah and I live on the east |
| | 41 | | side of the mountain (.) it's the sunrise side not the sunset |
| | 42 | | side< (.) it's the side to see the day that's coming not to |
| | 43 | | see the day that's gone (.) I <u>love</u> the optimism in that |
| {*2H palms touch* | 44 | | painting because that's how I {<u>feel</u> about America} (.) and |
| *heart*} | 45 | | we've been through a lot together during the last (.) three |
| | 46 | | and three quarter years (.) we've come through a recession |
| | 47 | | (.) a stock market decline (.) an <u>attack</u> on our country (.) |
| | 48 | | and yet (.) because of the hard work of the American |
| | 49 | | people and good policies this economy is growing (.) over |
| {*2H palms move* | 50 | | the next four years we'll make sure |
| *apart*} | 51 | | {the economy <u>continues</u> to grow} (.) we reformed our |
| {*2H palms come* | 52 | | school system and now there's an achievement gap that's |
| *together*} | 53 | | beginning to {close} (.) over the next four years we'll |
| | 54 | | <u>continue</u> to insist on <u>excellence</u> in every classroom in |
| | 55 | | America so that our children have a chance to realise the |
| | 56 | | great promise of America (.) >over the next four years |
| | 57 | | we'll <u>continue</u> to work to make sure health care is |
| | 58 | | available and affordable< (.) |
| | 59 | | >over the next four years we'll <u>continue</u> to rally the |
| | 60 | | armies of <u>compassion</u>< (.) to help heal the hurt (.) that |
| {*RH in clenched fist* | 61 | | exists in some of our country's neighbourhoods {(.) I'm |
| *moves back and forth*} | 62 | | optimistic that we'll <u>win</u> the war on terror (.)} but I |
| | 63 | | understand it requires firm resolve and clear purpose (.) |
| {*RH in clenched fist* | 64 | | we must |
| *moves back and forth*} | 65 | | {<<u>never</u> waver>} in the face of this enemy tha- these |
| {*RH held high, with* | 66 | | ideologies of hate (.) and as we pursue the enemy |
| *bounces*} {*RH on* | 67 | | wherever it exists (.) we'll also {spread <<u>freedom</u>> (.) and |
| *heart*} | 68 | | <u>liberty</u> (.)} we've got {great <u>faith</u> in the ability of liberty to |
| | 69 | | transform societies} to convert a host- hostile world to a |
| | 70 | | <u>peaceful</u> world (.) my hope for America is a <u>prosperous</u> |
| | 71 | | America (.) a <u>hopeful</u> America and a <u>safer</u> world (.) I want |
| | 72 | | to thank you for listening tonight (.) <I'm asking for your |
| | 73 | | vote> (.) God bless you |

to convey emotion (*pathos*) and/or moral character (*ethos*) to his speech than his referential ones. However, only twice did Kerry accompany these non-referential gestures with emphatic stress, and hence added poignancy (6 and 7). And his most expressive discursive gestures, namely raising either his right hand (7) or his right index finger (5), co-occurred with sentences that relayed elements of his proposed programme. As far as his hand-gesturing was concerned, then, Kerry underplayed emotion.

Table 12.1  Hand gestures and co-occurring verbal expressions in *Closing Statements by Kerry and Bush* (2004)

|  | Gestures | Verbal expressions |
|---|---|---|
| Kerry | 1. {RH out to S} | as you heard from {Bob (.) Schieffer} a moment ago |
|  | 2. {2H palms up and out} | a::nd (.) like {Franklin Roosevelt} |
|  | 3. {2H sway to R and L} | whether an idea is a {Republican idea or a Democrat idea} |
|  | 4. {2H palms towards chest} | {I believe} that we can (.) together (.) do things |
|  | 5. {Index finger of RH up} | {let me just make it clear} |
|  | 6. {2H palms up and out} | as I fought for our country [. . .]{(.) with the same passion (.)} |
|  | 7. {RH held high} | I will {fight} to defend this nation that I love |
|  | 8. {2H palms up and out} | and with conviction in the mission of {America (.)} |
|  | 9. {2H palms up and out} | <our dreams and our hopes> are out there just waiting for us {to grab onto them} |
| Bush | 1. {2H palms touch left side of chest} | I love [. . .] because that's how {I feel about America} |
|  | 2. {2H palms move apart} | we'll make sure {the economy continues to grow} |
|  | 3. {2H palms come together} | and now there's an achievement gap that's beginning to {close} |
|  | 4. {RH in clenched fist, moves back and forth} | {(.) I'm optimistic that we'll win the war on terror (.)} but I understand it requires firm resolve |
|  | 5. {RH in clenched fist, moves back and forth} | we must {<never waver>} in the face of this enemy tha-these ideologies of hate |
|  | 6. {RH held high, with bounces} | we'll also {spread <freedom> (.) and liberty (.)} |
|  | 7. {RH on left side of chest} | we've got {great faith in the ability of liberty to transform societies} |

In contrast, Bush used hand gestures primarily to actualise emotion. His only non-referential gesturing (repeated in 4 and 5) sought to infuse his words with strength and determination – note his clenched fist in motion. His metaphorical referential gesturing pointed to, and was well synced with, verbal references to the abstract entities of feelings: 'freedom and liberty' (6) and 'great faith' (7). In 1 and 7, he placed the palm(s) of his hand(s) on the left side of his chest. The first of these instances, in particular, is worth discussing further.

It occurred within a descriptive sequence at the onset of his closing statement, in which he compared America to a painting in the Oval Office (lines 37–44). During this description, he talked about both the artist's (lines 40–43) and his (lines 43–44) feelings towards the painting. The former were relayed through constructed dialogue ('and (.) he said this about it'>he said Sarah and I . . .', lines 39–40), which has the ability to make speech more vivid and to conjure up more easily the evoked world than indirect reported speech ('he said that . . .') has.[3] The latter were expressed in emotive terms ('I love', 'I {feel', lines

43–44) and co-occurred with Bush bringing both hands to his heart – to the part of the human body that symbolises one's feelings. This combination of emotional language and heartfelt gesturing sought to persuade viewers through *ethos* and *pathos* from within the currently valued political images of deeply held values and emotional expressiveness (see Chapter 11). The relevance of Bush's description to the argumentation (*logos*) of the remainder of this statement was next established in lines 44–47 through references to past hardships (the sunset side of the mountain) and, in lines 48–72, through the belief in a promising future (the sunrise side of the mountain).

So, both Kerry and Bush made strategic use of non-verbal behaviour in their closing statements to project particular political images that, respectively, underplayed and emphasised emotion. These images were also communicated through verbal behaviour, of course. Within the context of televised addresses to the public, they were indeed crucially constructed in and through the ways in which Kerry and Bush verbally positioned themselves in relation to their viewers, i.e. through their selection of forms of address.

Politicians need to make a number of important decisions in their televised addresses to the general public regarding how to relate to what, to all intents and purposes, is an incredibly diverse viewing audience. In doing so, they often postulate a subject position for a 'typified "ideal" hearer', that is, for someone who may represent the 'typical' views, aspirations and hopes of 'the people' and 'by implication the audience as well' (Fairclough 1989: 178).

In Extract 12.1, Kerry and Bush drew upon similar forms of address in order to relate to this typified ideal hearer. They used only sparingly direct forms of address, either the second-person pronoun 'you' or, in Kerry's case, the appellative 'my fellow Americans' (line 04). The former featured mainly at the end of their statements and was the direct object of the performative verbs 'to ask', 'to thank' and 'to bless'. Kerry's appellative set the tone of the rest of his closing statement as an exhortation.

Both politicians favoured indirect forms of address, either nominal references or the first-person plural pronoun 'we'. Nominal references were used eight times by each candidate. They included 'America', 'Americans', 'the United States of America', 'the American people' and various positively qualified versions of 'nation' or 'America', such as 'this nation that I love' (Kerry, line 22) and 'the great promise of America' (Bush, lines 55–56). Used as forms of address, nominal references signal the most distance between interactants, for they exclude any direct, explicit reference to their co-existence within a given interactional space. However, because the referents selected by Kerry and Bush conjure up images of a collective, they placed candidates and viewers together in the shared space of 'Americanness'.

More frequent than nominal references in both politicians' statements was their use of the first-person plural pronoun 'we' as a form of address: nineteen occurrences in Kerry's statement and fifteen in Bush's. This is hardly surprising given the vagueness that characterises this pronoun and that makes it one of the most strategic pronominal choices in political (and other) communication contexts. Biber et al.'s (1999) work, for instance, has shown that the referential vagueness of the pronoun 'we' can ultimately be resolved only by its intended addressee(s). In the context of televised presidential election debates, use of the intrinsically ambiguous pronoun 'we' can help politicians to cast their persuasion net as widely as possible.

From a grammatical perspective, one can distinguish up to eight different uses of 'we' (Quirk et al. 1985). From the perspective of political persuasion in televised addresses to the general public, two of these are the most interesting: exclusive and inclusive 'we'. Exclusive 'we' has the capacity to distance the speaker from the hearer. It is for this reason normally associated with power imbalance between interactants. Inclusive 'we', in contrast, positions speaker and hearer within the same group and is therefore associated with solidarity and egalitarian relations.[4]

In US politics, inclusive and exclusive 'we' potentially appeal to two different patterns of thinking, or metaphorical models, about the American nation: (1) the 'nurturant parent family', and (2) the 'strict father family'. Both models are subsumed beneath a more general one, which sees the nation as a family. The nurturant parent family model is generally associated with liberal, or left-wing, political views. It sees the family (the US nation) as a team working together and sharing household (nation-building) responsibilities. The strict father family metaphor, in turn, is generally associated with conservative, or right-wing, political views. It is built upon a patriarchal family model in which the father (the President and his administration) provides for the children (the citizens), who must learn to become self-sufficient (Lakoff 1996).

In his closing statement, Kerry used inclusive 'we', making emphatic, explicit references to politician–political party–citizenship togetherness: 'we can (.) together' + 'lift our schools up', 'create jobs', 'have health care for all Americans', 'reach higher', 'do better', and so forth. Kerry therefore related to his viewers from within the nurturant family model. Since 'we' was the subject of clauses about what would happen if he were elected, the alleged egalitarian position of this model implicated the audiences in his projections of the future. Rather than the site of the possible and the potential, the future was in this way constructed as an ideological site already shared and agreed upon by Kerry, his party and the American people.

Bush, too, used inclusive 'we' throughout his closing statement. In those clauses (a total of five) that referred to events in the past, he made a point of constructing President–administration–citizenship togetherness: 'we've been through a lot together . . .' (line 45) and 'we've come through a recession [. . .] an attack on our country' (lines 46–47). In this way, he specifically sought to present himself as just one more hard-hit American. The use of inclusive 'we' helped to project the image of an emotionally expressive leader touched by and in touch with his citizens' trauma after 9/11. When it came to constructing responsibility for the future, Bush was careful to list the two pillars upon which the American family/nation rested, namely the citizens and the President's administration: *'because of the hard work of the American people and good policies*, this economy is growing (.) over the next four years we'll make sure {the economy <u>continues</u> to grow} . . . over the next four years we'll <u>continue</u> to insist on <u>excellence</u> in every classroom in America . . . over the next four years we'll <u>continue</u> to rally the armies of <u>compassion</u> . . . we'll <u>win</u> the war on terror . . .' (lines 48–62). The causal subordinate clause with which he opened his list (italicised above) constructed, just as Kerry had done, an uncertain time period (the future) as an ideologically shared and agreed one by a leader seeking re-election, his administration and the American people.

This part of the chapter has identified and discussed some of the self-presentational work undertaken in Bush and Kerry's closing statements to the public in the third presidential debate of the 2004 US Presidential Election, specifically their use of hand gestures and forms of address. Through these, and other (non-)verbal resources, politicians like Kerry and Bush project their political images in public. This process, Corner and Pels (2003: 10) argue, 'is partly a matter of choice (a conscious "branding" exercise designed to sharpen profile) and partly a required reaction to the terms of media visibility that now frame and interpret political action in many countries'. And it is to the latter that this chapter now turns by looking at what one of the main media responsible for increased political visibility – television – makes of politicians' on-screen appearances. Special attention is paid to television's representation of their non-verbal behaviour and their projected relationships with viewers and fellow politicians.

## 12.2    Of television and its metalanguage on politicians

In 'Sound bite news', Hallin (1992) compared the coverage by CBS and ABC of two US presidential elections across time, focusing on sound-bites that featured politicians speaking. He found that the average length of the sound-bite had shrunk from over forty seconds in 1968 to less than ten seconds in 1988. This begged the question: Where had all the additional seconds from the televised coverage of politics in the late 1960s gone? The answer, Hallin's study revealed, was: to the journalists. By the late 1980s, journalists regularly treated politicians' public appearances as 'raw material to be taken apart, combined with other sounds and images, and reintegrated into a new narrative' (1992: 9–10): that of the journalists'.

Recurrent ways of combining and repackaging politicians' public appearances for television purposes included extensive use of visuals (film and graphics), a considerable rise in the number of evaluative 'wrap-ups' by journalists at the end of news items, and an increasing tendency to incorporate material from different settings simultaneously into news reports. As an example of the latter, Hallin provided the case of a CBS story during the 1984 presidential campaign that included a sound-bite in which a single sentence by George H. Bush was made up of five one-second sound-bites taken from five different speeches.

Reflecting upon his findings, Hallin concluded that the television coverage of politics in the 1980s was often more attention-grabbing than in the 1960s. It also offered, in a way, more serious journalism because it sought to uncover the image-making strategies deployed by politicians in what was already a political climate of increased visibility. Nonetheless, Hallin also described the new practices as disturbing on three grounds. First, showing candidates speaking for no longer than approximately twenty seconds made it difficult for the viewers to understand candidates' arguments. Secondly, journalists' evaluative wrap-ups denied viewers the ability to judge for themselves. Thirdly, television's predilection for reporting on the PR side of the political process contributed to enhancing viewer cynicism towards politics.

Hallin's findings regarding television's coverage of politics in the late 1980s are easily transposable to nowadays. Not only is the micro-sound-bite culture still going strong and the use of visuals more frequent and sophisticated than ever before but the role of the journalist as primary communicator has also grown exponentially in recent years. This has often led to the coverage of politicians' public appearances being edited in different ways so as to fit journalists' news stories.

Consider, in this light, Extract 12.2, which is part of the extensive UK media coverage following publication of *The Hutton Report* (see Chapter 6 for story background). The editing strategy was to introduce the news item (lines 01–04), then attach to it a sound-bite containing one of the politician's answers during a previously recorded interview (lines 05–12), and then move on to the next reportable fact in the 'complicating action' (Labov 1972a) of the reporter's story (line 13). The interview question that triggered Davis's sound-bite was

---

**EXTRACT 12.2**

### *ITV News (ITV, 2004)*

[This extract comes from a live news update and relays Lord Hutton's decision to exonerate the UK Labour Government of any responsibility regarding the death of WMD expert Dr Kelly. R: Reporter Paul Davies; D: Conservative Shadow Cabinet Member David Davis; BBC HQ: BBC Headquarters.]

| | | | |
|---|---|---|---|
| *LS – Lord Hutton* | 01 | R | although Lord Hutton's report clears the |
| *stepping out of car* | 02 | (vo) | Prime Minister of any blame (.) |
| *and walking* | 03 | | the Conservatives <u>insist</u> Michael Howard <u>won't</u> be |
| *towards building.* | 04 | | apologising to him |
| *CU – D, to camera,* | 05 | D | what <u>for</u>? for challenging Mr Blair's er er account of |
| *looking angry.* | 06 | | events? (.) it <u>changed</u> <u>actually</u> over the course of yesterday |
| | 07 | | (.) <u>before</u> Lord Hutton's report came out (.) er Mr Blair |
| | 08 | | had <u>famously</u> denied <u>any</u> responsi<u>bility</u> for the naming of |
| | 09 | | Dr Kelly (.) on the aircr- er (.) with the journalists |
| | 10 | | <u>yesterday</u> he completely <u>changed</u> his tune and he said it |
| | 11 | | was <u>his</u> duty to name him because <u>of course</u> the report |
| *LS – BBC HQ. To* | 12 | | <had <u>exonerated</u> him> |
| *camera, outside* | 13 | R | but this lunchtime all eyes are on the BBC |
| *BBC HQ.* | 14 | | [. . .] |

edited out but the reporter's own cue (lines 03–04) and Davis's questions (lines 05–06) imply it to be along the lines of 'Will Howard apologise to Blair?' In his sound-bite, Davis appeared openly annoyed. Note his first challenge in line 05. This was delivered as a question ('<u>what</u> for?'), given emphatic stress and filmed via a close-up of him looking angry. The rest of his contribution was equally adversarial. He, for example, made extensive use of emphatic stress (underlined in the extract) and used categorical expressions, such as 'had <u>famously</u> denied <u>any</u> responsi<u>bility</u>' (line 08) and 'com<u>pletely</u> <u>changed</u> his tune' (line 10).

That Davis's contribution in this sound-bite was far from conciliatory is beyond question. One wonders, however, was it representative of the interview in its entirety? Or was it carefully selected because it fitted a particular 'professional vision', that is, a specific set of 'socially organized ways of seeing and understanding events that are answerable to the distinctive interests of a particular social group' (Goodwin and Goodwin 1997: 293). In other words, the journalist's story may well have been filtered through the media's vision of politics as conflict and of politicians as more interested in exposing their opponents than in tending the interests of the general public. Van Zoonen (2003) has argued that politics is often portrayed in the media as a soap opera – one often about cabinet strife, personal conflicts and interparty and intraparty rivalries. She cites examples of journalistic commentary in the UK and the US in support of her argument. For the UK, for instance: 'This is politics as soap opera: A Downing Street tale of broken friendship, betrayal and revenge that would not be out of place on BBC or ITV' (Maguire 2001); and for the US: 'American primaries have witnessed soap opera-like drama' (Hicks 2000a); 'scripts for a soap opera' (Hicks 2000b). This vision is particularly appealing to television's confrontainment agenda.

Also beyond question is that editing practices such as the one in Extract 12.2 recontextualise politicians' discourse. Recontextualisation is a discourse practice whereby a stretch of text, whether spoken or written, is taken from its original context and put into another (Linell 1998). Because the meaning of any text always depends on the context in which it appears, recontextualisations inevitably carry a change of meaning. They are therefore not neutral accounts of what has been said. On the contrary, they reflect their author's control over what is being retold and how it is being restructured (Caldas-Coulthard 1994). They are always performed in accordance with the author's view of the world, which is not to say that their author's subjectivity is always acknowledged.

The reporter's recontextualisation in Extract 12.2 entailed, for example, an instance of the strategic use of metalanguage (see Chapter 11). In line 03, he framed the sound-bite featuring Davis's answer with the verb 'to insist'. *Verba dicenda* (e.g. 'to insist' 'to urge', 'to complain', 'to demand') do not merely relay others' words. Instead, they label and categorise them, thereby embedding their author's assumptions about what and who is being reported. On this occasion, the reporter's narrative transformed the Conservative Party's request for a public apology from the Labour Party into a personal clash between these parties' respective leaders: 'the Conservatives <u>insist</u> Michael Howard <u>won't</u> be apologising to him [Tony Blair]' (lines 03–04). It was the journalist's version of the political event being reported on that viewers received. Davis's discourse was transformed into argument-building evidence for the journalist's story.

The strategic recontextualisation of politicians' verbal behaviour through sound-bites in news reports such as the one in Extract 12.2 is a well-documented strategy in media communication (e.g. Ekström 2001; Nylund 2003). Less recognised is television's strategic representation of politicians' *non*-verbal behaviour, which nevertheless illustrates television's capacity to exploit the believability yet indeterminacy surrounding non-verbal signs of communication (see Chapter 11).

Jaworski and Galasiński (2002) examined the UK newspaper coverage of former US President Clinton's non-verbal behaviour during his Grand Jury video testimony about his relationship with Monica Lewinsky. Across 'quality' (broadsheet) and 'tabloid' newspapers, Clinton's non-verbal behaviour was linked to his moral character. In other words, his political image (*ethos*) was assessed on the basis of his non-verbal behaviour, as reproduced in a series of photographic images from his video testimony. The ambiguity yet credibility of these images was exploited by all the newspapers. The same images, however, were interpreted differently by different newspapers. A photograph of Clinton looking up from above his reading glasses, for instance, was metarepresented by the tabloid *Sun* ('Deceit: Specs can't hide his mounting desperation') as a sign of lying by the tabloid *Daily Mail* ('Anguished') and as a sign of distress . By anchoring these visual signs (photographs of Clinton) to such verbal captions, the newspapers 'disambiguated' the politician's non-verbal behaviour in ways that suited their ideological orientations. As might be expected, the evaluation of Clinton's non-verbal behaviour was more positive in the broadsheet and left-leaning newspapers than in the tabloids and right-leaning newspapers. This study also found that the newspapers regularly quoted non-verbal communication experts, whose views always matched the ideological preferences of their respective newspapers. These experts were clearly used to help to construct the newspapers' own professional vision of Clinton. Extract 12.3 (see p. 161) provides a further example, this time from television, of how the media's metalanguage on politicians' non-verbal behaviour projects particular ways of seeing and understanding politics and politicians to viewers.

In both Extracts 12.2 and 12.3, part of a text was taken out of its original context (a political interview in Extract 12.2 and a political speech in Extract 12.3) and transferred into a new one (a sound-bite in a live news report on both occasions). In both extracts, too, the re-contextualised text emphasised the 'human' (emotional) side of politics. In Extract 12.2, anger was displayed by Davis and strategically interpreted by the reporter. In Extract 12.3, Kerry appeared overwhelmed – an emotional display that was also strategically commented upon by Simpson. Specifically, the sound-bite in Extract 12.3 showed, in close-up, a politician apparently struggling to control his voice and to finish his sentence (lines 06–07). This was followed by a long-range shot of his supporters at the Boston Democrat Headquarters, offering him a long and loud round of applause (lines 08–09). Next, there was another close-up of a

### BBC News (BBC, 2004)

[The extract corresponds to the opening thirty seconds of a live two-way. It features BBC senior correspondent John Simpson at the Democrat Headquarters in Boston, where John Kerry has just made his speech of concession in the immediate aftermath of his defeat in the 2004 US Presidential Elction. S: John Simpson; K: John Kerry; DH: Democrat Headquarters.]

| | | | |
|---|---|---|---|
| LS – S, standing outside<br>DH in Boston. To<br>camera. | 01<br>02<br>03<br>04<br>05 | S | <from the <u>depths</u> of his<br>disappointment> (.) <in the <u>manner</u><br>of his leaving> (.) <u>tonight</u> America<br>saw a John Kerry it hadn't seen<br>before (.) |
| CU – Kerry, on stage, to live<br>audience. LS – K in DH.<br>CU – K acknowledges support with<br>head nod and smile. | 06<br>07<br>08<br>09 | K | I wish I could wrap you up in my<br>arms (voice breaks) a::nd =<br>= (5.0) loud round of applause from<br>audience |
| CU – S, looking down to a monitor<br>as though taken aback, then to<br>camera. | 10<br>11<br>12<br>13 | S | (2.0) John Kerry more moved than<br>he'd ever been (.) it was his <u>greatest</u><br>speech (.) Americans seeing the <u>raw</u><br><u>man</u> for the <u>first</u> time |
| LS – K, on stage being comforted. | 14<br>15 | (vo) | (2.0) he enjoyed the warm embrace<br>of his colleagues [. . .] |

visibly touched Kerry, in which he acknowledged with a nod and a smile his colleagues and supporters (lines 08–09). The sound-bite thus contained just one, incomplete, sentence by Kerry. Yet it contained non-verbal signs of communication that were constructed as especially newsworthy.

Simpson's decision to use the above sound-bite within the opening seconds of his live news report was probably determined by Kerry's display of emotion, which incidentally lasted no more than ten seconds within his sixteen-minute concession speech. Kerry's apparent difficulty in controlling his voice was treated as exceptional in the report. During the 2004 US presidential campaign, viewers were (over)exposed to Kerry's 'publicness' in a variety of television contexts, ranging from election debates to interviews. In these, he consistently projected a political image that underplayed emotion. The contrast between the hitherto emotionally inexpressive Kerry and the Kerry laying bare his feelings in public is what made the sound-bite in Extract 12.3 particularly newsworthy. Consider, for example, Simpson's mood reporting in lines 01–05: '*<from the depths of his disappointment> (.) <in the manner of his leaving> (.)* tonight America saw a John Kerry it hadn't seen before (.)'. The two adverbial clauses (in italics above) were delivered slowly, with emphatic stress, and were punctuated by micropauses.

Simpson projected his own mood, too, in his report. A two-second pause after Kerry's sound-bite offered a visual close-up of the reporter looking down in, presumably, the direction of a monitor that had just shown the sound-bite (lines 10–11). During this moment of live silence, Simpson appeared personally taken aback. This strengthened the impression that he and the viewers, through his report, had just witnessed an exceptional display of emotion.

In Extract 12.3, then, a politician's non-verbal behaviour was made salient both through the use of a particular sound-bite within the opening seconds of a live news report and through the news reporter's strategic metarepresentation of the non-verbal behaviour of its speaker. Yet the sound-bite did more than project Simpson's professional vision of Kerry's emotional expressiveness via his non-verbal behaviour. It treated the latter as indexical of Kerry's identity. Kerry's breaking voice was transformed into a signifier of the new 'John Kerry'. Note, in this respect, Simpson's explicit association of 'the manner of his [Kerry's] leaving (i.e. his emotional paralanguage) with 'a John Kerry it [America] hadn't seen before'. This new Kerry was, in turn, evaluated as more genuine than the old one: 'Americans seeing the raw man for the first time' (lines 12–13). Note, too, that just one feature of Kerry's non-verbal behaviour was held responsible for a politician's delivering 'his greatest speech' ever (line 11–12).

Simpson's metalanguage thus crafted a particular political image of Kerry – all the more persuasively so, given Simpson's professional standing as one of the UK's most senior and reputable editors. This image resonated with the contemporary emphasis on emotional expressiveness as a potential guarantor of moral worthiness. Simpson's report presented displaying emotion, verbally and/or non-verbally, as necessary behaviour for a member of a valued group: political leaders. Whilst this was extant in that group, by metarepresenting it in favourable terms, Simpson's report reinforced its social acceptability and further constructed social disapproval of 'deviant' forms of political behaviour, such as those of the 'old', 'un-emotional' Kerry.

## 12.3 Conclusion

Political persuasion on television reflects the strong synergetic relationship that exists between journalists and politicians. Both are locked in a process of mutual adaptation and influence. Politicians' ability to perform well on television is essential to their political survival. Coached by their PR teams, they try to sell to viewers what has effectively become a vital form of 'cultural capital' (Fairclough 1998: 150): their political image. And swept on by today's celebrity culture, they seek to capitalise upon the intense interest that their emotions and private lives generate.

This is not to say, however, that all politicians cultivate the same image on television, even if they often draw upon similar means of persuasion. As regards non-verbal behaviour, for example, the analysis of the closing statements by Kerry and Bush showed that the former opted for gestures that underplayed emotion. In contrast, Bush synced his hand gestures with emphatic, affectively rich language to project an image of a leader with deeply held personal values.

In addition to highlighting the salience of certain (non-)verbal signs of communication in televised political rhetoric, this chapter has examined television's extensive coverage of politicians' public appearances. That in a celebrity-obsessed era television constantly scrutinises politicians' performances is hardly surprising. It is arguably the price they pay for their increased visibility. But whilst politicians' behaviour is closely scrutinised on television, the ideological dimension of such scrutiny is rarely recognised. Instead, and as the examples of the two news reports containing sound-bites of politicians in the second half of this chapter have illustrated, journalists regularly construct subjective ways of seeing politics and politicians. The subjectivity of their professional visions is, however, not explicitly recognised, even if the style in which they are delivered is often openly so. Nowadays, for instance, the media often and openly refer to the image of politics as interpersonal conflict and politicians as individuals whose emotions and private lives are free for public consumption.

Television's coverage of politics and politicians reflects Cameron's (2004: 312) metaphor on metalanguage below:

> Metalanguage is like one of those supernatural wish-fulfilling creatures that so often appear in myths and fairy tales – a Genie, for example. Freed from the bottle, the Genie agrees to grant the liberator's every wish; at first the requests are for necessary, useful things, but as the story progresses they become more and more excessive. No-one can stop a person who has secured a Genie's services from using them for unnecessary and even ridiculous ends. The Genie's promise is unconditional, and it cannot be taken back ('you can't put the Genie back in the bottle').

Perhaps television's metalanguage on politicians was initially a 'necessary, useful' tool, namely to enable the watch-dog role of journalists to evolve. We should also take care not to over-state its influence. Television cannot imprint its professional vision of politics and politicians as if viewers were emotional and cognitive *tabula rasa* (Hall 1974). Nor, simply because it can sway some viewers, can television automatically influence policy-makers. For the latter to occur, policy-makers need to be influenced by mass citizenries. This is increasing in frequency but is still far from always the case (Louw 2005).[5] Nevertheless, just as with the Genie in Cameron's metaphor above, the chances of television's metalanguage on politicians returning to its bottle are remote in today's political climate of increased visibility – even if it does seem to be increasingly used to a number of 'unnecessary' ends, such as continuous (re)interpretation of the relationship between politicians' non-verbal behaviour and their political credibility.

# Persuasion and Lifestyle Television

13

Chapter 12 examined politicians' appearances before the cameras and television's metalanguage in relation to these appearances. It highlighted the part played by emotional expressiveness in the construction of appealing political images. Being able to share one's feelings with viewers, it was argued, is a symbolic good upon which many politicians draw in order to try to secure viewer support. It is also a symbolic good that political correspondents and pundits may use to persuade viewers to partake of their professional vision of the field of politics. Whilst this chapter also examines the part played by symbolic goods in television's persuasion, it does so in the context of lifestyle programming. This encompasses a range of programmes in which ordinary members of the public receive some expert advice or treatment in relation to a range of life domains: gardening, interior decoration, cooking, interpersonal skills, personal grooming, holiday habits, and so forth. The analysis focuses mainly on the lifestyle television variety of the property show, although it also makes reference to personal appearance make-over shows, and holiday and cookery programmes.

The first part of the chapter discusses lifestyle television's showcasing of tangible, consumer products as both reflecting and constituting desirable lifestyles and identities. In doing so, it reveals two central features of the discourse of these programmes: the celebration of superficiality and the construction and alleged democratisation of a 'universal notion of taste' (Moseley 2000). The second part moves on to explore the main participation frameworks through which lifestyles are constructed in these shows as desirable or otherwise. It pays particular attention to the figure of the presenter, in particular to its current status as an approachable 'personality-interpreter'. The latter requires presenters not only to dilute their previously authoritarian, detached teaching style, but also to be seen to engage in the same routine activities around the familiar spheres of the house and the garden, etc., as do the ordinary participants nowadays regularly featured in lifestyle shows. From within such positions of engagement, the presenters of lifestyle television programmes nevertheless seek to influence how ordinary participants and, potentially, viewers may come to assess particular lifestyles.

## 13.1   Lifestyle television: Celebrating superficiality and democratising taste

In the UK, lifestyle programmes began to replace situation comedies and 'high-status' genres, such as current affairs programmes and documentaries in the early 1990s (Brunsdon et al. 2001, Moseley 2000). Since then they have remained a popular form of broadcasting. One of the reasons for their continuing success is that they are low-budget programmes. Another reason is the strong symbiotic relationship that they enjoy with the powerful leisure and culture industries. In personal appearance make-over programmes, for instance, presenters advise ordinary people on how to change their outward appearance – a transformation that, amongst other things, tends to require a new wardrobe and a visit to the hairdresser's and beauty salon. At the beginning of many episodes old clothes are thrown away and new ones purchased. Old beauty regimes are abandoned, and new facial and hair treatments willingly embraced. The clothes and cosmetics used in the shows are not for sale, but the relevant brands and the businesses that stock them receive a certain amount of publicity, via footage of their products and premises and/or via explicit mention in the closing credits and the programme websites.

As well as acting as commercial intertexts for the goods and services of others (Bonner 2003; Meehan 1991), lifestyle shows promote their own products. These, however, tend to be of a symbolic nature. In one of the most popular varieties of the lifestyle genre in the UK, the home-improvement show, presenters (who are also the experts) show ordinary members of the public who are struggling to sell their properties how to give them a 'make-over' that will lead to a quick and lucrative sale. In the 2007 series of *Selling Houses* (Channel 4), for example, presenter Andrew Winter 'goes on an international rescue mission across Europe to help Brits who are having major problems selling their foreign properties [. . .] he leaves no stone unturned in his quest to secure that all important sale.'[1] The rationale in shows such as *Selling Houses* is that, by showing ordinary people being 'rescued' by the presenters' advice, viewers will be able to apply the lessons taught on the screen to their future real-life projects – that they will subsequently 'do it themselves'. This rationale is in line with what Rose (1999: 92) calls 'the pedagogies of expertise', whereby ordinary people are believed to internalise as codes of conduct knowledge and attitudes acquired from professionals or experts (see also Bonner 2003).

In their didactic ethos, home-improvement shows are the contemporary version of the leisure shows of the late 1960s–early 1970s, themselves a broadcast adaptation of the traditional DIY print manual. But, as Extract 13.1 (see p. 166) illustrates, there is significantly more to today's shows than DIY tips. Here, Winter gives Claire a lesson on how to show personal commitment to the product that one wants to sell (lines 01–03). A few moments later, Claire is filmed putting Winter's lesson into action (lines 05–08). Here, she discursively transforms a material space (a patio) into a symbolic place for stylish relaxation (drinking wine) and warmth (sitting outdoors on a summer evening). In the context of the UK, references to wine

---

**EXTRACT 13.1**

**Selling Houses (Channel 4, 2003)**

[Andrew Winter has conducted a one-week property make-over. He is now walking the house vendor, Claire, through the rooms of her house and explaining the changes made. Both stop in the kitchen, which has French-style double doors leading to a patio area. W: Andrew Winter; C: Claire; B: prospective buyer.]

| | | | |
|---|---|---|---|
| *MS – W and C* | 01 | W | it's just telling people how much <u>you</u>'ve |
| *standing in kitchen.* | 02 | | enjoyed living here so <u>they</u> get the feeling |
| *CU – W, to C.* | 03 | | that they will enjoy living here as well [. . .] |
| *LS – C showing house* | 04 | | |
| *rooms to B. CU – C* | 05 | C | [. . .] and then it's the patio (.) |
| *points at patio. MS –* | 06 | | we can sit out there (.) like in a summer |
| *C and B step on to* | 07 | | evening and (smiles) enjoy <u>far</u> too much wine |
| *patio. CU – B looks* | 08 | | [ giggles |
| *around pleased.* | 09 | B | [ <u>very</u> nice (nods in agreement) = |
| *LS – C and B stepping* | 10 | W | = <u>that's it</u> Claire (.) sell them the |
| *back into the house.* | 11 | (vo) | <<u>lifestyle</u> > [. . .] |

---

and outdoor living are resonant of appealing foreign lifestyles, as actively promoted in travel shows and the leisure industry. They conjure up, in particular, images of foreign destinations in countries that are seen as sophisticated, warm, relaxed and, on the whole, desirable: France and favourite Mediterranean destinations in Greece, Italy and Spain. The scene reproduced in Extract 13.1 ends with a close-up of the prospective buyer looking and sounding convinced by Claire's sales pitch (lines 08–09), which is immediately followed by the presenter's voice-over: '= <u>that's it</u> Claire (.) sell them the <<u>lifestyle</u> >' (lines 10–11). Winter's message could not be any clearer: (1) one sells lifestyles (here, a Mediterranean one) not houses; and (2) to do so, one wraps such lifestyles in easily recognisable and fashionable consumer choices (here, a patio area and a glass of wine). The mundane, safe and private domain of the home is thereby constructed as an enjoyable space and used to persuade viewers to partake of desirable lifestyles.

The permeability of material and symbolic goods in lifestyle television is particularly evident in the moment of revelation – or reveal – in many personal appearance make-over shows – the moment when the presenters unveil for the first time their finished 'product' both to the ordinary people concerned and to the viewers. Appropriate ambient music, camera close-ups of material (e.g. new make-up and accessories) and symbolic (e.g. younger, livelier personality) goods, and off-screen presenter descriptions of their achievements are offered simultaneously during these moments of revelation. At times, images of the person before and after the make-over are also provided simultaneously on the screen for greater effect. The left-hand side of the television, containing the before-make-over images, shows not just a person with a bad make-up style or a poor choice of accessories (by the shows' standards, that is), it also shows an unhappy looking person – a person who might have wanted to smile for the cameras (it is natural for most of us to do so) but was probably asked not to.

The after-make-over side of the screen, on the right-hand side, shows a trendier make-up style and outfit – once more, according to the shows' aesthetic criteria. It also shows a much happier person, one who poses confidently for the cameras as the proud recipient of not just a new wardrobe and cosmetics bag but also a 'better' personality. In a number of cases, too, this much happier person is also a person who, upon seeing the whole transformation 'for the first time', appears very surprised and highly emotional. Mosely (2000) argues that this merging of private experience and public display in the moment of revelation has the potential of making viewers uncomfortable. Yet, the extent to which the moment of revelation may become 'excessive' is carefully assessed by the shows' producers, who hold it 'just to the point of discomfort before it is cut' (Bonner 2003: 132).

Part of the persuasion potential of the reveal in make-over shows lies in the fact that viewers are not told either to purchase this or that hair product or kitchen appliance or to opt for this or that grooming regime or interior decoration style. Instead, the moment of revelation shows the persuader (the presenter) and the persuadee(s) (the ordinary person on the screen and, next, members of his/her family and/or friends) in agreement regarding the positive outcome of the make-over. Even if viewers disagree with the aesthetic choices involved in these make-overs, they will probably have to agree that the result (a house that sells, a happier person, a satisfied relative and/or friend) is a better option than the alternative of non-persuasion (a house still for sale, an unconfident person, a dissatisfied relative and/or friend). One is reminded at this point of Van Dijk's (1998) thesis that, for persuasion to work, persuader and persuadee(s) must agree that the implications of non-persuasion, as it were, are worse than those of persuasion. This agreement is grounded in an implicit threat and affirms the close connection that exists between persuasion and power.

Lifestyle television's ability to sell certain symbolic products, such as good aesthetic taste or a Mediterranean-home living style, relies on its ability to convince viewers that these can be acquired with little time, little effort and little capital. Property shows, for example, make an explicit point of highlighting how little time is needed to achieve one's dream-home lifestyle. Most of these programmes work to self-imposed deadlines of normally between three and seven days to help participants to achieve their goal of either buying or selling a property.[2] For instance, in Extract 13.2 (see p. 168), the presenter of *Selling Houses* flags the fact that incredible transformations to a property can be achieved within just one week.

As in Extract 13.1, Extract 13.2 contains a clear message – this time that it is easy to secure a quick sale so long as one follows the show's make-over rules. The persuasiveness of this message comes from a clever combination of (para-)language and camera angles, both of which emphasise the contrast between the situation before and after Winter's make-over. Starting with the situation before, the presenter describes the property as 'a tired shell' (line 01) that 'was <u>destined</u> to be on the market for a <<u>long long</u> time> (4.0)' (lines

**EXTRACT 13.2**

**Selling Houses (Channel 4, 2003)**

[The extract corresponds to the final three minutes of the episode. Winter and the owner of the made-over property are sitting in one of its newly decorated rooms. W: Andrew Winter; O: Owner.]

| MS, LS, CU – kitchen | 01 | W | <just a week ago> this house was a tired shell |
| and other rooms | 02 | (vo) | (.) it was destined to be on the market for |
| before make-over. | 03 | | a <long long time> (4.0) |
| CU – W to camera. | 04 | | since then things have changed |
| MS, LS, CU – kitchen | 05 | | dramatically [. . .] |
| and other rooms after | 06 | | [description of room changes over background |
| make-over. | 07 | | of soothing, classical music.] |
| LS – W and O in | 08 | O | so after a year of waiting and all the viewings |
| kitchen. CU – O, to | 09 | | (.) one week make-over and it sold on the first |
| camera, looks | 10 | | day (.) marvellous |
| satisfied. | 11 | | (laughs) [. . .] |

01–03). His use of emphatic stress, his repetition of the adjective 'long' and his markedly slow speech delivery in '<long long time>' all convey the impression that this situation has been not only lengthy but frustrating. The choice of the verbal phrase 'destined to be' also suggests that, without the presenter's help, the house would have been doomed not to sell. This impression is strengthened by the owner's remark: 'after a year of waiting and all the viewings (line 08).

As for the situation after the make-over, this is presented to viewers as entailing a comprehensive and exceptional transformation. Winter refers to 'things hav[ing] changed dramatically' (lines 04–05) and, in lines 09–11, the owner emphasises his favourable evaluation of the 'marvellous' make-over through positive paralanguage (laughter) and body language (satisfied look to camera). Both presenter and owner make the point that these results have been achieved within a week (line 01, line 09) and the owner refers also to the fact that the house 'sold on the first day' (lines 09–10) of its being back on the market.

The strength of the before–after contrast described above is visually reinforced by consecutive images of the rooms in the house prior to (lines 01–03) and after the make-over (lines 05–07). These images combine long-range shots, which capture the extent of the changes in their entirety, and medium-range and close-up ones, which strategically capture interior decoration features in the rooms. Images of the rooms after the make-over are also offered over the presenter's off-screen description of the many virtues achieved by the presenter and against a background of soothing classical music, all of which intends to persuade viewers of the stylishness of the make-over and, hence, of the show's notion of aesthetic taste.

As well as taking little time, desirable lifestyles are presented to viewers as requiring little effort. In personal make-over shows, a couple of new outfits and a new haircut and make-up often result – in the words of the presenters and the participants – in 'amazing' personal transformations. These, as noted earlier, go beyond physical appearance, often reaching aspects of people's personalities, such as their self-esteem. Minimum effort is likewise required to partake of appealing styles of 'doing tourism' abroad, according to the presenters of some holiday shows. These programmes tend to promote holiday habits based on convenience, both in terms of the activities that tourists may wish to undertake and, when in non-English-speaking countries, the language in which tourists may choose to communicate with local people.

Jaworski et al. (2003a, 2003b), for instance, found that across a number of holiday shows on British television a message was persuasively constructed: tourists abroad and local people needed to have little, if any, contact. In those cases where contact did take place, English was predominantly used, even if the destinations were non-English-speaking communities. Thus the languages of non-English-speaking local people featured in only 26 per cent of all inter-actions and were often displayed within brief, formulaic encounters that gave the impression that a couple of textbook phrases sufficed to satisfy tourist needs. The effect of such linguistic imbalance was a reduction of the local languages to the category of 'linguascapes'. They were exotic elements that adorned an otherwise tamed environment to which tourists could effortlessly adapt.

Similarly, in property shows in which presenters help ordinary people to find a house, the former make this possible after showing the latter only a few prop-erties and making only a couple of telephone calls to a handful of estate agen-cies. Property surveyors, solicitors and estate agents are generally available to talk to the presenters at short notice, which is quite remarkable considering the time limitations under which these presenters work.

In home improvement shows, for their part, the type of work conducted is seldom structural and, hence, relatively effortless. Interior decoration favourites in these programmes include wallpapering and/or painting, furniture rearrang-ing and strategic placing of ornamental features. By filming mainly the presen-ters at work, and only rarely the team of workers that the presenters actually use to carry out (most of) the work, the interior decorating in these shows appears particularly manageable. Consider in this respect Extract 13.3 (see p. 170), from the home improvement show *The House Doctor* (Five, UK).

During the course of this short extract, the presenter minimises on three occasions the nature and amount of work needed in the house about to undergo a make-over. First, when assessing the condition of the bathroom and bedrooms as 'tired' in lines 03 and 10, respectively, she pre-modifies this adjective with the emphatically delivered quantity hedges 'a little' and 'a bit', both of which soften its force. In fact, she further downplays the negative force of the (already miti-gated) adjectival phrase 'a little tired' (line 03) by using yet another mitigating device: 'it's just . . .' (line 03). Secondly, in line 04 she expresses her dissatisfac-tion with the bathroom cabinet. Yet next she explicitly refers to its requiring 'just a few light touches >I think< (.) to (.) erm (.) freshen it up a bit (.)' (lines 05–07). The work needed is therefore not only light but limited ('a few . . . touches') and purely cosmetic (to 'freshen it up') – even unimportantly so, for

### The House Doctor (Five, 2003)

[The owners of the house, two women, are showing presenter Ann Maurice the house that, for the past year, they have failed to sell. M: Ann Maurice; Wn: two women.]

| | | | |
|---|---|---|---|
| MS – M and Wn in bathroom. | 01 | M | o:: <u>kay</u> (.) this is a nice little bathroom = |
| CU – bathroom. | 02 | Wn | = yes |
| MS –M, to Wn. | 03 | M | it's just a <u>little</u> tired (.) |
| CU – M glances around | 04 | | >not happy about that dark cabinet< (.) |
| room disapprovingly. | 05 | | it kind of dates it (.) it needs <u>just</u> a <u>few</u> |
| CU – bathroom cabinet. LS – | 06 | | <u>light</u> touches >I think< (.) to (.) erm (.) |
| bathroom. | 07 | | freshen it up a bit (.) |
| LS – three bedrooms. | 08 | M | and <u>that</u> (.) essentially (.) is the problem |
| | 09 | (vo) | with the upstairs bedrooms too (.) |
| | 10 | | they're all looking a <u>bit</u> tired and in need |
| | 11 | | of some <u>light touches</u> to recapture that |
| | 12 | | <homely (.) lived-in> feeling [. . .] |

only 'a bit' of freshening up is needed in the presenter's view. Thirdly, in lines 08–11 she assesses the condition of the upstairs bedrooms as also being a 'problem' but one that can also easily be solved, for it requires 'light' and limited ('some') 'touches'. After listening to Maurice, both the viewers and the owners are likely to expect a small amount of work. Yet the results will, in the presenter's own words, manage to 'recapture that <homely (.) lived-in> feeling' (lines 11–12). The association between material (a cabinet, a bedroom) and symbolic (a homely, lived-in feeling) goods is thus not only seamlessly made but also persuasively constructed as effortless.

The accessibility of the lifestyles shown in these shows is also grounded in how inexpensive they are. In the US home-living show *Martha Stewart*, for instance, the presenter uses her own example as a self-made entrepreneur to promote an idealised, conventional, upper middle-class (white, heterosexual) lifestyle in which the woman happily fulfils the traditional role of homemaker. This upper middle-class lifestyle is explicitly constructed as the epitome of good taste. Crucially, Martha Stewart makes an equally explicit point of placing good taste within easy reach of those from lower socio-economic levels. She, for example, regularly combines within the same episode recipes for delicacies with those for inexpensive, simple dishes. In doing so, she seems to democratise taste, making it an essential yet affordable and accessible commodity within the lifestyle sector of home living (Evans Davies 2003).[3]

Property shows, too, allegedly democratise taste by emphasising the relatively low finances required to achieve a dream-home lifestyle. The home improvement variety, in particular, continually stresses that property makeovers which will secure quick sales do not require capital expenditure for anything which is not absolutely essential. In a radical departure from premodern aesthetic values that equated good taste with quality materials (and,

**EXTRACT 13.4**

### *Selling Houses* (Channel 4, 2003)

[Andrew Winter is in the middle of a make-over. The owner of the house, Judith, is with him in one of the rooms in the house. W: Andrew Winter; J: Judith.]

| | | | |
|---|---|---|---|
| *LS –W, painting and J,* | 01 | W | in the living room we are covering up the outdated |
| *standing next to him.* | 02 | (vo) | old cabinet with white paint |
| *MS – W, turns towards* | 03 | | Judith (.) I'm <u>always</u> telling people when they're |
| *J to speak to her.* | 04 | | selling their house (.) <u>you've got to</u> look for the |
| | 05 | | quickest option |
| *CU – J nods at W.* | 06 | | (1.0) |
| *MS – W and J.* | 07 | (to J) | ideally we'd like to rip all this panelling down but |
| *CU – W's hand resting* | 08 | | to me that's gonna take <a <u>lot</u> of time> (.) you |
| *on panelling.* | 09 | | don't know what's behind this = |
| *CU – J, to W.* | 10 | J | = no °you don't° |
| *LS – W and J in room.* | 11 | W | so we're painting this (.) let it <u>blend</u> into the wall (.) |
| *MS – W and J.* | 12 | (to J) | we will have done a <u>good</u> job without causing much |
| *CU – W, smiles at J.* | 13 | | hassle (.) it <u>looks good</u> and it's <u>MUCH</u> cheaper […] |

hence, high costs), inexpensive materials are generally preferred in these shows because – it is persuasively argued – they cost little but nevertheless look good. Aesthetic taste is therefore constructed as something both that one's home must have and that is financially attainable for most people. It is a form of 'symbolic capital' (Bourdieu 1984) that everyone can acquire, as Extract 13.4 illustrates.

The presenter in this extract distinguishes between what one should 'ideally' (line 07) do and what he has decided to do: to paint (line 11) rather than gut and rebuild (line 07). His cutting-corners policy does not cause 'much hassle' (lines 12–13), does not take much time (lines 04–05, 08) and, importantly, 'it's MUCH cheaper' (line 13). It nevertheless '<u>looks good</u>' (line 13) – it is indeed a policy that results in their 'hav[ing] done a <u>good</u> job' (line 12). Aesthetic taste is in this way persuasively presented to viewers and the house owner as something that is independent of cost and therefore within the reach of all budgets. It is, in fact, something that only in the ideal world entails considerable expense and/or quality of work. In the 'real' world, viewers' main consideration should be to limit the time, effort and capital that they spend on achieving an appealing home lifestyle. That is, after all, precisely what Winter is '<u>always</u> telling people when they're selling their house' (lines 03–04).

Make-over, cookery and holiday shows, then, are not simply about advice on interior decoration, fashion, cooking and travel destinations. Instead, they are about creating strong, positive associations in the minds of their viewers between certain material (a patio area, a haircut, a recipe, etc.) and symbolic (a Mediterranean-home lifestyle, a confident personality, a stylish, upper middle-class diet, etc.) choices. These shows do not force the participants – let alone the viewers – to partake of these lifestyles. Instead, by displaying them as quick, cheap and effortless, they persuasively invite viewers and participants to partake of them. We are here reminded of another aspect of Van Dijk's (1998) work, which sees power as closely connected to people's minds, specifically to our wanting to control the minds of others so that they may see things as we do and act as we want them to. Giving orders is one way to achieve power. Trying to convince others – to persuade them – is a more complex and subtle, yet often more effective, alternative.

The sheer number of verbal and non-verbal (e.g. music, images) resources used to showcase desirable material and symbolic goods and services in lifestyle television makes the discourse of these shows undoubtedly persuasive. The persuasive power of their discourse resides in its ability to convince viewers that they are the ones choosing the lifestyles that are simply being shown on their television screen. The programmes may thus be said to implement the rhetorical strategy of *occultatio* (see Chapter 11). They pretend not to do what they actually do: to sell ready-made, user-friendly lifestyle packages to viewers. The latter is a task in which the figure of the presenter is crucial, as the remainder of the chapter discusses.

## 13.2   From DIY lessons to melodrama

The leisure programmes in the late 1960s and early 1970s drew on a participation framework in which the experts (who were also the shows' presenters) were the only producers of talk. Ordinary members of the public were afforded the participatory role of ratified recipients of the presenters' talk. Within this participation framework, the purpose of the experts' talk was overtly didactic. Their mode of address and rhetoric were mainly authoritarian and expository. Verbally, they gave a succession of instructions on how to do certain tasks: 'this is how it is', 'this is what it looks like'. Visually, the shows used abundant camera close-ups to demonstrate step by step the tasks that their experts relayed (Brunsdon et al. 2001).

Today's lifestyle television has retained the didactic ethos that characterised its progenies. But contemporary distrust of expertise has contributed to their presenters being transformed in key ways, as Extracts 13.5 (see p. 173) and 13.6 (see p. 175) show.

In Extract 13.5 Winter's talk offers two lessons. One is the, by now, familiar conflation of the realms of the material and the symbolic. According to the presenter, '<trendy contemporary decor>' in general, and 'stainless steel appliances and a power shower' (lines 06–07) in particular, epitomise 'a <cool designer lifestyle>' (lines 04–05). This cool designer lifestyle performs, in turn, a given social identity, namely being '<affluent young professionals>' (line 03) – an identity that excludes other, possibly competing, identities, such as being 'first-time buyers' (line 03–04). Likewise, in lines 13–16, Winter explicitly connects 'a dining area in [the] kitchen' and 'practical desirable items like a nice dishwasher (.) big fridge freezer (.) a good cooker and task lighting' to 'show[ing] off' (line 14) a family lifestyle of stylish enjoyment (line 12). These appliances perform, too, a 'wealthy family' (line 10) identity. In contrast, the family 'on a tight budget' (line 20) identity is matched to a 'really user friendly

**EXTRACT 13.5**

## Selling Houses (Channel 4, 2003)

[Andrew Winter has completed a property make-over and described the changes made. He is now telling viewers about the 'dos and don'ts' of house improvements. The entire extract is spoken by Winter, either to camera (tc) or off-screen (vo). W: Andrew Winter.]

| | | | |
|---|---|---|---|
| MS – unfinished kitchen and bathroom. | 01 02 | (vo) | [. . .] never scare them off with rooms that need expensive refurbishment (2.0) |
| MS – W sitting on moulded chair. | 03 04 05 | (tc) | <affluent young professionals> who aren't first-time buyers demand a <cool designer lifestyle> |
| MS – modern-looking kitchen CU – stainless steel oven CU – through glass kitchen table from below. W wipes off dust. LS – W walks through main door into spacious hall, closes door and walks towards camera. Cut to LS – W walks into kitchen, towards table. CU – objects described. | 06 07 08 09 10 11 12 13 14 15 16 | (vo) (tc) (vo) (tc) (vo) (tc) (vo) | so go for <trendy contemporary decor> (.) stainless steel appliances and a power shower but (.) if anything's dirty (.) wave goodbye to your sale <wealthy family buyers> want a home that parents and kids can enjoy in style so if you can (.) create a dining area in your kitchen and show off practical desirable items like a nice dishwasher (.) big fridge freezer (.) a good cooker and task lighting (2.0) |
| LS – elegant hall. Cute toddler running towards camera. CU – Persian cat under table. LS – hall, then quickly CU/MS – W, standing by staircase. MS – stylish, tidy lounge. CU – bed. MS – bedroom, then cut to MS – staircase. CU – cracked window pane. CU – computer. MS – study desk. MS – rest of study with sofa bed. | 17 18 19 20 21 22 23 24 25 26 27 28 | (tc) (vo) | but don't let your <kids and pets> run around during viewings (.) it can spoil the presentation (.) family buyers on a tight budget want a really user friendly lifestyle [. . .] so get rid of clutter to maximise space and make sure the function of every room is <crystal clear> sort out unfinished jobs and (.) if you've got a large study put in a sofa bed to show off its potential as a guest room (.) |
| MS – hall, W facing mirror. | 29 30 31 | (tc) | finally (.) and this applies to all buyer groups (.) don't forget your part of the lifestyle package too (.) so (.) |
| MS – W straightens shirt, zips jacket up and smiles satisfied. | 32 33 | | present yourself immaculately before < every viewing > [. . .] |

lifestyle' (lines 20–21) that entails specific material decisions, such as getting rid of decorative items (defined as 'clutter' by Winter) and placing a sofa bed in a large study (lines 22–28). Throughout the extract, then, viewers are taught about the interdependence of consumer, lifestyle and identity choices.

The other lesson concerns the importance of aesthetics or, rather, its public display. This, as discussed earlier, is connected to the lack of interest in these shows in substantial work, for the latter is not seen as a prerequisite to achieving good taste. Note, for example, Winter's emphasis on, and markedly slower

'don't forget <u>your</u> part of the lifestyle package too (Extract 13.5, lines 30–31).

'present yourself <u>immaculately</u> before <every viewing>' (Extract 13.5, lines 32–33).

*Figure 13.1* **The importance of aesthetics (1)**

*Figure 13.2* **The importance of aesthetics (2)**

delivery of, key parts of his discourse on appearances in the extract above: 'if anything's <u>dirty</u>(.) wave <u>goodbye</u> to your sale' (lines 08–09); 'don't let your <<u>kids</u> and <u>pets</u>> run around during viewings (.) it can spoil the <u>presentation</u>' (lines 17–19); and 'don't forget <u>your</u> part of the lifestyle package too (.) so (.) present yourself <u>immaculately</u> before <every viewing>' (lines 30–33). In lines 08–10, a camera close-up from under a glass kitchen table of Winter wiping dust off it demonstrates his verbal instruction to keep the house clean. In lines 17–19, images of a cute toddler running across an elegant hall and of a Persian cat under an elegant table are presented in sync with Winter's mention of the risk of their 'spoil[ling] the <u>presentation</u>' – regardless of how cute the toddler and how high-bred the cat. And in lines 29–33, what he means exactly by immaculate self-presentation is visually clarified by a medium-range angle of Winter talking to the camera through a mirror (Figure 13.1). This co-occurs with his verbal reminder to viewers not to 'forget <u>your</u> part of the lifestyle package' (lines 30–31). Next, he is filmed demonstrating this instruction by straightening his shirt and zipping up his jacket (Figure 13.2). The presenter's shirt and jacket look new and smart-casual and he is clean-shaven and nicely groomed. Rather than being driven by structural, bricks-and-mortar considerations, in this extract Winter teaches viewers that selling a house is driven by aesthetic display.

Important as the actual lessons are, more so is the style of Winter's teaching. In Extract 13.5, he provides a number of verbal instructions, key aspects of which are subsequently demonstrated via camera close-ups (e.g. lines 07, 15–16, 19, 23, 25 and 26). He also uses 'incontrovertible truths' of the type 'X wants or demands Y', following them with specific courses of action: 'so you do Z' (lines 03–07; 10–16 and 20–28). His mode of address throughout is direct, the illocutionary force of his instructions (commands) explicit on virtually every occasion: 'never scare them off . . .' (line 01), 'go for . . .' (line 06), 'show off <u>practical</u> <u>desirable</u> items . . .' (line 14), '<u>don't</u> let . . .' (line 17), '<u>get rid</u> of . . . and make sure . . .' (lines 22–23) and '<u>sort out</u> unfinished jobs' (line 25). On the whole, Winter's teaching style is reminiscent of the paternalistic voice of the old public-service discourse of British terrestrial television, even if the content of his lessons targets consumer-based lifestyle choices rather than traditional ways of life.

But his teaching style differs from that of his predecessors in one crucial respect: he does not present himself as a distant, authoritarian expert. Instead, he constructs the image of a confident, well-researched consumer, who interprets currently fashionable lifestyle ideas for the benefit of other consumers, namely the show's participants and viewers. This is evident, for example, in his animating the various incontrovertible truths in the extract, but attributing their authorship to others. Thus, it is the 'young affluent professionals' (line 03), the 'wealthy family buyers' (line 10) and the 'family buyer on a tight budget' (line 20) who, respectively, 'demand' (line 04) and 'want' (lines 11 and 20) certain lifestyles.

In Extract 13.5, then, Winter is constructing the alleged aesthetic preferences of different social groups in ways that suit the lifestyles being showcased in the show. He is concomitantly distancing himself from the traditional position of detached expertise. Like the presenters of some holiday and gardening shows, the persuasion power behind Winter's performance relies partly on his ability to come across as an appealing personality-interpreter – as an informed person who willingly 'out-sources' the ideas with which their shows invite viewers to lead their lifestyles (Taylor 2002).

A similar attempt at shying away from the figure of the presenter being seen as a distant expert is evident in Extract 3.6, this time from the *Martha Stewart* home-living show. Martha Stewart leads her audience by the hand, as she goes through the dos and don'ts of baking substitutes. Her teaching style draws simultaneously from negative politeness (imposition-avoidance) and positive politeness (commonality-seeking) strategies. The former are compatible with the individualism of a number of Anglo-Saxon cultures, including that of the US. The latter fit in with a popular US ideology that denies class differences and

---

**EXTRACT 13.6**

### *Martha Stewart* (Martha Stewart TV Productions, 2004)

[This extract features a cooking segment of the *Martha Stewart* show. S: Martha Stewart.]

```
01  S   when you're baking (.) no matter how well-stocked you keep your pantry (.)
02      there's bound to be a time when you find yourself missing an important
03      ingredient (.) you could stop what you're doing and run out to the store (.) but
04      you may be able to save time and money by making a substitution (.) here are
05      some things that I find provide satisfactory results (2.0) for the equivalent of
06      one teaspoon of baking powder (.) combine one eighth of a teaspoon of cream
07      of tartar with a quarter of a teaspoon of baking soda (.) this is useful not only
08      when you're out of baking powder but also when the powder you have has lost
09      its effervescence (2.0) you should always test it before using it by dropping a
10      spoonful of it into hot water (.) if it doesn't bubble and foam actively (.) the
11      baking powder <shouldn't be used>
```

promotes the ideal of social equality and solidarity (Evans Davies 2003). Together they project the image of the lifestyle personality-interpreter as someone knowledgeable and helpful, willing to treat viewers as their equal and anxious to avoid imposing their advice upon them.

Thus, Stewart's negative politeness strategies in Extract 13.6 seek to give the impression that her audience can choose for themselves from the options – not rules – that she offers. She, for example, either premodifies her lessons with the modal verb 'should' ('you should <u>always</u> test it . . .', line 09) or uses the passive form ('the baking powder <shouldn't be used>', line 11). Both strategies try to minimise the degree of imposition that instructing others may carry. Also, rather than stating her own preferred course of action, she gives alternatives: '(.) you could stop what you're doing and run out to the store' (line 03).

As for her positive politeness strategies, these principally revolve around emphasising common ground between herself and her audience. The generic 'you' used throughout the extract, for instance, serves as a unifying pronoun that seeks to bring her and her audience together in the ordinary task of baking. In lines 01–03, her generic use of 'you' also makes the problem being described ('missing an important ingredient') inevitable ('bound to' happen) – 'no matter how well-stocked you keep your pantry'. Nobody is perfect, the underlying message goes. Only once in Extract 13.6 does Stewart use the first-person singular pronoun 'I': 'here are some things that <u>I</u> find provide satisfactory results' (lines 04–05). Therein, she seeks to get close to her audience by sharing with them, rather than imposing on them, her personal experience and expert know-how.

In addition to bringing the figure of the expert down from its previous pedestal, lifestyle television has also reduced his/her screen time. The consequent gaps have been filled by ordinary members of the public. Recall, for instance, Extract 13.1, where the presenter was filmed talking to an ordinary person, Claire, at her home. Claire was next filmed, seemingly unaware of the camera, showing her house to a prospective buyer (another ordinary person).

Make-over shows feature the ordinary person as a speaking subject, engrossed in a set of quotidian activities and practices, and interacting with the presenter and/or other ordinary people. Presenters, for their part, are also filmed in familiar, safe spaces, working together with the ordinary particiapants on the very same routine activities that viewers perform in their daily lives. And it is to these participant–presenter interactions within this shared space of mundanity, and to their persuasion potential, that the discussion turns in the final part of the chapter.

During the course of Extract 13.7 (see p. 177), taken from *Location, Location, Location*, the two presenters and the couple are filmed as they discuss the merits or otherwise of a property, in the course of either a conversation on camera (lines 01–09, 40–45) or a narrative voice-over (Allsopp's in lines 10–39). Regarding the former, the conversation between Jim and Allsopp is designed and articulated to come across as lively (see Chapter 5). Three factors in particular make it so. One is Jim's use of expresive language

**EXTRACT 13.7**

### Location, Location, Location (Channel 4, 2003)

[Presenters Kirstie Allsopp and Phil Spencer are about to show a young couple (Jim and Heather) a detached house located on an estate in the outskirts of Glasgow. All four walk into the property and stand in the hall. A: Kirstie Allsopp; J: Jim.]

| | | | |
|---|---|---|---|
| *MS from right –* | 01 | A | it's a blank canvas (.) everything is in <u>immaculate</u> |
| *group in hall.* | 02 | | condition (.) it's a <u>safe</u> (.) <u>secure</u> environment |
| *CU – J.* | 03 | J | I think it's <u>awful</u> (.) it's magnolia land (.) it's one point |
| | 04 | | seven children land (.) [it's |
| | 05 | A | [think [of |
| | 06 | J | [it's dreadful = |
| *LS – housing estate.* | 07 | A | = a very prestigious estate though (.) |
| *LS from above –* | 08 | J | prestigious for w-? (.) prestigious not in my eyes (.) I |
| *group. CU – A.* | 09 | | don't see it as a prestigious (*Allsopp smiles*) (1.0) |
| *MS, CU, MS, LS –* | 10 | A | <u>blimey</u> (.) we're not even out of the hall and things are |
| *elegant dining and* | 11 | (vo) | rapidly going downhill |
| *sitting room.* | 12 | | |
| | 13–17 | | [*Flattering description of rooms over range of MS,* |
| | | | *CU, LS of the rooms and decorative items therein.* |
| | | | *Soothing ambient music.*] |
| | 38 | (vo) | it'll no doubt be a beautiful house for many but it's |
| | 39 | | clearly not going to be for Jim and Heather |
| *MS from left – group.* | 40 | J | within a week I would be moving out (.) |
| *CU from above – J.* | 41 | | you wouldn't be able to lie in on a Sunday with the |
| *To group.* | 42 | | noises of the lawnmower and the pressure washes |
| | 43 | | (*Heather laughs*) and <u>all</u> that <u>malarkey</u> (.) we'd have to |
| | 44 | | join the bridge club (*all laugh*) (.) and <u>agh</u> (.) no (.) |
| *Cut to next scene* | 45 | | sorry [. . .] |

and of a delivery style that sounds unrehearsed. Examples of the former are the evaluative adjectives '<u>awful</u>' (line 03) and 'dreadful' (line 06), as well as the phrase '<u>all</u> that <u>malarkey</u>' (line 43). Instances of the latter are the marked stress in his adjectives and his expressive apology in lines 44–45 ('agh (.) <u>no</u> (.) sorry') with which he concludes a colourful description of his hypothetical lifestyle in that property (lines 40–45).

The second factor is Jim's use of fresh talk (see Chapter 4). In lines 03–04, 06 and 08–09 Jim verbalises his reaction to the property in the production roles of animator, author and principal. In lines 40–45, too, he starts by presenting himself as author, animator and principal: 'within a week I would be moving out' (line 40). Soon, though, he shifts to the positions of animator and author, with the principal position being occupied either by the generic second-person pronoun 'you' (line 41) or the first-person plural pronoun 'we' (line 43), which includes him and, for the first time in the extract, his co-present partner Heather. In the context of his use of seemingly unrehearsed, expressive language, Jim's apology at the end of this turn marks a shift back to fresh talk, albeit that his is not explicitly an 'I-apology'.

The third factor is of a visual nature. During the host–participant interaction in Extract 13.7, neither of them addresses or looks in the direction of the cameras. Instead, camera angles interchange rapidly during the extract. In the space of one sentence, for example, they move from a medium-range shot to a close-up shot, back to a medium-range shot and then to a long-range shot of two rooms (lines 10–12). Note, too, the various positions for the group shots in the hall in lines 01, 08 and 40. This all suggests the presence of several cameras simultaneously filming the rooms and the interaction between those on the screen. It also suggests that certain decisions have been made at post-recording time to include some camera angles at the expense of others. A case in point is lines 41–44, where the camera zooms in on Jim from above – an angle that positions the subject (Jim) as powerless relative to the camera and thus counteracts his co-occurring witty remarks. The cameras actually home in on Jim on several occasions, providing viewers with abundant close-ups as he verbally describes his reaction to the property. In lines 03–04 and 06, for example, the close-up angle extends over his entire response to Allsopp's prior sales pitch. And Jim's colourful description in lines 40–45 is also rendered to the viewers through a close-up of him which visually cuts out the reactions of the rest of the group.

Extensive use of camera close-ups in Extract 13.7 seeks to convey the impression of naturalness as well as to generate entertainment. Close-range shots foreground facial reactions at key moments in this type of show, such as the reveal. Lifestyle presenters, as noted earlier, provide ideas and symbolic repertoires from which participants, and viewers, select their lifestyle aspirations. Most likely, the producers' assumption in Extract 13.7 was that the viewers were wondering whether personality-interpreters Allsopp and Spencer as mediators would succeed in convincing Jim and Heather of their need for this home lifestyle. Homing in on Jim's reactions thus contributed to the shows' entertaining melodrama.

For the sake of analytic clarity, melodramatic and didactic participation frameworks have been kept apart so far in this section of the chapter. In practice, however, they often merge, for the entertaining, make-believe interactions performed in lifestyle programmes generally contain a lesson. In Extract 13.7, melodramatic value is provided by the expectancy created around the episode's reveal ('Will Jim and Heather like the property?') and the possibility of participant–presenter conflict. Didactics, for its part, is embedded in this possibility of conflict, specifically in the clashing lifestyle ideas of Allsopp and Jim. Allsopp's sales pitch in lines 01–02 that the property is in 'immaculate condition' and is a 'safe (.) secure environment', and in line 07 that it is situated in a 'prestigious' location, encapsulates a sensible, conservative and aestheticised lifestyle, which is favoured across many lifestyle programmes nowadays. Her flattering description of the rooms in the property, coupled with the strategic camera angles and soothing ambient music (lines 13–37), seek to persuade viewers that the material choices, lifestyles and identities being displayed are worth partaking of. As an off-screen, property-savvy Allsopp argues: 'it'll no doubt be a beautiful house for many' (line 38).

Jim's views are very different. For him buying this property is equivalent to joining a lifestyle where people show that they are house-proud by weekly mowing the lawn and cleaning their cars with a pressure washer (line 42) – something which he sees as unnecessary and a nuisance ('all that malarkey', line 43). It is also equivalent to buying into both a snob (hence his reference to joining the bridge club in lines 43–44) and a conformist, mainstream lifestyle. The latter is negatively evaluated through references to the house as 'magnolia land' and 'one point seven children land' (lines 03–04). In the currently fashionable British rhetoric of visual taste in interior decoration, the magnolia colour epitomises that which is middle class, bland and boring. As for 'one point seven', this is a reference to the frequently heard statistic for average child birth per family in the UK.

The clashing preferences of Jim and Allsopp with regard to home lifestyle augur well for confrontainment, especially since Extract 13.7 occurs within the first third of the episode and expectancy is thereby created about how they will continue to interact with one another. More importantly still, their interaction is broken into two parts (lines 01–09 and lines 40–45) by a narrative voice-over (lines 10–39) in which Allsopp steps out of her role in the episode's melodrama and adopts the role of 'mediator'. The latter is defined by Goffman (1974: 226–7) as:

> a specialised viewer who also participates as a staged character [and who] can comment on whole aspects of the production, treating as an object of direct attention what the projected characters have to treat as something in which they are immersed. He [sic] is a footnote that talks.

Within her mediator role, Allsopp strategically metarepresents Jim's discourse. Thus in lines 10–11 she suggests that Jim's reaction to the property is sharp-tongued and impulsive: 'blimey (.) we're not even out of the hall and things are rapidly going downhill'. It is worth noting that even though Allsopp's voice-over is performed *ex tempore*, it also aims to be perceived as lively. Expressive language, marked stress ('blimey'), and the colloquial idiom 'going downhill' are all used to represent Jim's speech. She uses fresh talk, too, in order to minimise the latter's previous criticism, whereby she moves to a solely animated but collectively authored production role, with all of them also involved as principals: 'we're not even out of the hall and . . .' (line 10). In lines 38–39, however, Allsopp's gloss emphasises the distance between 'us' (many people including, implicitly, her and Phil Spencer) and 'them' (Jim and Heather).

By stepping out of her role in the episode's melodrama in order to comment on one of its characters, Allsopp provides viewers with pointers as to what the lesson of the episode will be. In this respect, it is worth mentioning that Extract 13.7 comes from one of the few episodes of *Location, Location, Location* in which the participants fail to find their dream home. It is, for all the reasons discussed here, difficult not to conclude that such an unhappy ending is an integral part of the lesson that the viewers are expected to learn from Jim and Allsopp's otherwise rather entertaining make-believe interaction.

## 13.3 Conclusion

Lifestyle television is designed to be persuasive: Its communicative intention is to convince viewers that the goods and services on the screen are worth acquiring. These goods and services are primarily of a symbolic nature. Yet, they are strongly associated with tangible choices. As we saw in Extracts 13.1 and 13.5, respectively, a patio area became indexical of a desirable Mediterranean, outdoor living style and the size of one's fridge freezer became one of the chief markers of the identity some viewers may aspire to. Social identity is, incidentally, constructed in these shows in ways that combine traditional demographics and contemporary patterns of living and spending time and money.

Through the analysis of several typical extracts from mainly property make-over shows, this chapter has highlighted several defining aspects of the genre's persuasive showcasing of lifestyles. One of them is its emphasis on superficiality. According to Giddens (1991: 200), appearance has become 'the prime arbiter of value' in modern societies, where self-development has come to be seen primarily 'in terms of display'. Lifestyle television reflects and, given its synergy with the influential leisure and culture industries, further underscores the role of style over content in such societies. In personal make-over shows, changes to people's appearance are presented in terms of changes to their identity and, therefore, assigned particular salience. In property make-over shows, cosmetic improvements replace structural work and they are constructed as essential to the task of selling a house/lifestyle.

Related to the above, this chapter has also highlighted the ease with which the shows' lifestyles can allegedly be achieved. Not only is the work required to get one's dream-home lifestyle mainly superficial and hence relatively effortless, it is also, as a result, cheaper and quicker than substantial work. What is more, it looks good. Not only are the styles of doing tourism abroad promoted by presenters in holiday shows appealing, they are also hassle-free. Were they to be emulated by viewers, the latter would not need to 'bother' to learn about the culture, language and people of the places that they would visit. And not only are the transformations in personal make-over shows represented as aesthetically and psychologically desirable, they are also often the result of just a couple of new outfits and a different haircut and make-up. Ease and convenience arguments are regularly drawn upon across varieties of the lifestyle television genre. They are seemingly effective because of the implicit threat that the alternative of non-persuasion poses: spending more effort, time and money on renovating one's property, having to 'bother' with other languages and peoples whilst on holiday abroad, continuing to be a person who lacks confidence, and so forth.

This chapter has argued, moreover, that the current success of lifestyle television owes much to its having been able to move with the times, as it were. Coinciding with the socio-cultural shift from pre-modern ways of life to modern lifestyles, the genre has adapted its old didactics to fit the consumerism and multiplicity of options that characterise modern societies. Teaching continues to define the genre but the 'teachers' are no longer distant figures of authority. Instead, they have become personality-interpreters: informed consumers who either research and relay available market choices that are, in turn, likely to meet other consumers' demands (Extract 13.5) or share with others their expertise (Extract 13.6). The result is a participation framework that claims to bring those 'doing teaching' and those 'doing learning' closer than hitherto.

Concomitant to the shows' introduction of the figure of the presenter as a personality-interpreter has been their populating the studio sets with ordinary people. These have become important characters in the shows' melodramas. In theory, then, they have become more prominent than in the early DIY shows, in which they were largely unheard and unseen. In practice, they are often used simply to exemplify the presenters' teaching (Extract 13.1). At other times they are used to provide presenters with opportunities to prove these people wrong and, through this, to teach valuable lessons to the viewers (Extract 13.7). These lessons are predominantly about aesthetics. Given the salience of appearance to the self in modern societies (Giddens 1991), the presenters' talk is potentially very persuasive. Rather than contribute to creating a community of independently minded DIYers, this talk is intended to make viewers embrace their (the presenters'/ shows') notion of taste – a notion through which a number of different practices are articulated into a singular expression of identity (Bonner 2003).

# Conclusion . . . Television Discourse

14

> How do you think the Egyptians built the Sphinx? Surely, you don't think
> that a bunch of common Egyptians just got together one day and said:
> "Hey, why don't we build a Sphinx!" Of course not.
> Left to their own devices, the common Egyptians would have spent
> their time growing food. To get some real *culture*, to get the *Sphinx*,
> the Egyptians needed a government authority, someone with vision,
> someone with taste, someone with whips and spears.
> (Barry 1987: 164; original emphasis)

This book has examined neither Egyptian history nor the creation of the Sphinx.
The above quotation from US humorist and author Dave Barry may thus seem
an odd choice with which to begin to revisit the key arguments of *Television
Discourse*. However, the two are analogously linked by construction and agency.
The double articulation of television talk makes its performance anything but the
product of chance. Rather, just as Barry's Egyptians would not normally have
been expected to craft a Sphinx, television discourse is not 'built' just when a
group of ordinary people are made to gather in a purpose-built house – even if
this is the way that reality game shows like *Big Brother* try to portray it at times.
Nor are they built either just because a journalist and a politician meet in a television studio and talk about politics or because someone bares his/her soul on the
screen – be it through a confessional monologue to camera, an amiable chat with
a friendly host in a cosy studio set, or a testimony before a judge in a courtroom
show. Instead, each of these television talks, as with the others examined in the
pages of this book, is intentionally and carefully designed and articulated to be
broadcast. For Barry's government authority, then, substitute those responsible
for television discourse, including the people planning and performing it. And
substitute for Barry's whips and spears the semiotic resources through which television's discourse is implemented. Barring obvious differences, these 'authorities'
and 'tools' project the 'vision' and 'taste' that underpin the construction of the
Sphinx and television discourse respectively.

This book has examined television discourse from within a hermeneutics of
trust, and has sought, therefore, to remain suitably realistic (some might say

pragmatic) about television's (re-)mediation. The practices involved in 'building' television discourse have been shown to be considerable in number and variety. But they have not been treated as being indicative of television systematically levying its spears and cracking its whips at those upon whom it relies for its outputs. Rather, they have been regarded as manifestations of the jointly performed quality of television texts – of their emerging, in short, through far more than just a 'hey, why don't we create some television talk!' approach.

*Television Discourse* has identified and discussed, for example, some of the key semiotic resources through which television seeks to be a bard of reality, to be felt close to, to be enjoyed as confrontainment and to be persuasive. Television, as shown in Part I, often uses particular narrative structures and formal devices to establish a 'direct' link to the world out there, mediating in the process specific personal and social identities and particular visions of that world. It also uses different manifestations of sociability in order to create the impression of proximity. For instance, as discussed in Part II, television simulates interpersonal closeness amongst those on the screen, between them and the world about which they talk, and between them and the viewers. In doing so, television discourse tends to foreground emotions and, as the analyses in Part III revealed, in some contexts celebrates the explicit display of 'negative' emotions, such as anger, contempt and other-humiliation. These emotions are primarily offered as forms of spectacle, although they also point to television's projection of a new kind of mediated public sphere (see section 14.1). Furthermore, as seen in Part IV, television discourse tries to be sufficiently convincing of the desirability of the goods and services that it displays for us to want to partake of them. These goods and services are not necessarily material. They are, in fact, often of a symbolic nature, even if they remain rooted in pragmatic, consumer-dependent choices.

Of course, television discourse exhibits a significant degree of dynamicity, enabling it to hybridise, recycle, innovate, and so forth, which makes its development uncertain. This dynamicity is at times taken to mean a capacity for, as it were, accelerated evolution, which itself fuels much debate about what television (discourse) may be like (and look and sound like) in the future. Will the convergence of television and the information technology (IT) industry at the level of system be matched by a convergence in the use of domestic devices? Some see different patterns of domestic use and space as militating against this. Others believe that as CD, CD-Rom, telephone, television, internet use and computing applications become centralised in one device, single-device marketing will be the future of the mass media. And if *full* television/IT convergence did occur, what would be the implications? Corner, for one, suggests that it would probably increase the intensity and range of purposive use but would not reduce significantly 'the casual use of television' (1999: 124).

However, important and interesting though this is, more speculatively orientated research has been consciously eschewed here in favour of exploring television discourse's 'full communicative potential as a mode of interaction constitutive of its audience' (Montgomery 2007: 21). The medium's existence owes principally to its own forms and communicative structures and herein *Television Discourse* has explicitly examined the *what* vis-à-vis the *how* of television talk. Whilst it has done so around the features of storytelling, closeness, conflict and persuasion, a careful reading of its pages reveals that television discourse also reflects, encourages, shapes and depends upon three wider themes, namely emotion, morality and reality. It is to these that we now turn.

## 14.1   Television discourse and emotion

The purchase of emotional expressiveness on television is not only a matter of frequent instances of verbal sharing on our screens. It is also a matter of a preference for camera close-ups that allow detailed scrutiny of people's feelings of rage, sadness, disappointment, surprise, elation, and so on. It is, too, a matter of a visual flooding of the present in the guise of different screen windows simultaneously capturing live moments in all their auratic intensity. And it is a matter of presenters' direct look and address to camera, of upbeat/downbeat tunes that punctuate the happy/unhappy stages of stories told in documentaries and of a combination of concrete and metaphorical silence in live news to garner a particular mood. It is, all in all, a matter of television discourse drawing upon a wide range of semiotic resources in order to foreground emotion – to create the impression that it talks to us, with us and about us in ways which we can not only hear and see but also, and crucially, feel.

Resulting as it does from varied and sophisticated semiotic resources, emotion on television offers a paradigmatic example of the performativity of the medium's talk. The content and formal properties of verbal sharing are carefully planned and articulated across television programmes. In daytime talk shows, for example, ordinary people often relay personal-experience stories in highly emotive ways but these stories are always narrativised so as to maximise their potential for drama and entertainment. In celebrity chat shows, a parade of famous guests trade airtime for the disclosure of selective aspects of their 'true' selves. Their talk often includes explicit reference to their feelings and privateness. And across varieties of ordinary television, people reveal to camera their innermost fears, hopes, weaknesses and regrets. Their confessional monologues are constructed as direct gateways to these people's private selves, although they are often highly controlled performances of self in the presence of portable video cameras. Presenters of documentary and lifestyle programmes also at times talk directly to the camera about their views on, and feelings about, the situations in which they find themselves. These are generally performed as conversational, presenter–viewer asides, rather than as scripted speeches to closely positioned cameras and not necessarily contemporaneous with the talk sequences into which they are eventually broadcast.

In addition to the 'banal' contexts above, emotional talk is also commonplace in (traditionally held as) 'serious' television formats, such as the news and different forms of political talk. In this book, for instance, we have explored the role played by mood reporting in affiliated live two-ways, whereby the sharing of the feelings and opinions of the reporters and others with their colleagues in the news room and with the viewers is foregrounded over 'hard facts'. This may be accompanied by speech disfluencies and pauses, which give the impression that reporters are somehow taken aback – temporarily unable to perform their reporting duties because of emotion. In Chapter 6, for instance, we saw how – upon being asked to provide his 'gut feeling' on a news story – an on-location editor stumbled over his words as he conjectured about the future. Similarly, in Chapter 12 another on-location editor was shown momentarily speechless after sharing with the viewers the experience of watching the sound-bite of an unexpectedly emotional politician. Clearly, this editor was familiar with the sound-bite prior to its live broadcast. He was probably the one who had decided to insert it into his live two-way with the studio newsreader. Emotion, in the form of poignant silence, was likely to have been performed because of the cameras.

The relevance of verbal sharing in a mediaised political climate is both evident and one of the reasons why politics is also said to have undergone a process of emotionalisation (Bucy 2000; Corner and Pels 2003; Louw 2005; Richards 2004). Politicians' public displays of emotion are generally carefully planned by their PR teams and extensively metarepresented by journalists. Such is their prevalence that the importance of these displays is perhaps easier to see in relation to the portrayal by television (and other media) of emotionally *inex*pressive politicians as cold and robot-like. For instance, in Chapter 12 we saw that US Democrat presidential candidate John Kerry's finally sharing his emotions in his 2004 concession speech was positively metarepresented by the journalist covering it.

Yet verbalising emotions before the cameras can be a double-edged sword. For example, and as Chapter 10 showed, former British Prime Minister Blair's discourse of deeply held personal values was negatively appraised during a televised interview in which he was also subjected by the members of the general public acting as his interviewers to a different kind of emotional display: one that revolved around the explicit, unmitigated performance of adversarialness. Moreover, Blair actually fell victim to a paradox whereby emotions normally viewed as 'negative' in a number of societies are concomitantly celebrated in their televisation.

Across a range of contemporary television formats, ordinary folk and experts alike 'spontaneously' and unrestrainedly release their anger, frustration, disdain and contempt for others. Various chapters of this book have examined different realisations and degrees of this style of conflict talk as it is performed in 'tabloid' talk shows, courtroom shows, lifestyle coaching shows and political interviews. In Chapter 9, for instance, a confluence of semiotic resources was seen to render explicit the staging of 'negative' emotions before and because of the cameras. These included face-threatening linguistic (insults, direct accusations), paralinguistic (shouting, emphatic stress) and non-linguistic (springing from one's seat to invade another's physical space, finger-pointing) behaviour. They also included the rapid interweaving of camera angles that juxtaposed close-up shots of angry performers and long-range shots of amused audiences; and visual collages of angry participants over dramatic background music and a narrative description of events.

Regardless of the actual television format in which they occur, such performances of conflict talk seemingly thrive on the fact that they offer viewers instances of emotional decontrolling in the very controlled settings of television studios. This style of conflict talk constitutes, indeed, the money shot of these programmes and is guaranteed by the performances of ordinary folk and experts alike.

Explicit adversarialness, for example, is arguably becoming progressively politic behaviour in accountability interviews in the UK. This was suggested by the analysis offered in Chapter 10 concerning the use of openly hostile moves in interviews involving politicians and either journalists or members of the general public acting as interviewers. Here a number of overtly antagonistic (non-)verbal resources were identified in relation to the interactional tasks of doing asking and doing answering. The noticeable presence of overtly antagonistic styles of political interviewing on television, coupled with the fact they do not appear to jeopardise the actual interactional task at hand, signal significant changes regarding the kinds of allowable contributions within the activity type of interviewing politicians on television.

Montgomery (2007: 216) advances two explanations for the drift away from formal neutralism, namely (1) 'the erosion of areas of consensus in significant areas of social and political life (particularly around questions of value)', which means that 'more positions are contestable, fewer taken for granted', and (2) an evolution in the understanding of the role of the interviewer, who no longer plays the part of '"tribune of people", simply pursuing the truth on behalf of the audience through question and answer' but also that of 'arbiter of truth', assuming overt moral positions.

In this book, I have suggested a further explanation – one explicitly connected to performativity and spectacle. I have indicated, specifically, that the changes observed in, especially, the accountability political interview signal a 'formal coarsening' of this type of broadcast interview. The question–answer discourse structure has been superseded by one characterised by assertion–counter-assertion (Montgomery 2007). And within this discourse structure, interviewer and interviewee perform explicit antagonism almost as a 'matter of routine' – as expected-to-be-performed talk that panders to presumed demands for confrontainment. Writing on this interviewing style in the context of *Newsnight* (BBC2), for example, Born (2004: 416) observes: 'watching through the glass office walls as producers talked Paxman through his tactics prior to "doing battle" with Michael Portillo or Robin Cook was like observing a boxer being psyched up before a fight'. Training interviewers to produce neutralistic stances seems, at least in the case of British accountability interviews on television *à la Newsnight*, to have been replaced by training interviewers to perform explicitly coarse exchanges – at least at the formal level.

Whether or not under the same 'confrontainment spell', the performance of explicit adversarialness found in 'tabloid' talk shows, courtroom shows and political interviews suggests 'new' ways of managing expression, deliberation and reflection on television. It points, indeed, to television's projection of an emotional public sphere. For instance, in Chapter 9, the performance of conflict talk in courtroom shows was argued to offer another paradigmatic example of the current reversal of the principles of Habermas's bourgeois public sphere across television formats. The analysis offered in this chapter affirmed Lunt and Stenner's (2005: 70) thesis that 'rather than avoiding the potentially polluting effects of personal and institutional interests', some of today's television discourse 'embraces them and inverts the hierarchy between arguments and feelings'. In doing so, it adopts at times a playful, ironic tone, which makes crystal clear to viewers the staged status and entertainment value of the 'negative' emotions being released. This is why, just as Habermas's public sphere has been seen as 'an ideal speech situation in which the force of argument prevails', *The Jerry Springer Show* and like-minded programmes need to be seen as 'an ideal conflict situation in which the force of the spectacular succeeds.' (Lunt and Stenner 2005: 75). Both rely on an idealised set of circumstances that are seen to be conducive to the public expression of, respectively, rational and emotional public deliberation.

## 14.2   Television discourse and morality

Alongside its spectacle dimension, displays of emotion on television gain their purchase through their connection to moral worthiness. Emotional DIY, for example, is keenly promoted in a number of talk shows and lifestyle programmes. It is seen to surface in ordinary people advising, and receiving advice from others – often the host – on how to fix their lives in socially acceptable ways. A strong therapeutic and moralistic value is attached to their emotional expressiveness – especially when it involves self-disclosure of these people's efforts to overcome their problems and inner demons. Talking things through is not so much a 'cure' in these shows as a sign of being 'a good person'. It is the trying (to be good, to open up verbally) that seems to be indicative of moral worthiness, especially in programmes with markedly therapeutic overtones.

The moral dimension of emotional expressiveness is, though, far from restricted to the ordinary people who populate our television screens. It is instead a common denominator in the talk of various breeds of professional television performers, from small-screen (including presenters and news reporters) to big-screen celebrities. Traditional approaches to the study of celebrity regard their role to be the articulation of 'what it is to be a human being in contemporary society' (Dyer 1986: 8). From within such an 'exemplary human being' role, celebrities nowadays often seek to develop motivational/moral discourses of personal achievement. As might be expected, the latter relies heavily on the performance of emotional expressiveness. An emblematic example of this is Oprah Winfrey who, as we noted in Chapter 7, regularly discloses 'ordinary' personal experiences with a motto before the cameras. Celebrities' personal experiences are nowadays often constructed as 'exemplary narratives': as 'indisputable truths' for others to reflect upon and learn from (Tolson 2006).

Traditionally, small-screen celebrities have been seen to promote ordinary self-constructions that are consonant with the typified, ideal, ordinary television viewer, for whom these constructions are intended (Ellis 1982; Langer 1981). Big-screen celebrities – for their part – have been found to project 'larger than life' self-constructions. Yet how these small- and big-screen celebrities embed human exemplariness within their talk on television does vary across and between these categories. Consider, for example, the chat show interview of Hollywood film star Drew Barrymore that was examined in Chapter 7. Barrymore expectedly interpolated personal anecdotes and brief references to her feelings within clearly promotional talk. These anecdotes and feelings foregrounded her ordinary, rather than her celebrity, self and were related to the general subject of romantic relationships. They were nevertheless relayed partly as spectacle and partly as though they exemplified truths about people and about life for others (ordinary viewers) to learn from.

Talk show host Robert Kilroy-Silk adopted a different approach, as discussed in Chapter 4. He deliberately ironised his television persona through the sharing of a personal-experience anecdote that flagged the incongruity of his job possibly being like that of an ordinary man and, therefore, of him possibly being like an ordinary man. His anecdote succeeded in amusing his studio audience and in encouraging one member of that audience to continue to disclose her distressing experience of coping with sexual harassment.

Kilroy's self-mockery was characteristic of an emergent valorisation in the media of the 'relentlessly performing, public self' (Gamson 1994: 54) over the fleetingly available private self. Possibly fuelled by the unpredictably rapid mutability of celebrities' markers of sincerity and authenticity and the resulting growing audience scepticism, a number of small- and big-screen celebrities are opting for ironic discourse performances of selfhood on television.

As discussed in various sections of Chapters 7, 9 and 13, those television formats that attribute moral worth to emotional expressiveness tend also to use it to appraise those who perform it. Whether involving a health guru or a judge, reality shows in particular give the figure of the presenter the task of assessing the morality of ordinary people who have previously 'confessed' their hopes, views, fears and weaknesses, either to him/her or to the camera. These programmes thus perform a social regulation function similar in some respects to that identified by Foucault (1978) in his study of confession rituals in the Catholic Church. In both contexts, a lay person (a participant/a secular Catholic) would tell 'whatever is most difficult to tell' (1978: 59) to another, 'morally superior' person (a priest/a presenter).

Unlike in the penitent–priest confession ritual, however, the lay-person–expert confession ritual on television is flagrantly public and often cautionary. Listening, judging, punishing, forgiving, consoling and reconciling are first and foremost performed as spectacle in a number of reality programmes. Chapter 7, for instance, examined the use of clever editing practices whereby off-screen presenters punctuated the confessional monologues of ordinary people to camera with harsh but witty judgments on these people's claims to moral worthiness. And, as we saw in Chapter 9 in relation to courtroom shows, camera work was instrumental in maximising the dramatic potential of experts' appraisals of ordinary folk in their presence. The judges' brashness towards the litigants was captured in all its theatrical glory through, amongst other techniques, close-up angles of the judge that were immediately followed by either close-ups of the affected litigants looking humiliated, specific members of the audience looking positively amused and/or long-range shots of the courtroom audience laughing heartily.

It may be tempting to sweep such theatrical displays under the talk-as-spectacle carpet of factual entertainment (or reality) television – a hybrid programming category that is in any case regarded by some as of little worth. This would, however, wrongly disregard the discourse resources for doing surveillance that underlie experts' metarepresentations of ordinary people's discourse of moral worthiness. Unlike in the Catholic Church rite of confession, the 'mistakes' made by the ordinary people in the reality programmes examined in Chapters 7, 9 and 13 were treated as exemplary lessons – as cautionary tales – for viewers to learn from. The negative consequences of body-piercing were not, for example, seen to lie in the possibility of wound infection but in the fact that someone was making 'a hole in a place God did not give you one' (Extract 9.4). Similarly, the implications of not being persuaded by a presenter's sales pitch of prestigious housing estates were portrayed as causing failure to find one's dream-home lifestyle rather than as a clash of opinions about taste (Extract 13.7). The 'society of self-disclosure' (Thompson 2000) so keenly reflected and promoted by television, in short, was transformed in and through these forms of emotional talk into a society of 'spectacular' moral surveillance.

## 14.3 Television discourse and reality

The discourse forms examined in this book are embedded in non-fictional television formats which claim to varying degrees to be connected to the socio-historical world. They may draw more or less extensively upon semiotic resources traditionally associated with fiction but they all seek to assert some form of realism. I say 'some form' because television realism is a particularly slippery concept. It refers to one or more of the following elements: believability, plausibility, probability, actuality, naturalism, truthfulness and verisimilitude (Burton 2002). More importantly still, television realism is not simply about the believable, plausible, truthful and probable reproduction of the world out there. It is also about making sense of it (Fiske 1987), which is tantamount to saying that television discourse reflects and constructs particular values and beliefs about different aspects of 'reality'. Analysis of storytelling in documentaries (Chapter 3) and daytime talk shows (Chapter 4), for instance, revealed some of the means by which the taleworlds of these programmes are both constructed as 'mirrors' of the socio-historical world and as entertaining versions of it. Importantly, the entertainment dimension of storytelling in such television formats was also found to serve as an effective tool in the construction and promotion of particular values and beliefs about the documented and talked-about worlds.

The television discourse examined in this book has provided a number of other examples of how television mediates reality. In Part I, for example, the analysis of storytelling in talk shows revealed some of the verbal resources used by ordinary participants to construct their identities in socially appropriate ways, such as 'doing being ordinary' and 'doing emotional DIY'. And in Part III, the analysis of conflict talk in relation to the field of politics revealed a number of beliefs about the relationship between the media and politics. We saw, for example, how politicians are keen to perform various degrees of adversarialness, as determined by the activity type in which they find themselves. From the ritualised other-directed, face-threat and face-work of televised parliamentary debates to the explicitly challenging answers provided by spin-doctors during political interviews, 'politics as conflict' was seen to be actively projected on and by television.

However, the mediation of reality is perhaps most pronounced in our consideration of live news. Indeed, the increasing emphasis on speculating about the future, rather than reporting 'hard' facts (Chapter 6), has sparked considerable debate about what 'reality' news is actually delivering. For a start, as journalist Max Hastings (cited in McGregor 1997: 10) cautions, sometimes 'Images are being transmitted much quicker than any reporter, however brilliant, can possibly sensibly interpret them. In other words, viewers are in danger of being given the idea that they're being told what is going on whereas actually they're being given a wildly misleading impression of what's going on.'

The affective nature of live news may have positive, therapeutic effects for audiences (Zelizer and Allan 2002), especially when the moment captured and broadcast live involves unprecedented, unexpected, unpredictable and extreme events (Liebes 1998; Mellencamp 1990). Nevertheless, numerous instances of live speech that often include a highly emotional style of reporting are frequently used to fill airtime when there is little new to report about a disaster, and in doing so a different kind of socio-historical reality is focused on, which is built around viewers observing the trauma of those reporting on horrific events. Equally, reporters may take refuge in small talk and speculation to fill airtime, as we saw in Chapter 6, but focusing upon emotions risks cutting off events from their wider socio-political and historical contexts. Furthermore, the on-going present of live news and its constant search for what is about to happen creates permeable boundaries between the now and the future. Critics consequently see reported events becoming dislocated from the recent past, news degenerating into speculation and 'false' realities being presented. For instance, commenting on *Sky Television*'s coverage of the 2003 Iraq War, Martin Bell (2003) identifies an increase in the number of unverified, and therefore potentially inaccurate, reports of 'reality' that were broadcast as a result of the pressure to fill airtime.

## 14.4   Final words

This book has identified and elaborated upon four interconnected features of, and three themes within, television talk. It has examined these across a wide range of non-fictional programming. And in doing so it has drawn upon a substantial corpus of broadcasting from three English-speaking countries, at least two of which exert particular influence upon the international broadcasting landscape.

Yet the features and themes developed here cannot pretend to be a definitive summation of television discourse. Nor will they hold in perpetuity. Television discourse will be affected by technology, although to what extent remains to be seen. It will be affected by globalisation and global, national and subnational reactions to it. And it will be affected by societal changes as it seeks to devise new strategies and formats to reach different and evolving audiences.

This constant evolution may be an acknowledged frustration in studying television discourse but it is also a key reason to do so. Understanding its discourse now is essential if we are to understand how it has changed over the years and to engage intelligently in debate about how it might evolve in the future. Cast in this light, it is hoped that *Television Discourse* has whetted the appetite for research grounded in close description of how television talks to us, with us and about us now and that the analyses presented in its pages have equipped readers with the tools and insights necessary to investigate further the forms and communicative structures of this most fascinating medium.

# Notes

## 1 Introduction

1. Form refers to the various 'organisations of signification which constitute a given item *as communication*, for instance, an advertising hoarding, an episode of a situation comedy on television, an article in the local evening newspaper' (Corner 1998: 96; emphasis in the original).

2. Some authors within the 'hermeneutics of suspicion', such as Fowler (1981: 25), acknowledge that a critical dimension means 'acknowledging the artificial quality of the categories concerned' rather than 'intolerant fault-finding'.

3. This, as Corner (1998: 96–7) observes, is not necessarily welcome in some quarters of media research, in which the feeling is that the field 'has already suffered from an over-dose of inquiry into "form" (the term *formalism* has quite a long history as a label for distortion and limitation, especially in relation to literary and fine arts scholarship)' (original emphasis).

4. Further examples of recent (post-2000) books focused on television's form but outside of the broadcast talk research framework are Lury's (2005) *Interpreting Television* and O'Keeffe's (2006) *Investigating Media Discourse*.

5. Other definitions see discourse as regulated genres of expression, as ways of speaking about (and of constituting) particular aspects of reality: for example, the discourse of race, the discourse of gender, and so on.

6. Conversation analysis, for instance, sees the organisation of talk-in-interaction as its only necessary analytic source, whereas critical discourse studies make the socio-cultural and historical contexts of language use a *sine qua non* of their analyses. For critical discourse analysts, discourse is 'the instrument of the social construction of reality' (Van Leuwen 1993: 193). It not only reflects the social order but also constructs it, shaping in the process people's interaction with society.

7. The term 'non-fiction' is deliberately used here because, as we shall see in this book, even 'factual' genres par excellence, such as documentaries and the news, regularly draw upon semiotic resources typically associated with fiction.

8. This larger reference corpus consists of an extensive data set of video recordings and transcriptions of a wide range of non-fiction television formats, including children's television programmes (UK), quizzes (UK, US), breakfast television shows (New Zealand, UK), current affairs programmes (New Zealand, US, UK), political debates (UK) and interviews (New Zealand, UK), documentary varieties (New Zealand, UK, US), sports coverage shows (UK), news bulletins (New Zealand, UK, US), cookery programmes (New Zealand, UK, US), talk shows (UK, US), 'lifestyle coaching' shows (New Zealand, UK, US), courtroom shows (US), property shows (UK), talent shows (UK, US) and other types of reality television.

9. Significantly, Bonner (2003: 52) notes that 'ordinary people do not need to be present on screen for a programme to be ordinary television', although this is the most likely case.

## 2    Storytelling . . . or the Entertaining Construction of Reality

1. Whilst used interchangeably in this book, the terms 'story' and 'narrative' designate in narratology different dimensions of narrative discourse (see Glossary, under Story/narrative).
2. Interview conducted by the author in January 2007.
3. Narrative evaluation is 'the means used by the narrator to indicate the point of the narrative, its *raison d'être*: why it was told and what the narrator is getting at' (Labov 1972a: 375).
4. *Heartland* was originally screened in New Zealand in 1993. It continued and developed into a twenty-four-part series that won both a bronze medal at the 1994 Film and Television Awards in New York and the best factual series award at the 1994 New Zealand Film and Television Awards. A further series was produced and broadcast in 1995. Some *Heartland* episodes from the mid-1990s series were rescreened on New Zealand television in 2001.
5. Lay participant are those people who speak for themselves in talk shows. They do not include the experts who are invited to the studio in their professional capacity to speak for others and, often, 'in defence of "expertise" or "the profession"' (Livingstone and Lunt 1994: 129). They also do not include members of the studio audience, who are primarily involved in evaluating, through their applauding, jeering, etc., lay participants' contributions but who do not generally provide their own experiences.
6. Codas are defined by Labov (1972a: 365) as 'free clauses to be found at the end of narratives'. They wrap up narratives; they signal that they have finished and 'bring the narrator and the listener back to the point at which they entered the narrative' (1972a: 366).

## 3    Once Upon a Time in a Documentary

1. Examples of documentary varieties that do not claim to record reality are 'mock-documentaries' (Roscoe and Hight 2001). These parody the assumptions and expectations behind the genre. Some reality game shows *à la Big Brother* are less explicit about their mock-reality status. As will be discussed in Part II, they combine realist claims with the overt staging of different aspects of reality.
2. The conditions of 'liveness' created by the visual unfolding of an ongoing present on our television screens are discussed in Chapter 6 within the context of television newscasts.
3. This situation may of course change in the future (see Chapter 1).
4. This narrative feature can be explained also in part by reference to production considerations of scheduling, branding, audience-building and audience-holding (cf. Born 2004).

5.  On British television in the 1960s–1970s, for example, there was a famous presenter (Johnny Morris) whose comic impersonations of (mainly zoo) animals were very popular. Disney, too, was already anthropomorphising animals in films in the 1960s, which were subsequently shown on television.

6.  The practice of ventriloquising is not restricted to representing the speech of prelinguistic children, pets and other lovable objects. Its potential for representing others in an informal manner makes it a very useful resource, for example, in making critical yet seemingly innocent evaluations of linguistically able others (see Chapters 9 and 10).

7.  Since his early days in *Monty Python's Flying Circus*, Michael Palin has become one of the most popular television personalities in Britain. His popularity is attested to by a comprehensive website devoted to his travels (http://www.palinstravels.co.uk/index.php, last accessed March 2008) and a number of interviews on prime-time television celebrity talk shows such as *Parkinson* (UK).

8.  Fairclough's concept of conversationalisation is discussed in Chapter 5.

9.  The term 'small talk' is discussed in detail in Chapter 6.

10. The parody of the English male abroad was a running theme in the work in *Monty Python's Flying Circus* and in *Ripping Yarns* in the 1970s. In the latter, for example, Palin and Terry Jones (a fellow member of the monty *Python* group) wrote a series of parodies on the pre-war tales of daring-do and heroism 'oop north' on which they had been raised. Incidentally, it is also possible to interpret Palin's performance of the English male abroad as an instance of 'othering', similar to that at times identified in travel shows. Othering in these contexts refers to the conscious positioning of the peoples of the areas and cultures visited by tourists (epitomised by the shows' presenters) as forming a group which is distinctly different from the 'us' group (the presenters and the viewers) and unflatteringly portrayed in its difference (Jaworski et al. 2003a, 2003b).

# 4   Once Upon a Time in a Talk Show

1.  The terms 'orientation', 'complicating action' and 'result' are used here in the sense of Labov (1972a). (See Glossary, under Story/narrative.)

# 5   Closeness . . . or How Television Gets Up Close and Personal

1.  A further example, even if not of talk *per se*, is that of lay people sending in images that they have captured with their mobile phones and/or portable cameras. This is one of the manifestations of so-called 'citizen journalism' (Allan 2006; Gillmor 2006).

# 6   Live News and Closeness

1.  Montgomery (2007: 5) recently defined news values as 'particular principles of selection, paradigms of relevance, and frames for including and excluding material in news'.

2.  The notion of television's continuous flow was developed by Raymond Williams, who labelled it so when – on his own and bored in a hotel room in North America – he switched on the television set and noticed that the continual presentation of material (advertisements and programmes) exhibited no sequentiality but a sense of seamlessness instead. This owed, Williams argued, to the relentless 'interspersing' of shorter within longer segments of broadcasting. Ellis (1992: 122) took up the idea of television's flow, seeing it – just as Willliams did – as a core property of this medium. Ellis, however, characterised flow as the 'succession of segments, of internally coherent pieces of dramatic, instructional exhortatory, fictional, or documentary material'. Although viewers were able to customise to a certain degree their own flow before the advent of technological developments in, especially, the late twentieth century, these developments increased their ability to do so, so much so that the notion of flow has ceased to be, in the eyes of some (e.g. Grispud 2004), a core property of television.

3.  It is possible that the experience of watching the live version of a live event may be said to be 'fuller' than that of watching its live broadcast once it has been recycled as a news clip many times. Therefore, only those 'live viewers' who 'witnessed' the Hillarys' interview may have received the full experience of its live broadcast.

4.  In *Reading Images: The Grammar of Visual Design*, Kress and Van Leeuwen (1996, 2005 (2nd edn)) examine 'given/new visual structures'. These basically work on the premise that 'given' information is normally placed on the left side of a given space, whereas the right side tends to be reserved for, and associated with, information that is 'new'. In television interviews, for example, the interviewer is often seated to the left side of the interviewee (from the viewers' point of view). The intention behind such a seating arrangement, Kress and Van Leeuwen (2005: 184) explain, is to present interviewers as 'people whose views and assumptions viewers will identify and are already familiar, indeed as the people who ask questions on behalf of the viewers'. Interviewees, for their part, are normally seated to the right side of interviewers (from the viewers' point of view), that is, the side that represents new information. This is the case within the right-hand window frame in Figure 6.1.

5.  Alongside live coverage of commemorative and ceremonial events (Dayan and Katz 1992), 'live broadcasts of violent disruption' (Liebes 1998) offer another context in which mass-mediated witnessing becomes far more than just watching or seeing events unfold in real time.

6.  The term 'deixis' designates a set of language features that refer directly to the personal, locational or temporal characteristics of a given situation. (See Glossary, under Deictic expressions.)

7.  In British news broadcasting (BBC and ITV), the title 'editor' is used for those senior journalists who possess special expertise in specific areas, such as foreign affairs, economics or, in Bradby's case, politics. Editors are thus differentiated from reporters and correspondents in that they have more leeway to interpret and comment on the news (Montgomery 2007).

# 7  'Close' Talk and Moral Worthiness

1.  Bonner (2003) observes, though, that good looks are no disqualification at all for women.

2. Although *Rove Live* is produced and broadcast in Australia, it is also shown on New Zealand television (NZ3), which is where the programme from which Extract 7.1 comes was recorded. Throughout the interview between Rove and Barrymore, and as illustrated in Extract 7.1, Barrymore makes some concessions to the satirical style of the show but otherwise appears to perform as though she were being interviewed for a 'serious' celebrity talk show.

3. Goffman's theatrical metaphor is not intended to characterise social life as amoral, manipulative game-playing. Instead, performances are seen as an expression of deference to the social order (i.e. moral) through strategic gamesmanship. Goffman also accepts limits to the model of social life as drama ('all the world is not, of course, a stage' (1959: 72)), but he adds the caveat that it is not always easy to specify the key ways in which it is not.

4. This is the case for most but not all forms of reality television. Mock documentaries and reality shows like *Big Brother* challenge to different degrees the assertive stance to the specific realities that they 'record' (Chapters 2 and 3).

5. The entire confessional monologue is filmed via a medium-range shot, with Gregor's upper body the dominant image but also allowing for relevant background elements (e.g. the cucumber juice being prepared on the kitchen surface) to be shown.

6. The Diary Room is a small space within the house and comprising a chair to which participants can 'retreat' or 'be summoned' to talk to an invisible other (Big Brother) about their emotions, actions, relationships with the other housemates, and so forth. Their talk is directly addressed to a camera, which is placed at eye level and in front of the chair. The voice of this invisible other in the Diary Room is not always performed by a single individual and can be female as well as male.

7. *Kitchen Nightmares* is the US adaptation of the UK original *Ramsay's Kitchen Nightmares*, which is one of the many incarnations of UK-born chef Gordon Ramsay's television career. Other shows include the fly-on-the-kitchen-wall documentaries *Boiling Point* and *Beyond Boiling Point* and the reality series *Hell's Kitchen* and *The F-Word*.

8. Discourse politeness, including the notion of 'face needs', is discussed in detail in Part III.

9. The term 'exploited' is used here in a descriptive (rather than analytic) sense for, clearly, the producers of these shows do not market their shows in such a way.

# 8   Conflict ... or the Rise of Spectacular Incivility

1. ZB stands for *Newstalk ZB*: a national New Zealand talkback radio network operated by the Radio Network of New Zealand.

2. See, for example, Clayman and Heritage (2002), Fetzer and Weizman (2006), Heritage (2002), Hutchby (1996), Piirainen-Marsh (2005) and Thornborrow (2002).

3. The term 'raw' is used here in a descriptive manner.

4. Brown and Levinson's positive and negative politeness strategies are one of the four options (number 2 below) available to speakers in interaction. These are:

   1. Do the FTA, bald on-record, without redress.
   2. Do the FTA, on-record, with redressive action and using either positive or negative politeness strategies.

3. Do the FTA off-record.
4. Don't do the FTA.

5. Several criticisms of Brown and Levinson's model, however, have been made over the years. See, amongst others, Eelen (2001), Mills (2003) and Watts (2003).
6. This is not to say, though, that presenters do not try to develop their own idyosyncratic styles when it comes to the performance of face-threat.

# 9    Emotional Conflict Talk and Reality Television

1. These features were culled by Scott (2002) from a comprehensive review of the literature on disagreement (Grimshaw 1990), stance (Biber and Finegan 1988, 1989), voice (Bakhtin 1981, 1984), genre (Briggs and Bauman 1992) and orders of discourse (Foucault 1978). Backgrounded and foregrounded disagreements were located in Scott's study at the poles of a continuum. Between the two poles was a third category, 'mixed disagreements', which, as its name indicates, combined features of the other two.
2. For simplicity, I use the term 'modern' society to designate the various terms used by different scholars, e.g. 'late or high modernity' (Giddens 1991), 'modernity' (Chaney 1996, 2001, 2002) and 'postmodernity' (Livingstone and Lunt 1994).
3. See, for instance, www.judgejudy.com; www.judgejoebrown.com; www.texasjusticetv. com (last accessed April 2008).
4. See Glossary for a concise explanation of the term 'public sphere'.

# 10    Conflict Talk and Politics

1. Exceptions to this come in the form of supportive questions from members of one political party to their leader. In some cases, though, MPs may also attack their leader/peer MPs over particularly controversial political decisions. During the months preceding Tony Blair's decision to send combat troops to Iraq in 2003, for example, several of his MPs repeatedly used *PMQs* to challenge any such development.
2. See Glossary, under Forms of address, for a definition.
3. This point is also made by Blas-Arroyo (2003) in the context of political debates on Spanish television.
4. Example taken from Clayman and Heritage (2002: 153).
5. Montgomery (2007: 202–16), on the contrary, argues that the kind of aggressive interviewing in some accountability interviews on television has already attracted negative comment and is 'increasingly received as inappropriately rude'.

# 11    Persuasion … or the Art of *Occultatio*

1. Cicero (1988: 83).
2. The terms 'disabling' and 'enabling' constitute the two respective broad perspectives on the media–politics relationship, as per Corner and Pels (2003: 3–5).

3. *Washington Post*, 27 January 1998, p. 1, cited in Thompson (2000: 154)
4. In order to maintain the original terminology in Bakhtin's work, the terms 'language' and 'metalanguage' are used in this part of the book to refer to a general 'meta' dimension that encompasses verbal and non-verbal modes of communication. Also, utterance is used here in the sense of Bakhtin (1986: 61) to refer to structural units containing the turn of one individual. The length of these structural units can vary from a single word turn to a (written) novel or longer.

## 12    Persuasion, Politics and Television

1. The Fireside Chats were a series of 30 evening radio addresses given by US President Franklin D. Roosevelt between 1933 and 1944. They reportedly attracted more listeners than contemporaneous popular radio shows during what is believed to have been the Golden Age of radio in the US (Burite and Levy 1992).
2. Space limitations preclude a discussion of classic oratory strategies in this chapter (see Guide to Further Reading).
3. Constructed dialogue can poeticise the message that it contains (Baynham 1996, 1999; Johnstone 1994; Tannen 1987, 1989), foregrounding it for its own sake. This is in fact what Jakobson (1960) refers to as 'the poetic function of language', that is, the use of language such that it is the formal qualities of language that draw the user's attention and produce special (generally, aesthetic) effects through an 'excess' of meaning.
4. There are, however, instances in which inclusive 'we' can sound condescending, for example when used by doctors to talk to patients about the latters' medical conditions.
5. The ability of the television medium to feed into and shape a specific event at a specific moment in time by news programmes is often referred to as 'the CNN effect' (see Glossary).

## 13    Persuasion and Lifestyle Television

1. www.channel4.com/4homes/ontv/sellinghouses/index.html (last accessed April 2008).
2. In addition to providing narrative interest, authors such as Bonner (2003: 135), see in these self-imposed deadlines an attempt by the shows to 'reflect a world in which there is never enough time for what work has to be done'.
3. In the UK a similar 'cookery educative' style, although obviously adapted to British socio-cultural values, is displayed by Delia Smith (see Strange (2004) for an analysis of the discourse of four cookery shows on British television, including *Delia Smith's Christmas*).

# Glossary

The following is a list of basic terms and concepts that are used in this book, with a brief explanatory definition for each of them.

**Actuality footage:** As a general concept, 'actuality' designates what is actually done, what actually happened, and what is actually perceived. Actuality footage refers to pictures of news events that represent events that were filmed live.

**Adjacency pair:** This is a single sequence of stimulus–utterance response–utterance produced by two different speakers. Examples of adjacency pairs include question–answer and greeting exchanges.

**Activity type:** This is any type of social activity that is conventionally recognised as such and that social members are likely to categorise in similar ways (cf. Levinson's definition in Chapter 7).

**CNN effect:** Also known as 'CNN-isation' (McGregor 1997), this refers to the arrival of global television and its having altered the nature of foreign relations through the media-isation of policy-decision making. The name stems from CNN coverage of the first Gulf War, when this channel provided all the parties concerned with 24/7 information which seemed to provide real-time visual intelligence for both sides of the conflict, 'a vehicle for delivering mis-information; a vehicle for back channel negotiations [. . .] and a means for delivering PR/psy-ops messages directly to the other side's population' (Louw 2005: 285).

**CNN look:** This is the term originally coined by Bolter and Grusin (2000) to refer to news programmes' tendency to fill up the television screen with visible 'evidence' of the power of the television medium to gather events. The CNN look offers a busy screen in which 'the televised image of the newscaster is coordinated with a series of graphics and explanatory captions, until the broadcast begins to resemble a web site or multimedia application'. Unlike in the 1980s, when news programmes generally offered 'a unified screen', the change in presentation that the CNN – and since then other channels – have adopted means that viewers 'experience such hypermedia not through an extended and unified gaze, but through directing their attention here and there in brief moments' (Bolter and Grusin, 2000: 198).

**Conversationalisation:** The term is principally associated with the work of Norman Fairclough within critical discourse studies and designates both 'the colonization of the public domain by the practices of the private domain, an opening up of public orders of discourse to discursive practices which we can all attain rather than the elite and exclusive traditional practices of the public domain' and the 'appropriation of private domain practices which are needed in post-traditional public settings for the complex processes of negotiating relationships and identities' (Fairclough 1995: 138).

**Deictic expressions:** These are language features that refer directly to the personal, locational or temporal characteristics of a given situation. According to Lyons (1977: 637), deixis designates 'the location and identification of persons, objects, events, processes and activities being talked about or referred to, in relation to the spatiotemporal context created and sustained by the act of the utterance and the participation in it, typically, of a single speaker and at least one addressee'. Not all expressions of time and place are deictic. In the sentence 'John is scheduled to arrive in London at 16:00 on 20 October', for instance, the time and date of John's arrival, as well as his destination, are non-deictic expressions because their interpretation does not depend on the context of the utterance in which they appear. Conversely, in the sentence 'John is meeting us here any minute now', 'here' and 'any minute now' can only take their reference from the context in which they are used, for example outside the cinema ('here') at 19:30 ('any minute now').

**Documentary:** This is a screen form that is seen as most able to portray the social world accurately and truthfully: 'Documentary suggests fullness and completion, knowledge and fact, explanations of the social world and its motivating mechanisms' (Nichols, 1993: 174). Documentary is a varied genre that includes, and draws upon, five main modes of representation: expositional, observational, interactive, reflexive and performative (Nichols 1991). The use of narrative in the expositional and observational modes of representation is examined in *Television Discourse*. The former builds in an explicit manner an argument about the socio-historical world, although it also uses narrative. It addresses viewers directly and seeks to convey the impression that the film-maker is an objective outsider. The latter provides a detailed depiction of everyday life, rather than an argument around the social world. To suggest that the documentary is produced as though it had a direct, unmediated access to the real world, the film-maker does not appear to intervene. Viewers are provided with a 'window on reality – an idealistic (voyeuristic) spectator position' (Roscoe and Hight 2001: 19).

**Face:** This is one of the three main tenets of P. Brown and S. Levinson's (1987) politeness theory, which they borrowed and adapted from the work of E. Goffman. Face designates the kind of social standing or esteem that individuals are believed to claim for themselves and to want other individuals to respect.

**Footing:** This is the stance adopted by a participant towards other participants in verbal interaction (cf. Goffman's definition in Chapter 4).

**Forms of address:** A range of (pro)nominal choices through which speakers not only display but also (re)define existing interpersonal relations. Choosing one form of address over another – say a formal title over a first name or a nickname – is a discursive act that carries important ideological implications: it situates one speaker as more or less powerful than another, as an in-group or out-group member, and so forth (Van Dijk 1998). This makes forms of address a key gauge of the 'power and solidarity semantics' (Brown and Gillman 1972) that exist between interactants.

**Frame:** This refers to particular sets of principles of organisation that define the meaning and significance of social events (Goffman 1981).

**Fresh talk:** This is a participation framework for the production of talk in which the speaker occupies the roles of animator, principal and author (cf. Chapter 1 for an explanation of these terms and their usage in the context of television discourse).

**Given/new visual structures:** These are visual arrangements that work on the premise that 'given' information is normally placed on the left side of a given space, whereas the right side tends to be reserved for, and associated with, information that is 'new' (Kress and Van Leeuwen 2001).

**Hedge:** This is a linguistic expression that softens the force of a speaker's utterance in some way. Examples of hedging expressions include 'sort of', 'I mean' and 'more or less'.

**Identity:** This is the sense of self that individuals construct and perform in and through discourse.

**Ideology:** There are numerous definitions of this term. In this book, ideology is used in the sense outlined by Jaworski and Coupland (1999: 496) who, drawing on the work of authors such as Van Dijk (1998) and Fowler (1985), describe it as the 'social (general and abstract) representations shared by members of a group and used by them to accomplish everyday social practices: acting and communicating. These representations are organised into systems which are deployed by social classes and other groups "in order to make sense of, figure out and render intelligible the way society works"' (Hall 1996: 26).

**Indirect speech (also known as reported/constructed speech or dialogue):** A construction in which the speaker's words are presented as 'subordinate' to a verb of 'saying', for example: 'They said/reported/explained that she had not been able to finish the report in time for the meeting.'

**Intertextuality:** In (critical) discourse studies, this term designates borrowing among genres of discourse. In the context of media discourse, it describes the ways in which media texts and their meaning are intertwined, from one medium to another or even within a genre. Intertextuality thus refers to our ability to understand one media text partly from what we already know about other texts.

**Live two-way:** This is a journalistic term used to describe an interactional exchange which is broadcast in real time and which is between a newsreader normally in the television studio, and a news reporter at the scene.

**Marked:** This designates that which tends to occur less frequently and therefore appears unusual and salient when it occurs. Similarly, 'unmarked' designates that which occurs most frequently and therefore seems normal and neutral.

**Media event:** This is a term that emphasises the functional features of 'the festive viewing of television' (Dayan and Katz 1992: 1) and is used to refer to live coverage of events such as the Olympics, state weddings, state funerals, and the moon landing. For Dayan and Katz (1992: 1), such coverage constitutes 'a new narrative genre that employs the unique potential of the electronic media to command attention universally and simultaneously in order to tell a primordial story about current events'.

**Metalanguage:** This is language used for talking about language (cf. Chapter 11 for a discussion of the origins of the term and its relevance to the study of media discourse).

**Multi-modal discourse analysis/Multimodality:** This is an approach to social discourse analysis developed mainly by G. Kress and T. Van Leeuwen (e.g. 2001) in which all semiotic resources (colour, language, music, etc.) play an equal role. It seeks to answer the question: how do people use a range of communicative modes and media in actual, concrete, interactive instances of communicative practice?

**Naturalisation:** This refers to representation practices through language and/or visual images which suggest that the reality being presented is the result of 'the way things are', rather than the outcome of social practices. Naturalisation practices obscure the fact that '"the way things are" is not inevitable or unchangeable' (Cameron, 2001: 123).

**Neutralistic stance:** '[A] manner or style of interviewing, it refers to patterns of IR [interviewer] conduct which can escape formal charges of bias – whether in the interview context itself or beyond' (Greatbatch 1998: 167).

**Presupposition:** This is a speaker's assumption that he/she and the addressee share knowledge of certain facts that will enable an interpretation of an utterance or piece of discourse.

**Public sphere:** The term was originally coined by the German philosopher and sociologist Jürgen Habermas. It designates 'a domain of our social life where such a thing as public opinion can be formed', where citizens are able to 'deal with matters of general interest without being subject to coercion', and where they can 'express and publicize their views.' (1997: 105). For Habermas, newspapers, radio and television are the media of the public sphere, which is not to say that he is entirely optimistic about citizens' ability to circulate and form opinion freely in each and every one of these mass media.

**Reality TV:** Also known as 'popular factual entertainment' and 'ordinary television', this is a catch-all term that includes a wide range of programmes about real people which allow viewers to 'see for themselves'. The main formats of reality television are infotainment, docusoaps, lifestyle shows and reality gameshows. The diversity of programmes within and across these formats is due to the fact that reality television consists 'of a number of distinctive and historically based TV genres [. . .] which have merged with each other to create a number of hybrid genres' (Hill 2005: 55).

**Rhetoric:** This is one of the oldest defined concepts and broadly designates the art of persuasive discourse. Aristotle (1926: 15) defines it as 'the faculty of discovering the possible means of persuasion in reference to any subject whatsoever'. The actual language of persuasion involves a range of lexical choices, syntactic structures and sound patterning that comprise the persuasive repertoire of rhetorical figures.

**Self-presentation:** In a general sense, self-presentation refers to the discursive process whereby the self tries to manage how he/she is perceived by others. The systematic study of self-presentation started with the work of the North American sociologist Erving Goffman. One of Goffman's basic premises is that many of the most revealing insights into social behaviour can be found in the surface appearances that people create for one another in daily interaction, i.e. in their public presentations of self.

**Sound-bite:** This term that originates from radio, where it is also known as 'actuality' and designates a film or tape segment, within a news story, that includes someone speaking. A sound-bite is a line or sentence that is taken from a longer speech or piece of text and is used as indicative of the broader content. Former US President John F. Kennedy was the first politician to use sound-bites strategically, a famous example being his 'Ich bin ein Berliner' (I am a Berliner), through which he sought to offer solidarity to West Germans living in the shadow of the Berlin Wall. UK Prime Minister Harold Wilson 'picked up' on this style and used it effectively in successful election campaigns in 1964 and 1966 (Lilleker 2006).

**Speech act:** This is an utterance (locution) that is defined in terms of both the intentions of the speaker (illocution) and the effect that it has on the listener (perlocution).

**Story/narrative:** This is a discursive account of one or more factual or fictitious events which have either taken place, are taking place or will take place at a given time. Jaworksi and Coupland (1999: 30) define narratives as 'structural representations of events in a particular temporal order'. The terms 'story' and 'narrative' are used in narratology to designate different dimensions of narrative discourse. A story (known as *fabula* in the work of early Russian formalists such as Propp and Tomashevsky and as *histoire* in the work of French scholars such as Benveniste and Barthes) is 'a series of logically and chronologically related events that are caused or experienced by actors' (Bal 1985: 5). Narrative (or *sjuzhet* in the work of early Russian formalists, and *discours* in the work of French scholars) is the telling of a story – its rendering in a particular narrative context.

According to sociolinguists Labov and Waletzky (1967), all verbal narratives share a basic structure, which comprises the following elements (although not all narratives display all of them) and provides answers to a series of underlying questions:

1. Abstract: what was it about?
2. Orientation: who, when, what, where?
3. Complicating action: then what happened?
4. Evaluation: so what?
5. Coda: what finally happened?

In literary contexts, Vladimir Propp (1975) examined the narrative structure of fairytales, that is, oral or written stories aimed at children. Propp examined one hundred fairytales and found, at an abstract level, the same underlying story. Propp also identified eight basic 'character roles' – such as villain, victim, helper, heroine – and thirty-two 'fixed elements of narrative functions', which he subsumed under six stages or sections that were always present in the same order (and which are parallel to Labov and Waletzky's categories), namely: preparation, complication, transference, struggle, return and recognition.

**Spin-doctor:** This term was used originally to refer to Ronald Reagan's media team in a *New York Times* editorial on 21 October 1984. A spin-doctor is a professional impression manager who is skilled in using the media to influence public opinion. He/she is involved in trying to (a) get journalists to see the world from an angle that suits the spin-doctor's agenda; (b) deflect attention away from issues and stories he/she wants to 'bury'; and (c) plant and leak stories. Spin-doctors are experts in using the media to 'steer' public opinion (Louw 2005: 297–8).

**Symbolic capital:** This is a term coined by French sociologist Pierre Bourdieu (1930–2002). Bourdieu identifies four, to some extent interdependent, forms of 'capital' that characterise class positions, namely economic, cultural, social and symbolic. Symbolic capital entails possessing a good reputation and is similar to the idea of status. It is seen by Bourdieu as an important indicator of social class in contemporary society.

**Televisuality:** This concept used by Caldwell to define North American television in the 1980s can nevertheless be applied to subsequent periods and other countries in many respects. According to Caldwell (1995: 5–11), six principles defined and delimited the extent of televisuality:

1. Stylizing performance – an exhibitionism that utilizes many different looks. (This is the aspect examined in *Television Discourse*).
2. A structural inversion between narrative and discourse.
3. An industrial product resulting from new technological developments.
4. A programming phenomenon – a distinctive increase in showcase television: 'Everything on television now seems to be pitched at the viewer as a special event [. . .] so much so in fact, that the term special is now almost meaningless' (1995: 9).

5.  A function of the audience. The cultural abilities of audiences were considered to have changed by the 1980s: 'Many viewers expected and watched programs that made additional aesthetic and conceptual demands not evident in earlier programmes' (1995: 9)
6.  A product of economic crisis: the crisis that network television underwent after 1980 and that led to 'downsizing'. 'Stylist exhibitionism and downsizing were obviously very different organizational tactics' (1995: 11) that attempted to solve the same problem: the declining market share of the networks.

# Guide to Further Reading

*Television Discourse* is designed to be read and used as a whole. The further reading indicated below reflects this and the intertwined nature of much of the work it covers. It is also accepted, though, that some readers will be more interested in certain aspects of the research than others. To facilitate this, guided reading is grouped thematically as far as possible.

- On **television and narrative**, see Holland, P. *The Television Handbook,* 2nd edn (London: Routledge, 2000). The book's emphasis is on the production of television. Its second part, though, contains relevant work on narrative and documentary on television and explains critical approaches used in its study.
- For a case study of **the use of narrative on television from a discourse/sociolinguistic approach**, see Montgomery, M. 'Television news and narrative. How relevant are narrative models for explaining the coherence of television news?', in J. Thornborrow and J. Coates (eds), *The Sociolinguistics of Narrative* (Amsterdam and Philadelphia, PA: John Benjamins, 2005) 239–57.
- For **an application of Todorov's work on narrative structure to documentary discourse**, see Smith, P. 'Raising anxiety to construct the nation: Heartland – A case study', *Working Papers, Centre for Communication Research* (Auckland: Auckland University of Technology, 2006), http://www.aut.ac.nz/research/research_institutes/ccr/publications/working_papers/archive.htm (last accessed April 2008).
- On **archive footage in news reports and its ability to create an impression of realism** (or at least a sufficient likeness of the world), see Machin, D. and Jaworski, A. 'Archive video footage in news: Creating a likeness and index of the phenomenal world', *Visual Communication,* 5 (2006) 345–66.
- In addition to the substantial body of research on **documentary** discussed in Part I of this book, readers may also find the following of particular interest:
  - Barnouw, E. *Documentary: A History of the Non-Fiction Film,* 2nd edn (New York and Oxford: Oxford University Press, 1993).
  - Roscoe, J. *Documentary in New Zealand. An Immigrant Nation* (Palmerston, North: Dunmore Press, 1999).
  - Bruzzi, S. *New Documentary: A Critical Introduction* (London: Routledge, 2000). Examining non-fiction output in the 1980s–1990s, Bruzzi's work challenges some of the prevailing axioms of documentary critique and appraisal. The second part of the book in particular is useful to contextualise further the analysis of the discourse of docusoaps offered in Chapter 3 of *Television Discourse,* in which amongst other things, Bruzzi discusses the hybrid UK television docusoap variety (e.g. *Lakesiders, Hotel, Driving School and The Cruise*).
- For the **current factual television environment** (news, current affairs, documentaries and reality TV), and using research on audiences in primarily Sweden and the UK but also the US, see Hill, A. *Restyling Factual TV* (London: Routledge, 2007).
- For a **history of reality television**, from *Candid Camera* to *The Osbournes,* see Holmes, S and Jermyn, D., *Understanding Reality Television* (London: Routledge, 2003).

- For **temporality in news and the future in news reporting**, see Jaworski, A. and Fitzgerald, R. "'This poll has not happened yet": Temporal play in election predictions', *Discourse & Communication*, 2 (2008) 5–27. In this article, the authors draw upon media coverage of the 2001 UK General Election campaign to explore the manipulation of temporal relations during its course.
- As noted in Chapter 6, **liveness** is a much debated concept in media research. In addition to the studies referred to in *Television Discourse*, readers may want to consult a couple of recent journal issues themed on liveness, namely:
  - *The Communication Review*, 7 (2004), edited by P. Lunt and including papers by N. Couldry and J. Roscoe on liveness in reality TV, by J. Corner on liveness in documentaries, and by J. Thornborrow and R. Fitzgerald on live events in news reports.
  - *Media, Culture & Society*, 23 (2001), edited by P. Scannell and including a case study by S. Marriott of the live coverage of a lunar eclipse: 'In pursuit of the ineffable: How television found the eclipse but lost the plot', 725–42. Marriott has made a most significant contribution to our understanding of the ways that television produces effects of liveness for absent viewers. Some of this work has been drawn upon in Chapter 6 of this book but also noteworthy is her article on the live broadcasting of the 1997 funeral of Princess Diana on two British terrestrial channels: 'The BBC, ITN and the funeral of Princess Diana', *Media History*, 13 (2007), 93–110.
  - For the effect of liveness in political news reports on viewers, see Snoijer, R., de Vreese, C.H. and Semetko, H.A 'The effects of live television reporting on recall and appreciation of political news', *European Journal of Communication*, 17 (2002) 85–101.
  - On media leaks and their 'live' coverage in news, see Jaworski, A., Fitzgerald, R. and Morris, D. 'Radio leaks: Presenting and contesting leaks in radio news broadcasts', *Journalism*, 5 (2004) 183–202. For a wider discussion of media leaks and their importance in political communciation, see Tiffin, R, *News and Power* (Allen Unwin: Sydney, 1989).
- For a history of how the term 'spin' has been documented, see Pitcher, G. *The Death of Spin* (London: John Wiley, 2002). For case studies of spin in specific countries, see (on the US) Hurtz, H. *Spin Cycle: Inside the Clinton Propaganda Machine* (New York: Free Press, 1998) and (on the UK) Moloney, K. 'The rise and fall of spin: Changes in fashion in the presentation of UK politics', *Journal of Public Affairs*, 1 (2002) 124–35.
- A thorough overview of '**small talk**', including a history of the term and of its different interpretations, together with a number of case studies, is provided in Coupland, J. (ed.) *Small Talk* (London: Pearson Education, 2000).
- For a series of discussions on the '**meta' dimension of language**, as well as parallel terms such as metadiscourse, metapragmatics and metacommunication, see the various chapters in Jaworski, A., Coupland, N. and Galasiński, D. (eds) *Metalanguage. Social and Ideological Perspectives* (Berlin: Mouton de Gruyter, 2004).
- On **silence in the media**, see Jaworski, A., Fitzgerald, R and Constantinou, O. 'Busy saying nothing new: Live silence in TV reporting of 9/11', *Multilingua* 24 (2005): 121–44. (Special issue, Adam Jaworski (ed.) *Silence in Institutional and Intercultural Contexts*).
- On the **CNN effect**, see Livingston, S. 'Clarifying the CNN effect: An examination of media effects according to the type of military intervention', *Research Paper R-18* (The Joan Shorenstein Center: Harvard University, 1997); Robinson, P. *The CNN*

*Effect. The Myth of News, Foreign Policy and Intervention* (London: Routledge, 2002), especially Chapter 4 ('The CNN effect in action', 72–92); and Volkmer, I. *News in the Global Sphere. A Study of CNN and its Impact on Global Communication* (Luton: University of Luton Press, 1999). For a detailed case study, and in addition to those offered in McGregor, B.B. *Live, Direct and Biased? Making Television News in the Satellite Age* (London and New York: Arnold, 1997), see Livingston, S. and Eachus, T. 'Humanitarian crises and US foreign policy: Somalia and the CNN effect reconsidered', *Political Communication*, 12 (1995) 413–29.

- Classic work on **media events** includes Dayan, D. and Katz, E. *Media Events: The Live Broadcasting of History* (Cambridge, MA: Harvard University Press, 1992); and Liebes, T. 'Television's disaster marathons: A danger for democratic processes?', in T. Liebes and J. Curran (eds) *Media, Ritual and Identity* (London: Routledge, 1998) 71–84. In the latter, Liebes discusses live disaster marathons as a type of media event in the context of the murder of Israeli athletes during the 1972 Munich Olympics. More recent case studies of major events (9/11) can be found in Zelizer, B. and Allan, S. (eds) *Journalism after September 11* (London and New York: Routledge, 2002) and in Hoskins, A. 'Television and the collapse of memory', *Time & Society*, 13 (2004b) 109–27. Herein and drawing upon data from three media events (the 1991 Gulf War, 9/11 and the 2003 Iraq War), Hoskins examines how these events have acted as markers of the transformation of the relationship between television, the present and the past.

- On **therapeutic discourse** and television, see Peck, J. 'TV talk shows as therapeutic discourse: The ideological labor of the television talking cure', *Communication Theory*, 5 (1995) 58–81. Using data from the US talk shows *Sally Jessy Raphael* and *Oprah Winfrey*, Peck's article shows how therapeutic discourse is used to help organise and thereby manage social conflict into narratives of individual psychological dysfunction. See also Shattuc, J. *The Talking Cure: TV Talk Shows and Women* (London: Routledge, 1997) and White, M. *Tele-Advising: Therapeutic Discourse in American Television* (Chapel Hill: University of North Carolina Press, 1992).

- For recent work on **celebrity charisma/rhetoric of authenticity**, see:
  ○ Tolson, A. 'Celebrity Talk' in *Media Talk: Spoken Discourse on TV and Radio* (Edinburgh: Edinburgh University Press, 2006) 149–66. This provides a detailed analysis and discussion of a range of forms of talk regularly performed by celebrities on television, from 'celebrity rehab' to self-reflexive irony. Further case studies of celebrity talk by the same author include an article in a special issue of the journal *Discourse Studies* (2001) on authenticity in media discourse based on a documentary on the former Spice Girl Gerri Haliwell, '"Being yourself": The pursuit of authentic celebrity', 433–57.
  ○ Marshall, P.D. *The Celebrity Culture Reader* (London: Routledge, 2006) provides a combination of classic essays and contemporary writings that together paint a clear picture of the cultural underpinnings and implications of the complex phenomenon of the celebrity culture.

- For **an application of Goffman's dramaturgical metaphor to gender research**, see Coates, J. 'Women behaving badly: Female speakers backstage', *Journal of Sociolinguistics*, 3 (1999) 65–80. This explores how females perform backstage talk as an arena where norms can be subverted and challenged and alternative selves explored.

- For **applications of Foucault's work on confession rituals and moral surveillance to media research** see:

- ○ Holland, S. 'Our ladies of the airwaves', in E.M. Mazur and K. McCarthy (eds) *God in the Details: American Religion in Popular Culture* (London: Routledge, 2006) 217–23.
- ○ Aldridge, M. 'Confessional culture, masculinity and emotional work', *Journalism*, 29 (2001), 91–108. The author discusses confessional culture as a particularly controversial aspect of news tabloidisation, which many within the media industry condemn as trivial and even degrading. For others, including the author of the article, it 'provides positive audience responses and an important flexing of the boundary between the public/rational/masculine and the private/affective/female domain.'
- ○ Shugart, H. 'Ruling class: Disciplining class, race and ethnicity in television reality court shows', *The Howard Journal of Communications,* 17 (2006) 79–100. This examines ways in which moral excess and authority television courtroom shows are inscribed in ways that cultivate the normalisation of hegemonic dominant discourses of discipline which revolve around class and race/ethnicity.
- On **impoliteness in the media**, especially in reality television, see the following recent studies:
  - ○ Bousfield, D. 'Beginnings, middles and ends: Towards a biopsy of the dynamics of impoliteness.' *Journal of Pragmatics,* 39 (2007) 2185 – 216.
  - ○ Bousfield, D. *Impoliteness in Interaction,* (Amsterdam and Philadelphia, PA: John Benjamins, 2008).
  - ○ Bousfield, D. and Locher, M. (eds) *Impoliteness in Language* (Mouton de Gruyter: Berlin, 2007).
  - ○ Culpeper, J. 'Impoliteness and entertainment in the television quiz show: The Weakest Link', *Journal of Politeness Research,* 1 (2005) 35–72.
  - ○ Culpeper, J., Bousfield, D. and Wichmann, A. 'Impoliteness revisited: With special reference to dynamic and prosodic aspects', *Journal of Pragmatics,* 35 (2003) 1545–79.
- Part III of this book contains a discussion of the role of recontextualisation in political news reports, but for a more general discussion of **recontextualisation as a discourse practice**, see Linell, P. *Approaching Dialogue: Talk, Interaction and Contexts in Dialogical Perspectives* (Amsterdam and Philadelphia, PSA John Benjamins, 1998).
- On the **coarsening of political and mediated discourse**, see the following chapters in D. Tannen, *The Argument Culture* (London: Virago Press, 1999):
  - ○ 'A plague on both your houses!: Opposition in our political lives' (Chapter 4, 100–37). This examines conflict talk in politics and the media as a form of spectacle.
  - ○ 'Fast forward: Technologically enhanced aggression' (Chapter 8, 244–63). This chapter looks at verbal aggression in e-mail communication.
- On **news interviews in the UK and the US that do not abode by the principle of the neutralist stance**, see Chapter 7 ('Adversarial questioning: Setting agendas and exerting pressure') in Clayman. S. and Heritage, J. *The News Interview* (Cambridge: Cambridge University Press, 2002) 188–237. For an Australian perspective, see Rendle-Short, J. 'Neutralism and adversarial challenges in the political news interview', *Discourse & Communication,* 1 (2007) 387–406. The article examines journalists' adversarial challenges within the Australian political news interview and shows how, although politicians do not overtly accuse interviewers of bias or impartiality, they clearly orient to the challenging nature of the journalists' turns.

- For a comprehensive, reader-friendly overview of **rhetoric** containing numerous examples from political communication, see Cockcroft, R. and Cockcroft, S. *Persuading People. An Introduction to Rhetoric*, 2nd edn (Basingstoke: Palgrave Macmillan, 2005).
- On **the relationship between politics and the media (news) in the UK,** see Chapters 6 ('News', 145–75) and 7 ('The Government and news management', 176–202) in Kuhn, R. *Politics and the Media in Britain* (London: Palgrave Macmillan, 2007).
- Of the numerous studies available on **political discourse**, those worth considering include:
  - Fetzer, A. and Lauerbach, G. (eds) *Political Discourse in the Media* (Amsterdam and Philadelphia, PA: John Benjamins, 2007). This edited volume has contributions that examine political discourse in the media from a cross-culturally comparative perspective in a wide range of contexts, including Arab, British, Dutch, US American, French, British, and Israeli.
  - Other comparative political discourse work includes the book on parliamentary discourse by Bayley, P. (ed.) *Cross-cultural Perspectives on Parliamentary Discourse* (Amsterdam and Philadelphia, PA: John Benjamins, 2004). Of special interest to readers of *Television Discourse* is the chapter by D. Miller, 'Truth, justice and the American way: The appraisal system of judgment in the U.S. House debate on the impeachment of the President, 1998', 271–300. The analysis shows the varying meanings given to 'truth' according to the position of the individual speaker, and the overlapping of the concepts of truth and justice.
  - On the synergies of public discourses and specifically the discourse of politics and the discourse of the media, see Fairclough, N. (1998) 'Political discourse in the media: An analytical framework', in A. Bell and P. Garrett (eds) *Approaches to Media Discourse* (Oxford: Blackwell, 1998) 142 – 62.
  - For the strategic use of forms of address and, specifically, the pronoun 'we' in parliamentary discourse, see Iñigo-Mora, I. 'On the uses of the personal pronoun we in communities', *Journal of Language and Politics*, 3 (2004) 27–52.
  - For a discourse analysis of politics and deception, see Galasiński, D. *The Language of Deception: A Discourse Analytic Approach* (London: Sage, 2000), especially Chapter 5 'Metadiscursive deception', 71–86.
  - An accessible yet comprehensive study of political persuasive discourse with numerous practical examples of, especially, metaphor in political discourse is: Charteris-Black, J. *Politicians and Rhetoric* (London: Palgrave Macmillan, 2004).
  - On politicians' images, in addition to the studies referred to in Chapter 12, readers may find useful Fairclough, N. *New Labour, New Language* (London: Routledge, 2000) and J. Street, 'Celebrity politicians: Popular culture and political representation', *British Journal of Politics and International Relations*, 6 (2004) 435–52.
  - For an overview of global trends in the media reporting of image politics, see Stanyer, J. and Wring D. 'Public images, private lives: The mediation of politicians around the globe', *Parliamentary Affairs*, 57 (2004) 1–8. See also Bucy, E.P. 'Emotional and evaluative consequences of inappropriate leader displays', *Communication Research*, 27 (2000) 194–226.
  - On aspects of the interface between media and politics, see the special issue of *Journal of Pragmatics*, 2006, *Pragmatic Aspects of Political Discourse in the Media*, edited by A. Fetzer and E. Weizman. Of particular interest therein are A. Fetzer's '"Minister, we will see how the public judges you". Media references in political

interviews', 180–95, G. Lauerbach's 'Discourse representation in political interviews: The construction of identities and relations through voicing and ventriloquizing', 196–215, and T. Ensik's 'Pragmatic aspects of televised texts: A single case study of the intervention of televised documentary program in party politics', pp. 230–49, which focuses on how the media affect the composition and interpretation of political messages.

o On the mediaisation of politics, see Davies, A. *The Mediation of Power* (London: Routledge, 2007). The book provides a critical exploration of the debates surrounding the idea of mediated politics and is enlivened by first-hand accounts taken from interviews with relevant parties – politicians, spin doctors, campaigners, and so forth.

o Two comprehensive studies of public relations in Britain are Davies, A. *Public Relations and the Mass Media in Britain* (Manchester: Manchester University Press, 2002) and Franklin, B. *Packaging Politics: Political Communications in Britain's Media Democracy* (London: Arnold, 2004). For a critical account of the relationship between the public relations industry and democracy, see Moloney, K. 'Democracy and public relations', *Journal of Communication Management*, 9 (2004) 89–92.

• On **non-verbal communication**, and specifically its importance vis-à-vis verbal behaviour, see Richmond, V.P. and McCroskey, J.C. *Nonverbal Behaviour in Interpersonal Relations,* 4th edn (Boston, MA: Allyn and Bacon, 2000) and Remland, M.S. *Nonverbal Communication in Everyday Life* (Boston, MA: Houghton Mifflin, 2000).

• On **'doing tourism' from a sociological perspective**, see Urry's study *The Tourist Gaze*, 2nd edn (London: Sage, 2000). For a more sociolinguistic approach, see the chapter by Gieve, S. and Norton, J. 'Dealing with linguistic difference in encounters with others on British television', in S. Johnson and A. Ensslin (eds) *Language in the Media* (London: Continuum, 2007) 188–212. These authors examine the ways in which many represented encounters between English-speaking television presenters and their foreign interlocutors on holiday shows eschew complex attempts to communicate. The study centres on the production and editorial practices that often result in the scorning of those foreigners who attempt to cross the linguistic divide.

• For **the relationship between lifestyles and the media**, see a special issue of the *Journal of European Communication*, 17 (2002) edited by D. McQuail. Of particular interest to the points discussed in Chapters 11 and 13 of this book are: Taylor, L. 'From ways of life to lifestyles: The "ordinari-ization" of British gardening lifestyle television' 479–94 and Vyncke, P. 'Lifestyle segmentation: From attitudes, interests and opinions, to values, aesthetic styles, life visions and media preferences' 445–64.

• An introductory text on **the Habermasian concept of the public sphere** is McKee, A. *The Public Sphere: An Introduction* (Cambridge: Cambridge University Press, 2005). The book offers a clear overview of the current functioning of the public sphere and also traces both popular and academic contributions to discussion about the issue. A more advanced book, full of insightful analysis of amongst other things the language of the public sphere, is P. Dahlgren, *Television and the Public Sphere: Citizenship, the Public Sphere and National Identity* (London: Sage, 1995).

• For a study of **media discourse (print media) that draws upon the concept of 'symbolic capital'**, see Thurlow, C. and Jaworski, A. 'The alchemy of the upwardly mobile: Symbolic capital and the stylization of elites in frequent-flyer programs', *Discourse & Society*, 17 (2006) 131–67.

# Bibliography

Aldridge, M. 'Confessional culture, masculinity and emotional work', *Journalism,* 29 (2001) 91–108.

Allan, S. *News Culture,* 2nd edn (Buckingham: Open University Press, 2004).

Allan, S. *Online News: Journalism and the Internet* (Maidenhead: Open University Press, 2006).

Argyle, M., Slater, V., Nicholson, H., Williams, M. and Burgess, P. 'The communication of inferior and superior attitudes by verbal and non-verbal signals', *British Journal of Social and Clinical Psychology,* 9 (1970) 221–31.

Aristotle, *The 'Art' of Rhetoric,* translated by J.H. Freese, Loeb Classical Library (London: Heinemann, 1926).

Aslama, M. and Pantii, M. 'Talking alone. Reality TV, emotions and authenticity', *European Journal of Cultural Studies,* 9 (2006) 167–184.

Atkinson, J.M. and Heritage, J. 'Jefferson's transcript notation', in J.M. Atkinson and J. Heritage (eds) *Structures of Social Action: Studies in Conversation Analysis* (Cambridge: Cambridge University Press, 1984) ix–xvi.

Austin, J.L. *How to Do Things with Words: The William James Lectures Delivered at Harvard University in 1955,* edited by J.O. Urmson (Oxford: Claredon, 1962).

Bakhtin, M.M. *The Dialogic Imagination,* edited by M. Holquist, translated by C. Emerson and M. Holquist (Austin: University of Texas Press, 1981).

Bakhtin, M.M. *Problems in Dostoyevsky's Poetics* (Minneapolis: University of Minnesota Press, 1984).

Bakthin, M.M. *Speech Genres and Other Late Essays.* Edited by C. Emerson and M. Holquist, translated by V.M. McGee (Austin: University of Texas Press, 1986).

Bal, M. *Narratology: Introduction to the Theory of Narrative* (Toronto: University of Toronto Press, 1985).

Barnouw, E. *Documentary: A History of the Non-Fiction Film,* 2nd edn (New York and Oxford: Oxford University Press: 1993).

Barry, D. *Bad Habits* (New York: Henry Holt, 1987).

Bayley, P. (ed.) *Cross-cultural Perspectives on Parliamentary Discourse* (Amsterdam and Philadelphia, PA: John Benjamins, 2004).

Baynham, M. 'Direct speech: What's it doing in non-narrative discourse', *Journal of Pragmatics,* 25 (1996) 61–81.

Baynham, M. 'Double-voicing and the scholarly "I": On incorporating the words of others in academic discourse', in M. Baynham and S. Slembrouck (eds) *Speech Representation and Institutional Discourse,* special issue of *Text* (1999) 485–504.

Bell, A. 'Styling the other to define the self: A study in New Zealand identity', *Journal of Sociolinguistics,* 3 (1999) 523–41.

Bell, A. 'Poles apart. Globalization and the development of news discourse across the twentieth century', in J. Aitchison and D. Lewis (eds) *New Media Language* (London: Routledge, 2003) 7–17.

Bell, M. *Through Gates of Fire* (London: Phoenix, Orion, 2003).

Bell, P. and Van Leeuwen, T. *The Media Interview: Confession, Contest, Conversation* (Kensington: University of New South Wales Press, 1994).

Benjamin, W. 'The work of art in the age of mechanical reproduction', in H. Arendt (ed.) *Illuminations* (New York: Harcourt Brace Jovanovich, 1968).

Bernstein, B. *Class, Code and Control,* vol. 1 (London: Routledge and Kegan Paul, 1971).

Biber, D. and Finegan, E., 'Adverbial stance types in English', *Discourse Processes,* 11 (1988) 1–34.

Biber, D. and Finegan, E. 'Styles of stance in English: Lexical and grammatical marking of evidentiality and affect', *Text,* 9 (1989) 93–165.

Biber, D., Johansson, S., Leech, G., Conrad, S. and Finegan, E. *Longman Grammar of Spoken and Written English* (London: Longman, 1999).

Biressi, A. and Nunn, H. *Reality TV. Realism and Revelation* (London and New York: Wallflower Press, 2005).

Blas-Arroyo, J.L. 'Perdóneme que se lo diga, pero vuelve usted a faltar a la verdad, señor González: Form and function of politic verbal behaviour in face-to-face Spanish political debates', *Discourse & Society,* 4 (2003) 395–424.

Blum-Kulka, S. '"You gotta know how to tell a story": Telling, tales and tellers in American and Israeli narrative events at dinner', *Language in Society,* 22 (1993) 361–402.

Blum-Kulka, S. *Dinner Talk: Cultural Patterns of Sociability and Socialization in Family Discourse* (London and Mahwah, NJ: Lawrence Erlbaum Associates, 1997).

Blum-Kulka, S. 'The many faces of *With Meni:* The history and stories of one Israeli talk show', in A. Tolson (ed.) *Television Talk Shows. Discourse, Performance, Spectacle* (London and Mahwah, NJ: Lawrence Erlbaum Associates, 2001) 89–116.

Bolter, J.D. and Grusin, R. *Remediation: Understanding New Media,* 3rd printing (London: MIT Press, 2000).

Bonner, F. *Ordinary Television* (London: Sage, 2003).

Born, G. *Uncertain Vision. Birt, Dyke and the Reinvention of the BBC* (London: Secker & Warburg, 2004).

Bourdieu, P. *Distinction: A Social Critique of the Judgement of Taste* (London: Routledge and Kegan Paul, 1984).

Bourdon, J. 'Live television is still alive: On television as an unfulfilled promise', *Media, Culture & Society,* 22 (2000) 531–52.

Bousfield, D. 'Beginnings, middles and ends: Towards a biopsy of the dynamics of impoliteness', *Journal of Pragmatics,* 39 (2007) 2185–216.

Bousfield, D. *Impoliteness in Interaction* (Amsterdam and Philadelphia, PA, John Benjamins, 2008).

Bousfield, D. and Locher, M. (eds) *Impoliteness in Language* (Mouton de Gruyter: Berlin, 2007).

Briggs, C.L. and Bauman, R. 'Genre, intertextuality and social power', *Journal of Linguistic Anthropology,* 2 (1992) 131–72.

Brown, G. and Yule, G. *Discourse Analysis* (Cambridge: Cambridge University Press, 1983).

Brown, P. and Levinson, S. *Politeness: Some Universals in Language Usage* (Cambridge: Cambridge University Press, 1987).

Brown, R. and Gillman, A. 'The pronouns of power and solidarity', in P.P. Giglioli (ed.) *Language and Social Context* (Harmondsworth: Penguin, 1972), 265–82. (First published in T.A. Sebeok (ed.) *Style in Language* (Cambridge, MA: MIT Press) 253–77).

Brunsdon, C., Johnson, C., Moseley, R. and Wheatley, H. 'Factual entertainment on British television: The Midlands TV Research Group's "8–9 Project"', *European Journal of Cultural Studies,* 4 (2001) 29–62.

Bruzzi, S. *New Documentary: A Critical Introduction* (London: Routledge, 2000).

Bucholtz, M. 'The politics of transcription', *Journal of Pragmatics*, 32 (2000) 1439–65.

Bucy, E.P. 'Emotional and evaluative consequences of inappropriate leader displays', *Communication Research*, 27 (2000) 194–226.

Burite, R. and Levy, D.W. (eds) *FDR's Fireside Chats* (Norman, OK: University of Oklahoma Press, 1992).

Burton, G. *More than Meets the Eye*, 3rd edn (London: Arnold, 2002).

Caldas-Coulthard, C.R. 'On reporting reporting: The representation of speech in factual and fictional narratives', in M. Coulthard (ed.) *Advances in Written Text Analysis* (London: Routledge, 1994) 295–308.

Caldwell, J.T. *Televisuality: Style, Crisis and Authority in American Television* (New Brunswick, NJ: Rutgers University Press, 1995).

Cameron, D. *Verbal Hygiene* (London: Routledge, 1995).

Cameron, D. 'Performing gender identity: Young men's talk and the construction of heterosexual identity', in S. Johnson and U.H. Meinhof (eds) *Language and Masculinity* (Oxford: Blackwell, 1997) 47–64.

Cameron, D. *Good to Talk? Living and Working in a Communication Culture* (London: Sage, 2000).

Cameron, D. *Working with Spoken Discourse* (London: Sage, 2001).

Cameron, D. 'Globalizing "communication"', in J. Aitchison and D. Lewis (eds) *New Media Language* (London: Routledge, 2003) 27–35.

Cameron, D. 'Out of the bottle: The social life of metalanguage', in A. Jaworski, N. Coupland and D. Galasiński (eds) *Metalanguage. Social and Ideological Perspectives* (Berlin: Mouton de Gruyter, 2004) 311–21.

Carpignano, P., Andersen, R., Aronowitz, S. and Difazio, W. 'Chatter in the age of electronic reproduction: Talk television and the "public mind"', *Social Text*, 25 (1990) 33–55.

Chaney, D. *Lifestyles* (London: Routledge, 1996).

Chaney, D. 'From ways of life to lifestyles: Rethinking culture as ideology and sensibility', in J. Lull (ed.) *Culture in the Communication Age* (London: Routledge, 2001) 75–88.

Chaney, D. *Cultural Change and Everyday Life.* (Basingstoke: Palgrave Macmillan, 2002).

Charteris-Black, J. *Politicians and Rhetoric* (Basingstoke: Palgrave Macmillan, 2004).

Chibnall, S. *Law-and-Order News: An Analysis of Crime Reporting in the British Press* (London: Tavistok, 1977).

Chouliaraki, L. 'Watching 11 September: The politics of pity', *Discourse & Society*, 15 (2004) 185–98.

Cicero, *Selected Political Speeches of Cicero* (translated and introduced by M. Grant, Harmondsworth, Penguin Classics, 1988).

Cienki, A. 'Bush's and Gore's language and gestures in the 2000 US Presidential debates', *Journal of Language and Politics*, 3 (2004) 409–40.

Clayman, S. 'Footing in the achievement of neutrality: The case of news-interview discourse', in P. Drew and J. Heritage (eds) *Talk at Work: Interaction in Institutional Settings* (Cambridge: Cambridge University Press, 1992) 163–98.

Clayman, S. and Heritage, J. *The News Interview* (Cambridge: Cambridge University Press, 2002).

Coates, J. 'Women behaving badly: Female speakers backstage', *Journal of Sociolinguistics*, 3 (1999) 65–80.

Coates, J. and Thornborrow, J. 'Myths, lies and audiotapes: Some thoughts on data transcripts', *Discourse & Society*, 10 (1999) 594–7.

Cockcroft, R. and Cockcroft, S. *Persuading People. An Introduction to Rhetoric*, 2nd edn (Basingstoke: Palgrave Macmillan, 2005).

Cook, G. 'Transcribing infinity. Problems of contextual presentation', *Journal of Pragmatics*, 14 (1990) 1–24.

Cook, G. *The Discourse of Advertising*, 2nd edn (London; Routledge, 2001).

Corner, J. *Television Form and Public Address* (London: Edward Arnold, 1995).

Corner, J. *Studying Media. Problems of Theory and Method* (Edinburgh: Edinburgh University Press, 1998).

Corner, J. *Critical Ideas in Television Studies* (Oxford: Claredon Press, 1999).

Corner, J. 'Mediated persona and political culture', in J. Corner and D. Pels (eds) *Media and the Re-Styling of Politics* (London: Sage, 2003) 67–84.

Corner, J. and Pels, D. (eds) *Media and the Re-Styling of Politics* (London: Sage, 2003).

Couldry, N. *Media Rituals: A Critical Approach* (London: Routledge, 2003).

Couldry, N. 'Liveness, "reality", and the mediated habitus. From television to the mobile phone', *The Communication Review*, 7 (2004) 353–61.

Coupland, J. (ed.) *Small Talk* (London: Pearson Education, 2000).

Culpeper, J. 'Towards an anatomy of impoliteness', *Journal of Pragmatics*, 29 (1996) 173–91.

Culpeper, J. 'Impoliteness in dramatic dialogue', in J. Culpeper, M. Short and P. Verdonk (eds) *Exploring the Language of Drama: From Text to Context* (London: Routledge, 1998) 83–95.

Culpeper, J. 'Impoliteness and entertainment in the television quiz show: The Weakest Link', *Journal of Politeness Research*, 1 (2005) 35–72.

Culpeper, J. Bousfield, D. and Wichmann, A. 'Impoliteness revisited: With special reference to dynamic and prosodic aspects', *Journal of Pragmatics*, 35 (2003) 1545–79.

Dahlgren, P. *Television and the Public Sphere: Citizenship, the Public Sphere and National Identity* (London: Sage, 1995).

Davies, A. *Public Relations and the Mass Media in Britain* (Manchester: Manchester University Press, 2002).

Davies, A. *The Mediation of Power* (London: Routledge, 2007).

Dayan, D. and Katz, E. *Media Events: The Live Broadcasting of History* (Cambridge, MA: Harvard University Press, 1992).

Debrett, M. 'Branding documentary: New Zealand's minimalist solution to cultural subsidy', *Media, Culture & Society*, 24 (2004) 5–23.

Doane, M.A. 'Information, crisis, catastrophe', in P. Mellencamp (ed.) *Logics of Television: Essays in Cultural Criticism* (Bloomington, IND: Indiana University Press, 1990) 222–39.

*Dominion Post, The* (Wellington, New Zealand, 2004).

Dovey, J. *Freakshow: First Person Media and Factual Television* (London and Sterling, VA: Pluto Press, 2000).

Dyer, R. *Stars* (London: British Film Institute, 1979).

Dyer, R. *Heavenly Bodies* (New York: St Martin's Press, 1986).

Dyer, R. 'A star is born and the construction of authenticity', in C. Gledhill (ed.) *Stardom: Industry of Desire* (London: Routledge, 1991) 132–40.

Eelen, G. *A Critique of Politeness Theories* (Manchester: St Jerome, 2001).

Ellis, J. *Visible Fictions* (London: Routledge, 1982, updated 2nd edn pub 1992).

Ekström, M. 'Politicians interviewed on television news', *Discourse & Society*, 12 (2001) 563–84.

Ensik, T. 'Pragmatic aspects of televised texts; a single case study of the intervention of televised documentary program in party politics', *Journal of Pragmatics*, 38 (2006) 230–49.

Evans, J. and Hesmondhalgh, D. *Understanding the Media: Inside Celebrity* (Maidenhead, England and New York: Open University Press in association with the Open University, 2005).

Evans Davies, C. 'Language and American "good taste". Martha Stewart as mass-media role model', in J. Aitchison and D. Lewis (eds) *New Media Language* (London: Routledge, 2003) 146–55.

Fairclough, N. *Language and Power* (Harlow: Longman, 1989).

Fairclough, N. 'What might we mean by "enterprise discourse"', in K. Russell and N. Abercrombie (eds) *Enterprise Culture* (London: Routledge, 1991) 38–58.

Fairclough, N. (ed.) *Critical Language Awareness* (London: Longman, 1992).

Fairclough, N. *Media Discourse* (London and Mahwah, NJ: Lawrence Erlbaum Associates, 1995).

Fairclough, N. 'Political discourse in the media: An analytical framework', in A. Bell and P. Garrett (eds) *Approaches to Media Discourse* (Oxford: Blackwell, 1998) 142–62.

Fairclough, N. *New Labour, New Language* (London: Routledge, 2000).

Fasold, R. *Sociolinguistics of Language* (Oxford: Blackwell, 1990).

Felski, R. 'The invention of everyday life', *New Formations*, 39 (2000) 15–31.

Fetzer, A. and Lauerbach, G. (eds) *Political Discourse in the Media* (Amsterdam and Philadelphia, PA: John Benjamins, 2007).

Fetzer, A. and Weizman, E. (eds) *Pragmatic Aspects of Political Discourse in the Media*, special issue of *Journal of Pragmatics*, 38 (2006).

Feuer, J. 'The concept of live television', in E. Kaplan (ed.) *Regarding Television* (Los Angeles: American Film Institute, 1983) 12–22.

Fiske, J. *Television Culture* (London: Routledge, 1987).

Fiske, J. and Hartley, J. *Reading Television* (London: Methuen, 1978).

Foucault, M. *Discipline and Punish: The Birth of the Prison* (New York: Pantheon Books, 1977).

Foucault, M. *The History of Sexuality: An Introduction* (New York: Random House, 1978).

Fowler, R. *Literature as Social Discourse: The Practice of Linguistic Criticism* (London: Batsford Academic, 1981).

Fowler, R. 'Power', in T. Van Dijk (ed.) *Handbook of Discourse Analysis*, vol. 4 (London: Academic Press, 1985), 61–8.

Fowler, R. *Language in the News: Discourse and Ideology in the Press* (London: Routledge, 1991).

Franklin, B. *Packaging Politics: Political Communications in Britain's Media Democracy* (London: Arnold, 2004).

Furedi, F. *Therapy Culture: Cultivating Vulnerability in an Uncertain Age* (London: Routledge, 2004).

Galasiński, D. *The Language of Deception: A Discourse Analytic Approach* (London: Sage, 2000).

Galtung, J. and Ruge, M.H. 'The structure of foreign news', *Journal of Peace Research*, 2 (1965) 64–91.

Gamson, J. *Claims to Fame: Celebrity in Contemporary America* (Berkeley and Los Angeles: University of California Press, 1994).

García, A. 'Dispute resolution without disputing: How the interactional organization of mediation hearings minimizes argument', *American Sociological Review*, 56 (1991) 818–35.

Geraghty, C. and Lusted, D. (eds) *The Television Studies Book,* 2nd edn (London: Arnold, 2004).

Giddens, A. *Modernity and Self-Identity* (Cambridge: Polity Press, in association with Blackwell, 1991).

Gieve, S. and Norton, J. 'Dealing with linguistic difference in encounters with others on British television', in S. Johnson and A. Ensslin (eds) *Language in the Media* (London: Continuum, 2007) 188–212.

Giles, D. 'Keeping the public in their place: Audience participation in lifestyle television programming', *Discourse & Society,* 13 (2002) 603–28.

Gillmor, D. *We the Media: Grassroots Journalism by the People, for the People* (Sebastopol, CA: O'Reilly, 2006).

Gitlin, T. *Media Unlimited* (New York: Metropolitan Books, 2001).

Goffman, E. *The Presentation of Self in Everyday Life* (New York: Anchor Books, 1959).

Goffman, E. *Encounters: Two Studies in the Sociology of Interaction* (Indianapolis: Bobbs-Merritt, 1961).

Goffman, E. *Behaviour in Public Places* (New York: Free Press, 1963).

Goffman, E. *Interactional Ritual: Essays on Face-to-Face Behaviour* (Garden City, NY: Anchor, 1967).

Goffman, E. *Strategic Interaction* (Philadelphia, PA: University of Pennsylvania Press, 1969).

Goffman, E. *Frame Analysis: An Essay on the Organization of Experience* (New York: Harper & Row, 1974).

Goffman, E. *Forms of Talk* (Oxford: Blackwell, 1981).

Goodwin, C. and Goodwin, M.H. 'Contested vision: The discursive constitution of Rodney King', in B.L. Gunnarsson, P. Linell and B. Nordberg (eds) *The Construction of Professional Discourse* (London: Longman, 1997) 292–316.

Goodwin, M.H. *He-Said-She-Said: Talk as Social Organisation among Black Children* (Bloomington: Indiana University Press, 1990).

Greatbatch, D. 'Conversation analysis: Neutralism in British news interviews', in A. Bell and P. Garrett (eds) *Approaches to Media Discourse* (Oxford: Blackwell, 1998) 163–85.

Gregori-Signes, C. 'Heroes and villains: Metacognition in tabloid talk-show storytelling', in A. Sánchez Macarro (ed.) *Windows on the World: Media Discourse in English* (Valencia: University of Valencia Press, 2001) 153–76.

Grimshaw, A.D. (ed.) *Conflict Talk: Sociolinguistic Investigations of Arguments in Conversations* (Cambridge: Cambridge University Press, 1990).

Grindstaff, L. 'Producing trash, class and the money shot', in J. Lull and S. Hinerman, (eds) *Media Scandals* (Cambridge: Cambridge University Press, 1997) 164–201.

Grindstaff, L. *The Money Shot. Trash, Class, and the Making of TV Talk Shows* (Chicago and London: University of Chicago Press, 2002).

Grispud, J. 'Television, broadcasting, flow: Key metaphors in TV theory', in C. Geraghty and D Lusted (eds) *The Television Studies Book,* 2nd edn (London: Arnold, 2004) 17–32.

Gruber, H. 'Political language and textual vagueness', *Pragmatics,* 3 (1993) 1–28.

Habermas, J. *The Structural Transformation of the Public Sphere: An Inquiry into a Category of Bourgeois Society* (Cambridge, MA: MIT Press, 1989 (1962)), translated by T. Burger and F. Lawrence.

Habermas, J. 'The public sphere', in R.E. Goodin and P. Pettit (eds) *Contemporary Political Philosophy: An Anthology* (Oxford: Blackwell, 1997) 105–8.

Hall, S. 'The television discourse – Encoding and decoding', *Education and Culture,* 25 (1974) 8–14.

Hall, S. 'The problem of ideology: Marxism without guarantees', in D. Morley and K.H. Chen (eds) *Stuart Hall: Critical Dialogues in Cultural Studies* (London: Routledge, 1996) 25–46.

Hallin, D. 'Sound bite news. Television coverage of elections', *Journal of Communication,* 42 (1992) 5–24.

Hardy, B. 'Towards a poetics of fiction', *Novel,* 2 (1968) 5–14.

Harris, S. 'Being politically impolite: Extending politeness theory to adversarial political discourse', *Discourse & Society,* 12 (2001) 451–72.

Hartley, J. 'Housing television: Textual traditions in TV and Cultural Studies', in C. Geraghty and D. Lusted (eds) *The Television Studies Book,* 2nd edn (London: Arnold, 2004) 33–50.

Hawkins, G. 'The ethics of television', *International Journal of Cultural Studies,* 4 (2001) 412–26.

Heller, D. (ed.) *Makeover Television. Realities Remodelled* (Basingstoke: Palgrave Macmillan, 2007).

Heritage, J. 'Analyzing news interviews: Aspects of the production of talk for an overhearing audience', in T.A. Van Dijk (ed.) *Handbook of Discourse Analysis, Volume III: Discourse and Dialogue* (London: Academic Press, 1985) 95–116.

Heritage, J. 'The limits of questioning: Negative interrogatives and hostile question content', *Journal of Pragmatics,* 34 (2002) 1427–46.

Heritage, J. and Greatbatch, D. 'On the institutional character of institutional talk: The case of news interviews', in D. Boden and D.H. Zimmerman (eds) *Talk and Social Structure* (Berkeley: University of California Press, 1991) 93–137.

Heritage, J. and Roth, A.L. 'Grammar and institution: Questions and questioning in broadcast news interviews', *Research on Language and Social Interaction,* 28 (1995) 1–60.

Hetch, M.L., De Vito, J.A. and Guerrero, L.K. 'Perspectives on nonverbal communication', in L.K. Guerrero, J.A. De Vito and M.L. Hetch (eds) *The Nonverbal Communication Reader* (Prospect Heights, IL: Waveland Press, 1999) 3–18.

Hicks, J.P. 'Bitter primary contest hits ethnic nerve among blacks', *The New York Times,* 31 August (2000a).

Hicks, J.P. 'Vitriol flows in race for Congress', *The New York Times,* 8 September (2000b).

Hill, A. *Reality TV: Audiences and Popular Factual Television* (London: Routledge, 2005).

Hill, A. *Restyling Factual TV* (London: Routledge, 2007).

Hodge, R. and Kress, G. *Social Semiotics* (Cambridge: Polity, 1988).

Holland, S. 'Our ladies of the airwaves', in E.M. Mazur and K. McCarthy (eds) *God in the Details: American Religion in Popular Culture* (London: Routledge, 2006) 217–23.

Holmes, J. 'Doing collegiality and keeping control at work: Small talk in government departments', in J. Coupland (ed.) *Small Talk* (London: Pearson Education, 2000) 32–61.

Holmes, S and Jermyn, D. *Understanding Reality Television* (London: Routledge, 2003).

Horton, D. and Wohl, R.R. 'Mass communication and para-social interaction', *Psychiatry,* 19 (1956) 215–29.

Hoskins, A. 'Mediating time: The temporal mix of television', *Time & Society,* 10 (2001) 333–46.

Hoskins, A, *Televising War: From Vietnam to Iraq* (London: Continuum, 2004a).

Hoskins, A. 'Television and the collapse of memory', *Time & Society,* 13 (2004b) 109–27.

Hoskins, A. and O'Loughlin, B. *Television and Terror: Conflicting Times and the Crisis of News Discourse* (Basingstoke: Palgrave Macmillan, 2007).

Hunter, L. *Rhetorical Stance in Modern Literature: Allegories of Love and Death* (Basingstoke: Macmillan, 1984).

Hurtz, H. *Spin Cycle: Inside the Clinton Propaganda Machine* (New York: Free Press, 1998).

Hutchby, I. *Confrontation Talk* (Mahwah, NJ: Lawrence Erlbaum, 1996).

Hutchby, I. 'Building alignments in public debate: A case study from British TV', *Text*, 17 (1997) 161–79.

Hutchby, I. 'Confrontation as a spectacle: The argumentative frame of the Ricki Lake Show', in A. Tolson (ed.) *Television Talk Shows. Discourse, Performance, Spectacle* (London and Mahwah, NJ: Lawrence Erlbaum Associates, 2001) 155–72.

Hutchby, I. *Media Talk. Conversation Analysis and the Study of Broadcasting* (Maidenhead: Open University Press, 2006).

Illie, C. 'Question-response argumentation in talk shows', *Journal of Pragmatics*, 33 (1999) 209–54.

Iñigo-Mora, I. 'On the uses of the personal pronoun we in communities', *Journal of Language and Politics*, 3 (2004) 27–52.

Jakobson, R. 'Closing statement: Linguistics and poetics', in T.A. Sebeok (ed.) *Style in Language* (Cambridge, MA: MIT Press, 1960) 350–77.

Jamieson, K.H. *Packaging the Presidency. A History and Criticism of Presidential Campaign Advertising* (Oxford: Oxford University Press, 1984).

Jamieson, K.H. *Dirty Politics. Deception, Distraction and Democracy* (Oxford: Oxford University Press, 1992).

Jaworski, A. *The Power of Silence: Social and Pragmatic Perspectives* (Newbury Park, CA.: Sage, 1993).

Jaworski, A. (ed.) *Silence: Interdisciplinary Perspectives* (Berlin: Mouton de Gruyter, 1997).

Jaworski, A. and N. Coupland (eds) *The Discourse Reader*, 1st edn/2nd edn (London: Routledge, 1999/2005).

Jaworski, A., Coupland, N. and Galasiński, D. (eds) *Metalanguage. Social and Ideological Perspectives* (Berlin: Mouton de Gruyter, 2004).

Jaworski, A. and Fitzgerald, R '"This poll has not happened yet": Temporal play in election predictions', *Discourse & Communication*, 2 (2008) 5–27.

Jaworski, A., Fitzgerald, R. and Constantinou, O. 'Busy saying nothing new: Live silence in TV reporting of 9/11', *Multilingua*, 24 (2005) 121–44.

Jaworski, A. and Galasiński, D. 'The verbal construction of non-verbal behaviour: British press reports of President Clinton's grand jury testimony video', *Discourse & Society*, 13 (2002) 629–49.

Jaworski, A. and I. Sachdev, 'Teachers' beliefs about students' talk and salience: Constructing academic success and failure through metapragmatic comments', in A. Jaworski, N. Coupland and D. Galasiński (eds) *Metalanguage. Social and Ideological Perspectives* (Berlin: Mouton de Gruyter, 2004) 227–46.

Jaworski, A., Thurlow, C., Lawson, S. and Ylänne-McEwen, V. 'The uses and representations of local languages in tourist destinations: A view from British television holiday programmes', *Language Awareness*, 12 (2003b) 5–29.

Jaworski, A., Ylänne-McEwen, V., Lawson, S. and Thurlow, C. 'Social roles and negotiation of status in host–tourist interactions: A view from British television holiday programmes', *Journal of Sociolinguistics*, 7 (2003a) 135–63.

Johnstone, B. *Repetition in Discourse: Interdisciplinary Perspectives*, vols 1 and 2 (Norwood, NJ: Ablex, 1994).

Joyner Priest, P. *Public Intimacies: Talk Show Participants and Tell-all TV* (Cresskill, NJ: Hampton Press, 1995).

Katriel, T. and Philipsen, G. '"What we need is communication": Communication as a cultural category in some American speech', in D. Carbaugh (ed.) *Cultural Communication and Intercultural Contact* (London and Mahwah, NJ: Lawrence Erlbaum Associates, 1990) 77–93.

Kendon, A. 'Do gestures communicate? A review', *Research on Language and Social Interaction,* 27 (1994) 175–200.

Kilborn, R. and Izod, J. *An Introduction to Television Documentary.* (Manchester: Manchester University Press, 1997).

Knapp, M.L. *Nonverbal Communication in Human Interaction* (New York: Holt, Rinehart and Winston, 1972).

Kozloff, S. 'Narrative theory and television', in R.C. Allen (ed.) *Channels of Discourse, Reassembled* (London: University of North Carolina Press, 1992) 67–100.

Kress, G. and Van Leeuwen, T. *Reading Images: The Grammar of Visual Design* (London: Routledge, 1996 and 2005 (2nd edn)).

Kress, G. and Van Leeuwen, T. *Multimodal Discourse* (London: Arnold, 2001).

Kuhn, R. *Politics and the Media in Britain* (Basingstoke: Palgrave Macmillan, 2007).

Labov, W. 'The transformation of experience in narrative syntax', in W. Labov, *Language in the Inner City* (Philadelphia, PA: University of Philadelphia Press, and Oxford: Blackwell, 1972a) 354–96.

Labov, W. 'Rules for ritual insults', in W. Labov, *Language in the Inner City* (Philadelphia, PA: University of Philadelphia Press and Oxford: Blackwell, 1972b) 297–353.

Labov, W. and Fanshel, D. *Therapeutic Discourse: Psychotherapy as Conversation.* (New York: Academic Press, 1977).

Labov, W. and Waletzky, J. 'Narrative analysis', in J. Helm (ed.) *Essays on the Verbal and Visual Arts* (Seattle: University of Washington Press, 1967) 12–44.

Lakoff, G. *Moral Politics: What Conservatives Know the Liberals Don't* (Chicago: University of Chicago Press, 1996). [2nd edn (2002) published as *Moral Politics: How Liberals and Conservatives Think*].

Lakoff, R. *Language and Woman's Place* (New York: Harper Collins Publishers, 1975).

Lakoff, R. 'The new incivility: Threat or promise?', in J. Aitchison and D. Lewis (eds) *New Media Language* (London: Routledge, 2003) 36–44.

Langer, J. 'Television's "personality system"', *Media, Culture & Society,* 3 (1981) 351–65.

Lauerbach, G. 'Discourse representation in political interviews: The construction of identities and relations through voicing and ventriloquizing', *Journal of Pragmatics,* 38 (2006) 196–215.

Lavandera, B. 'Argumentatividad y discurso', *Voz y Letra. Revista de Filología,* 3 (1992) 3–18.

Laver, J. 'Linguistic routines and politeness in greeting and parting', in F. Coulmas (ed.) *Conversational Routines: Explorations in Standardized Communication Situations and Prepatterned Speech* (The Hague: Mouton de Gruyter, 1981) 289–304.

Levinson, S.C. 'Putting linguistics on a proper footing: Explorations in Goffman's concepts of participation', in P. Drew and A. Wooton (eds) *Erving Goffman: Exploring the Interaction Order* (Cambridge: Polity, 1988) 161–227.

Levinson, S.C. 'Activity types and language', in P. Drew and J. Heritage (eds) *Talk at Work. Interaction in Institutional Settings* (Cambridge: Cambridge University Press, 1992) 66–100.

Liebes, T. 'Television's disaster marathons: A danger for democratic processes?', in T. Liebes and J. Curran (eds) *Media, Ritual and Identity* (London: Routledge, 1998) 71–84.

Lilleker, D.G. *Key Concepts in Political Communication* (London: Sage, 2006).

Linell, P. *Approaching Dialogue: Talk, Interaction and Contexts in Dialogical Perspectives* (Amsterdam and Philadelphia: John Benjamins, 1998).

Livingston, S. 'Classifying the CNN effect: An examination of media effects according to the type of military intervention', *Research Paper R-18* (The Joan Shorenstein Center: Harvard University, 1997).

Livingston, S and Eachus, T. 'Humanitarian crises and US foreign policy: Somalia and the CNN effect reconsidered', *Political Communication*, 12 (1995) 413–29.

Livingstone, S. and Lunt, P. *Talk on Television: Audience Participation and Public Debate* (London: Routledge, 1994).

Lorenzo-Dus, N. 'Up close and personal: The narrativization of private experience in Media Talk', *Studies in English Language and Linguistics*, 3 (2001a) 125–48.

Lorenzo-Dus, N. 'Compliment responses among British and Spanish university students: A contrastive study', *Journal of Pragmatics*, 33 (2001b) 107–27.

Lorenzo-Dus, N. 'Emotional DIY and proper parenting in Kilroy', in J. Aitchison and D. Lewis (eds) *New Media Language* (London and New York: Routledge, 2003) 136–45.

Lorenzo-Dus, N. 'A rapport and impression management approach to public figures' performance of talk', *Journal of Pragmatics*, 37 (2005) 611–31.

Lorenzo-Dus, N. 'Buying and selling: Mediating persuasion in British property shows', *Media, Culture & Society*, 28 (2006a) 739–61.

Lorenzo-Dus, N. 'The discourse of lifestyles in the broadcast media', in P. Bou Franch (ed.) *Ways into Discourse* (Granada: Comares, 2006b) 135–50.

Lorenzo-Dus, N. '(Im)politeness and the Spanish media: The case of audience participation debates', in M.E. Placencia and C. García (eds) *Research on Politeness in the Spanish-Speaking World* (Mahwah, NJ and London: Lawrence Erlbaum Associates, 2007) 145–66.

Lorenzo-Dus, N. '*Real* disorder in the court: An investigation of conflict talk in US courtroom shows', *Media, Culture & Society*, 30 (2008) 81–107.

Louw, E. *The Media and Political Process* (London: Sage, 2005).

Lunt, P. and Stenner, P. '*The Jerry Springer Show* as an emotional public sphere', *Media, Culture & Society*, 27 (2005) 59–82.

Lury, K. *Interpreting Television* (London and New York: Hodder Arnold, 2005).

Lyons, J. *Semantics* (Cambridge: Cambridge University Press, 1977).

Machin, D. and Jaworski, A. 'Archive video footage in news: Creating a likeness and index of the phenomenal world', *Visual Communication*, 5 (2006) 345–66.

Maguire, K. 'Masters of the political black arts go to war', *Guardian*, 10 March (2001).

Macdonald, M. *Exploring Media Discourse* (London: Arnold, 2003).

Malinowski, B. 'The problem of meaning in primitive languages', supplement to C.K. Ogden and I.A. Richards, *The Meaning of Meaning* (London : Routledge and Kegan Paul, 1923) 146–52.

Marriott, S. 'Time and time again: "live" television commentary and the construction of replay talk', *Media, Culture & Society*, 22 (1996) 131–48.

Marriott, S. 'Election night', *Media, Culture & Society*, 18 (2000) 69–86.

Marriott, S. 'In pursuit of the ineffable: How television found the eclipse but lost the plot', *Media, Culture & Society*, 23 (2001) 725–42.

Marriott, S. 'The BBC, ITN and the funeral of Princess Diana', *Media History*, 13 (2007), 93–110.

Marshall, P.D. *Celebrity and Power: Fame in Contemporary Culture* (Minneapolis: University of Minnesota Press, 1997).

Marshall, P.D. *The Celebrity Culture Reader* (London: Routledge, 2006).

May, T.E. *The Thomas Erskine May Treatise on the Law, Privileges, Proceedings and Usage of Parliament* (London: Butterworths, 1989).

Maynard, D. 'How children start arguments', *Language in Society,* 14 (1985) 1–30.

McGregor, B.B. *Live, Direct and Biased? Making Television News in the Satellite Age* (London and New York: Arnold, 1997).

McGuiran, J. *Cultural Populism* (London: Routledge, 1992).

McKee, A. *The Public Sphere: An Introduction* (Cambridge: Cambridge University Press, 2005).

McNair, B. *An Introduction to Political Communication* (London: Routledge, 1999, 2nd edn).

McQuail, D. 'The media and lifestyles. Editor's Introduction', *European Journal of Communication,* 17 (2002) 427–28.

Meehan, E. 'Holy commodity fetish Batman', in R.R. Pearson and W. Uricchio (eds) *The Many Lives of Batman: Critical Approaches to a Superhero and his Media* (London: Routledge, 1991) 47– 65.

Mellencamp, P. (ed.) *Logics of Television: Essays in Cultural Criticism* (Bloomington, IND: Indiana University Press, 1990).

Messaris, P. *Visual Persuasion. The Role of Images in Advertising* (London: Sage, 1997).

Mestrovic, S. *Postemotional Society* (London: Sage, 1997).

Miller 'Truth, justice and the American way: The appraisal system of judgment in the U.S. House debate on the impeachment of the President, 1998', in P. Bayley (ed.) *Cross-Cultural Perspectives on Parliamentary Discourse* (Amsterdam and Philadelphia, PA: John Benjamins, 2004) 271–300.

Mills, S. *Gender and Politeness* (Cambridge: Cambridge University Press, 2003).

Moloney, K. 'The rise and fall of spin: Changes in fashion in the presentation of UK politics', *Journal of Public Affairs*, 1 (2002) 124–35.

Moloney, K. 'Democracy and public relations', *Journal of Communication Management*, 9 (2004) 89–92.

Montgomery, M. *An Introduction to Language and Society* (London: Methuen, 1986).

Montgomery, M. '"Our Tune": A study of a discourse genre', in P. Scannell (ed.) *Broadcast Talk* (London: Sage, 1991) 138–77.

Montgomery, M. 'Speaking sincerely: Public reactions to the death of Diana', *Language and Literature*, 8 (1999) 5–33.

Montgomery, M. 'Defining "authentic talk"', *Discourse Studies,* 3 (2001) 397–405.

Montgomery, M. 'Television news and narrative. How relevant are narrative models for explaining the coherence of television news?', in J. Thornborrow and J. Coates (eds) *The Sociolinguistics of Narrative* (Amsterdam and Philadelphia, PA: John Benjamins, 2005) 239–57.

Montgomery, M. 'Broadcast news, the live "two-way" and the case of Andrew Gilligan', *Media, Culture & Society*, 28 (2006) 233–59.

Montgomery, M. *The Discourse of Broadcast News. A Linguistic Approach* (London: Routledge, 2007).

Moores, S. *Media and Everyday Life in Modern Society* (Edinburgh: Edinburgh University Press, 2000).

Moseley, R. 'Makeover takeover on British television', *Screen*, 41 (2000) 299–314.

Munson, W. *All Talk: The Talk Show in Media Culture* (Philadelphia, PA: Temple University Press, 1993).

Murdock, G. 'Talk shows: Democratic debates and tabloid tales', in J. Wieten, G. Murdock and P. Dahlgren (eds) *Television Across Europe: A Comparative Introduction* (London: Sage, 2000) 198–220.

Nichols, B. *Representing Reality* (Bloomington, IND: Indiana University Press, 1991).

Nichols, B. '"Getting to know you . . ."; Knowledge, power and the body', in M. Renov (ed.) *Theorizing Documentary* (New York: Routledge, 1993) 174–92.

Nichols, B. *Introduction to Documentary*, (Bloomington, IND: Indiana University Press, 2001).

Nylund, M. 'Asking questions, making sound-bites: Research reports, interviews and television news stories', *Discourse Studies*, 5 (2003) 517–33.

Ochs, E. 'Transcription as theory', in E. Ochs and B.B. Schiefflen (eds) *Developmental Pragmatics* (New York: Academic Press, 1979) 43–72.

Ochs, E. and Taylor, C. 'Family narrative as political activity', *Discourse & Society*, 3 (1992) 301–40.

Ochs, E., Taylor, C., Rudolph, D. and Smith, R. 'Storytelling as a theory-building activity', *Discourse Processes*, 15 (1992) 37–72.

O'Connell, D. and Kowal, S. 'Transcription systems for spoken discourse', in J. Verschueren, J. Otsman and J. Blommaert (eds) *Handbook of Pragmatics* (Amsterdam and Philadelphia, PA: John Benjamins, 1995) 645–56.

O'Keeffe, A. *Investigating Media Discourse* (London: Routledge, 2006).

Pardo, L. 'Linguistic persuasion as an essential political factor in current democracies: Globalization discourse in Argentina at the turn and the end of the century', *Discourse & Society*, 12 (2001) 91–118.

Partington, A. *The Linguistics of Political Argument* (London: Routledge, 2003).

Peck, J. 'TV talk shows as therapeutic discourse: The ideological labor of the television talking cure', *Communication Theory*, 5 (1995) 58–81.

Pérez de Ayala, S. 'FTAs and Erskine May: Conflicting needs? – Politeness in Question Time', *Journal of Pragmatics*, 33 (2001) 143–70.

Peters, J. 'Witnessing', *Media, Culture & Society*, 23 (2001) 707–23.

Piirainen-Marsh, A. 'Managing adversarial questioning in broadcast interviews', *Journal of Politeness Research*, 3 (2005) 193–218.

Pitcher, G. *The Death of Spin* (London: John Wiley, 2002).

Plantiga, C.R. *Rhetoric and Representation in Nonfiction Film* (Cambridge: Cambridge University Press, 1997).

Pountain, D. and Robins, D. *Cool Rules: Anatomy of an Attitude* (London: Reaktion, 2000).

Propp, V. *Morphology of the Folk Tale* (Austin: University of Texas Press, 1975).

Quirk, R., Greenbaum, S., Leech, G. and Svartvik, J. *A Comprehensive Grammar of the English Language* (London: Longman, 1985).

Rach, C.D. 'Live/life: Television as a generator of events in everyday life', in P. Drummond and R. Paterson (eds) *Television and its Audience* (London: British Film Institute, 1988) 32–8.

Remland, M.S. *Nonverbal Communication in Everyday Life* (Boston, MA: Houghton Mifflin, 2000).

Rendle-Short, J. 'Neutralism and adversarial challenges in the political news interview', *Discourse & Communication*, 1 (2007) 387–406.

Rentschler, C. 'Witnessing: US citizenship and the vicarious experience of suffering', *Media, Culture & Society*, 26 (2004) 296–304.

Richards, B. 'The emotional deficit in political communication', *Political Communication*, 21 (2004) 339–52.

Richardson, K. and Meinhof, U. *Worlds in Common? Television Discourse in a Changing Europe* (London and New York: Routledge, 1999).

Richmond, V.P. and McCroskey, J.C. *Nonverbal Behavior in Interpersonal Relations*, 4th edn (Boston, MA: Allyn and Bacon, 2000).

Riddell, P. 'Members and Millbank: The media and parliament', in J. Seaton (ed.) *Politics and the Media* (Oxford: Blackwell, 1998) 8–17.

Robinson, P. *The CNN Effect. The Myth of News, Foreign Policy and Intervention* (London: Routledge, 2002).

Rojek, C. *Celebrity* (Reaktion Books: London, 2001).

Roscoe, J. *Documentary in New Zealand: An Immigrant Nation* (Palmerston North: Dunmore Press, 1999).

Roscoe, J. and Hight, C. *Faking it. Mock-documentary and the Subversion of Factuality* (Manchester: Manchester University Press, 2001).

Rose, N. *Powers of Freedom: Reframing Political Thought* (Cambridge: Cambridge University Press, 1999).

Ross, K. 'Political talk radio and democratic participation: Caller perspectives on *Election Call*', *Media, Culture & Society*, 26 (2004) 785–801.

Russell, K. and Abercrombie, N. (eds) *Enterprise Culture* (London: Routledge, 1991).

Sacks, H. 'On doing "being ordinary"', in G. Jefferson (ed.) *Structures of Social Action: Studies in Conversation Analysis* (Cambridge: Cambridge University Press, 1984) 413–29.

Sacks, H. *Lectures on Conversation* (vols 1 & 2) (Cambridge, MA and Oxford: Blackwell, 1992).

Saussure, F. de (1916) *Cours de linguistique générale*, edited by C. Bally and A. Sechehaye, in collaboration with A. Riedlinger (Paris: Éditions Payot).

Scammell, M. *Designer Politics. How Elections are Won* (London: Macmillan, 1995).

Scannell, P. 'Public service broadcasting and modern public life', *Media, Culture & Society*, 11 (1989) 134–66.

Scannell, P. (ed.) *Broadcast Talk* (London: Sage, 1991).

Scannell, P. *Radio, Television and Modern Life* (Oxford: Blackwell, 1996).

Scannell, P 'Media-language-world', in A. Bell and P. Garrett (eds) *Approaches to Media Discourse* (Oxford: Blackwell, 1998) 251–67.

Scannell, P. 'For-anyone-as-someone structures', *Media, Culture & Society*, 22 (2000) 5–24.

Schiffrin, D. 'The management of a co-operative self during argument: The role of opinions and stories', in A.D. Grimshaw (ed.) *Conflict Talk* (Cambridge: Cambridge University Press, 1990) 241–59.

Schiffrin, D. 'Narrative as self-portrait: Sociolinguistic constructions of identity', *Language in Society*, 25 (1996) 167–203.

Scott, S. 'Linguistic feature variation within disagreements: An empirical investigation', *Text*, 22 (2002) 301–28.

Seaton, J. (ed.) *Politics and the Media* (Oxford: Blackwell, 1998).

Sebeck, T.A. *A Sign is Just a Sign* (Bloomington, IND: Indiana University Press, 1991).

Shannon, C.E. and Weaver, W. *The Mathematical Theory of Communication* (Urbana: University of Illinois Press, 1949).

Shattuc, J. *The Talking Cure: TV Talk Shows and Women* (London: Routledge, 1997).

Shugart, H.A. 'Ruling class: Disciplining class, race and ethnicity in television reality court shows', *The Howard Journal of Communications*, 17 (2006) 79–100.

Smith, P. 'Rebuilding New Zealand's national identity: A critical discourse analysis of the role of the charismatic documentary presenter', in *Proceedings of the International*

*Conference on Critical Discourse Analysis: Theory into Research* (Tasmania, 2005) 660–7.

Smith, P. 'Raising anxiety to construct the nation: Heartland – A case study', *Working Papers, Centre for Communication Research* (Auckland: Auckland University of Technology, 2006) 1–14.

Snoeijer, R., de Vreese, C.H. and Semetko, H.A. 'The effects of live television reporting on recall and appreciation of political news', *European Journal of Communication*, 17 (2002) 85–101.

Sontag, S. *Regarding the Pain of Others* (New York: Farrer, Straus and Giroux, 2003).

Sperber, D. and Wilson, D. *Relevance: Communication and Cognition*, 2nd edn (Oxford: Blackwell, 1995).

Spigel, L. 'The Reveal', in D. Heller (ed.) *The Great American Makeover* (Basingstoke: Palgrave Macmillan, 2006) 227–41.

Squire, C. 'Empowering women? The Oprah Winfrey show', in C. Brunsdon, J. D'Acci and L. Spigel (eds) *Feminist Television Criticism* (Oxford: Clarendon Press, 1990) 98–113.

Squire, C. 'AIDS panic', in J.M. Usher (ed.) *Body Talk: The Material and Discursive Regulation of Sexuality, Madness and Reproduction* (London and New York: Routledge, 1997) 50–69.

Stanyer, J. and Wring D. 'Public images, private lives: The mediation of politicians around the globe', *Parliamentary Affairs*, 57 (2004) 1–8.

Strange, N. 'Perform, educate, entertain: Ingredients in the cookery programme genre', in C. Geraghty and D. Lusted (eds) *The Television Studies Book*, 2nd edn (London: Arnold, 2004) 301–14.

Street, J. 'Celebrity politicians: Popular culture and political representation', *British Journal of Politics and International Relations*, 6 (2004) 435–52.

Stubbs, M. *Discourse Analysis* (Oxford: Blackwell, 1983).

Swain, J. 'War doesn't belong to the generals', *British Journalism Review*, 14 (2003) 23–9.

Tannen, D. 'Repetition in conversation: Toward a poetics of talk', *Language*, 63 (1987) 574–605.

Tannen, D. *Talking Voices: Repetition, Dialogue and Imagery in Conversational Discourse* (Cambridge: Cambridge University Press, 1989).

Tannen, D. *The Argument Culture* (London: Virago Press, 1999).

Taylor, L. 'From ways of life to lifestyles. The 'ordinari-ization' of British gardening lifestyle television', *European Journal of Communication*, 17 (2002) 479–94.

Thompson, J. *The Media and Modernity* (Oxford: Polity Press, 1995).

Thompson, J. *Political Scandal* (Cambridge: Polity Press, 2000).

Thornborrow, J. 'Having their say: The function of stories in talk show discourse', *Text*, 17 (1997) 241–62.

Thornborrow, J. '"Has it ever happened to you?": Talk show stories as mediated performance', in A. Tolson (ed.) *Television Talk Shows. Discourse, Performance, Spectacle* (London and Mahwah, NJ: Lawrence Erlbaum Associates, 2001) 117–38.

Thornborrow, J. Power *Talk: Language and Interaction in Institutional Discourse* (London: Longman, 2002).

Thornborrow, J. and Fitzgerald, R. 'Storying the news through category, actor and reason', *The Communication Review*, 7 (2004), 345–52.

Thornborrow, J. and Morris, D. 'Gossip as strategy: The management of talk about others on reality TV show "Big Brother"', *Journal of Sociolinguistics*, 8 (2004) 246–71.

Thurlow, C. and Jaworski, A. 'The alchemy of the upwardly mobile: Symbolic capital and the stylization of elites in frequent-flyer programs', *Discourse & Society*, 17 (2006) 131–67.

Tiffin, R. *News and Power* (Sydney: Allen Unwin, 1989).

Todorov, T. *The Poetics of Prose*, translated by Jonathan Culler (New York: Cornell University Press, 1971).

Todorov, T. *Fantastic: A Structural Approach to a Literary Genre*, translated by R. Howard (Ithaca, NY: Cornell University Press, 1975).

Todorov, T. *Introduction to Poetics*, translated by R. Howard (Brighton: Harvester Press, 1981).

Tolson, A. 'Televised chat and the synthetic personality', in P. Scannell (ed.) *Broadcast Talk* (London: Sage, 1991) 179–87.

Tolson, A. *Mediations* (London: Arnold, 1996).

Tolson, A. (ed.) *Television Talk Shows. Discourse, Performance, Spectacle* (London and Mahwah, NJ: Lawrence Erlbaum Associates, 2001a).

Tolson, A. '"Being yourself": The pursuit of authentic celebrity', *Discourse Studies*, 3 (2001b) 433–57.

Tolson, A. *Media Talk. Spoken Discourse on TV and Radio* (Edinburgh: Edinburgh University Press, 2006).

Toolan, M. *Narrative: A Critical Linguistic Introduction* (London: Routledge, 1988).

Tuggle, C.A., Carr, F. and Huffman, S. *Broadcast News Handbook: Writing, Reporting and Producing in a Converging Media World* (Boston and London: McGraw-Hill, 2004).

Turner, G., Bonner, F. and Marshall, P.D. *Fame Games. The Production of Celebrity in Australia* (Cambridge: Cambridge University Press, 2000).

Urry, J. *The Tourist Gaze*, 2nd edn (London: Sage, 2000).

Van Dijk, T.A. *Ideology* (London: Sage, 1998).

Van Leeuwen, T. 'Genre and field in critical discourse analysis', *Discourse & Society*, 4 (1993) 193–225.

Van Zoonen, L. '"After Dallas and Dynasty we have . . . democracy': Articulating soap, politics and gender', in J. Corner and D. Pels (eds) *Media and the Re-Styling of Politics* (London: Sage, 2003) 99–116.

Volkmer, I. *News in the Global Sphere. A Study of CNN and its Impact on Global Communication* (Luton: University of Luton Press, 1999).

Vyncke, P. 'Lifestyle segmentation: From attitudes, interests and opinions, to values, aesthetic styles, life visions and media preferences', *European Journal of Communication*, 17 (2002) 445–64.

Watts, R. *Politeness* (Cambridge: Cambridge University Press, 2003).

White, M. *Tele-Advising: Therapeutic Discourse in American Television*, (Chapel Hill: University of North Carolina Press, 1992).

White, M. 'Television, therapy and the social subject; or, the TV therapy machine', in J. Friedman (ed.) *Reality Squared. Televisual Discourse on the Real* (New Brunswick, NJ.: Rutgers University Press, 2002) 313–21.

Wieten, J. and Pantii, M. 'Obsessed with the audience; breakfast television revisited', *Media, Culture & Society*, 27 (2006) 21–39.

Winston, B. *Claiming the Real: The Documentary Film Revisited* (London: British Film Institute, 1995).

Winston, B. *Lies, Damn Lies and Documentaries* (London: British Film Institute, 2000).

Winston, B. 'Towards tabloidization? Glasgow revisited, 1975–2001', *Journalism Studies*, 3 (2002) 5–20.

Wood, H. '"No, YOU rioted!": The pursuit of conflict in the management of "lay" and "expert" discourses on *Kilroy*', in A. Tolson (ed.) *Television Talk Shows. Discourse, Performance, Spectacle* (London and Mahwah, NJ: Lawrence Erlbaum Associates, 2001) 65–88.

Yatziv, G. *Introduction to Normative Sociology* (Claremont, CA: Foundation for California, 2000).

Yawn, M. and Beatty, B. 'Debate-induced opinion change. What matters?', *American Politics Quarterly*, 28 (2000) 270–85.

Young, K.G. 1987. *Taleworlds and Storyrealms: The Phenomenology of Narrative* (Dordrecht: Martinus Nijhoff, 1987).

Zelizer, B. 'Photography, journalism and trauma', in B. Zelizer and S. Allan (eds) *Journalism after September 11* (London and New York: Routledge, 2002) 48–69.

Zelizer, B. and Allan, S. (eds) *Journalism after September 11* (London and New York: Routledge, 2002).

# Index